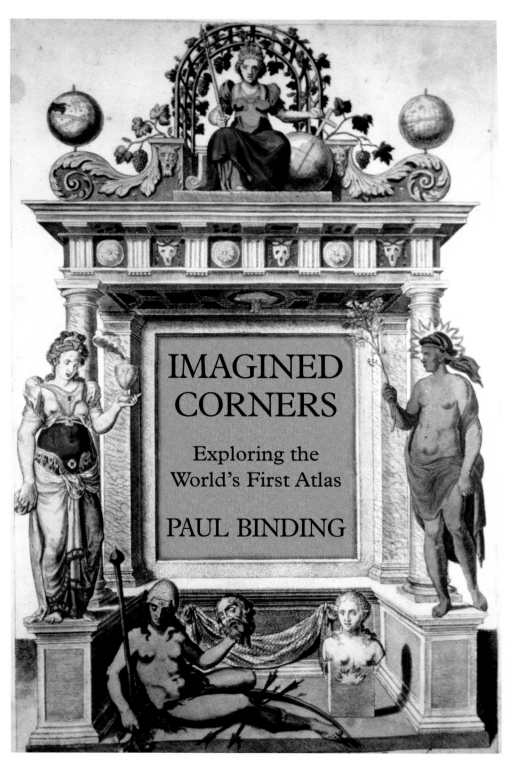

IMAGINED CORNERS

Exploring the
World's First Atlas

PAUL BINDING

Also by Paul Binding

Separate Country
St Martin's Ride
Harmonica's Bridegroom
My Cousin the Writer

First published in 2003
by REVIEW

An imprint of Headline Book Publishing

10 9 8 7 6 5 4 3 2 1

Every effort has been made to fulfil requirements with regard to reproducing copyright
material. The author and publisher will be glad to rectify any omissions at the earliest
opportunity.

Endpapers: *Typus Orbis Terrarum*, or World Map, from the 1570 *Theatrum*.

A CIP catalogue record for this title is available from the British Library

ISBN 0 7472 3040 4

Designed and typeset by Ben Cracknell Studios
Picture research by Mia Stewart-Wilson
Printed and bound in Italy by Canale & C.S.p.A.

Headline Book Publishing
A division of Hodder Headline
338 Euston Road
London NW1 3BH

www.reviewbooks.co.uk
www.hodderheadline.com

To Jonny Gathorne-Hardy and Nicky Loutit

CONTENTS

PART ONE

BACKCLOTH   1

PART TWO

THE *THEATRUM* COMES

INTO BEING   65

PART THREE

THE *THEATRUM* AS

A REALITY   165

PART FOUR

INSIDE THE *THEATRUM*   231

SELECT BIBLIOGRAPHY   303

ACKNOWLEDGEMENTS   306

PICTURE CREDITS   308

INDEX   310

ANVERPIA.

PARS FLANDRIAE

SCALDIS FLV.

Les noms des Bou:
leuerts & ra:
pars.
A. Buluardo del Duc.
B. Buluardo de Ernado
C. Buluardo de Toledo
D. Buluardo de Alua
E. Buluardo de Paciotto

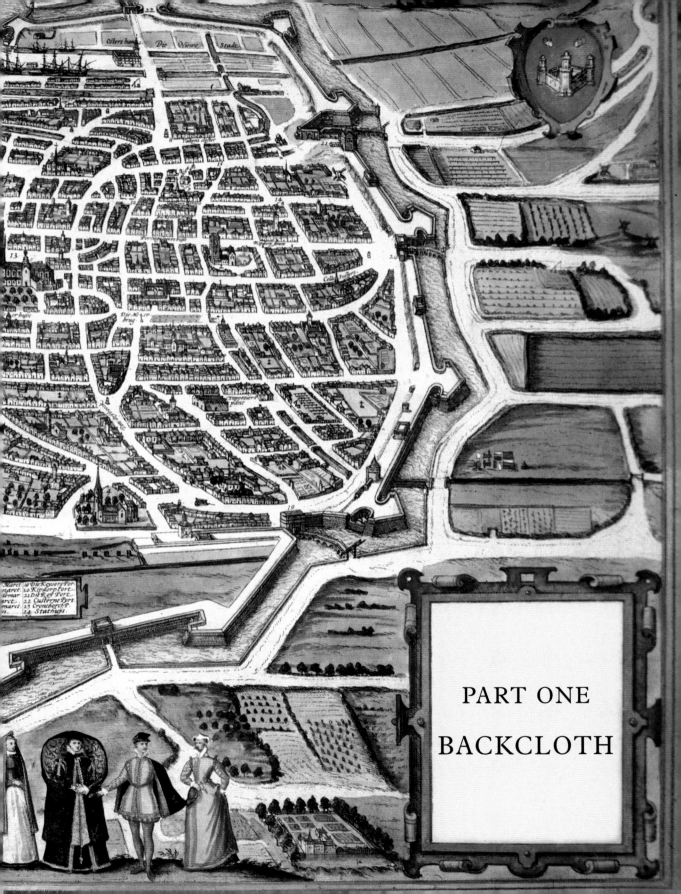

PART ONE

BACKCLOTH

Previous page:
Included in Braun and Hogenberg's Civitates orbis terrarum *of 1572, this view of Antwerp from the south, showing its newer fortifications and the might of its river, is a woodcut previously used for Antwerp resident Lodovico Guicciardini's* Descrittio di tutti i Paesi Bassi *('Description of all the Low Countries') of 1567.*

CHAPTER ONE

The most successful book of the entire sixteenth century – the first century to open with the printed book as a fact of western life – was *Theatrum orbis terrarum* (*Theatre of the countries of the world*). It did something no previous book had done. Here was the world itself, with its many component parts, and it was shown to be both a place of extraordinary varieties and a singular whole. The *Theatrum*, published in Antwerp on 20 May 1570, was the world's first-ever atlas.

An atlas is both a book of maps and far more than a book of maps. The maps are its body, the prime reason for its existence – however excellent the text, however interesting its information tables. But just as lands and seas unite to make up our planet, so, in an atlas, all the maps must cohere. They must have correspondences – in scale, symbols, names, lettering, figures – one with another, so that never, even in our most engrossed particular examinations, do we forget the greater picture. This does not mean that every map in an atlas is made to the same measurements, but that there's a rationalised consistency throughout the book enabling us to compare like with like – large country with large country, smaller island with smaller island – while seeing them all as constituents of the same one world.

Gratitude for this novel and needed undertaking was expressed in every possible way – in the *Theatrum*'s unprecedentedly high sales figures, in the numerous editions it went through (including pocket ones), in all the languages it appeared in (Latin, Dutch, French, German, Spanish, Italian, English) and – this above all – in the enthusiastic tributes paid to it right from the very start. Royalty, statesmen, clerics, merchants, explorers, young scholars – they all praised it, often rapturously. A leading Italian poet and historian thought the *Theatrum* positively amounted to a new invention, a 'world-machine'; an eminent French orientalist considered it humanity's most important book after the Bible.

As for its creator, its conceiver, compiler, editor – after the success of the *Theatrum*, Abram Ortel, known as Ortelius, was lauded for his scholarship, originality and 'singular humaneness'. 'I shall live a worshipper of your name,' wrote one ecstatic contemporary.

The *Theatrum* was handsome to hold and to look through. The first edition contained 69 maps on 53 sheets. These maps were printed from engravings on copper-plate, and the book is often credited with being the first to use only this process throughout its extent, another way in which it imparted the desired sense of cohesion. On the versos of the maps the often quite ample text was placed, the work of the editor himself, a man of prodigious reading as his lists of sources indicate.

Not just in its extent was this atlas so considerable, it was also very tall. In fact, when the book came out in England in 1606, it was declared the tallest seen in the country to date, its trimmed pages measuring 49 × 33cm.

The production and dimensions of the *Theatrum* matched the scope of its subject. If its readers were heirs to a century-long tradition of printing and publishing, they were heirs also of an unprecedented opening-up of the world by their own kind, the inhabitants of Europe. Now the gigantism of European operations the world over, continuous and ongoing, was given a visible, tangible analogue – a book in all probability the costliest of the century, the most expensive to produce, the most expensive to buy.

Awareness of the extraordinary uncovering of the world that had taken place in less than a hundred years and curiosity about its next developments account, beyond doubt, for much of the *Theatrum*'s immediate appeal. Back at the beginning of the century, Columbus, in fact unusually learned in cartography, was still under the impression, when in Caribbean territory, that he was exploring Asia. 'Ten journeys away,' he wrote in 1503 from present-day Guatemala, 'is the river Ganges,' and shortly afterwards he was to describe a district of Cuba as 'border[ing] on Cathay'. For the readers of the *Theatrum* in 1570 these words would have rung almost as quaintly as they do for us now. Many of them would have had dealings with second-generation American colonists; they might even have known that there'd been a printing press in Mexico City since 1539. The first continental map the *Theatrum* offers us is of the Americas: the *Novus Mundus* or New World. But its discovery – and now its scientific mapping – had, in a sense, made the whole world 'new'. Assumptions had been challenged and removed; expectations had been raised and vindicated; intellectual problems had been solved, and new moral and political ones had risen in their stead – thanks to the unremitting enterprises of Portuguese and Spaniards, and now of French, English and Dutch.

The *Theatrum* reminded its readers of what even the biblical and classical pasts had not known and of the unparalleled opportunities of the present. And it pointed towards an even more exciting future. It can be seen as a standard for the advancing European domination of the world that was to last into the twentieth century.

The book was not only first published in Antwerp, it continued to be published there throughout its 'life'. Ortelius himself was an Antwerper, Dutch was his first language, just as it is for Antwerpers today, and his career is indissoluble from his native city.

The place of origin of any significant enterprise can never be accidental. In the case of the *Theatrum* there are especially strong reasons why Antwerp, and nowhere else, should be the city which produced the first atlas. Today its visitors invariably go to the handsome house, in an equally handsome square, that is the Plantin-Moretus Museum. Here lived and worked the sixteenth century's greatest printer/publisher, Christophe Plantin, a Frenchman who made Antwerp his home. He was closely associated with the production of the *Theatrum*, and was not only a good friend of Ortelius, but of Ortelius' own older friend and mentor, Gerard Mercator, the pre-eminent geographer of his age. The association of three men of such calibre with one city – in which two of them made their permanent homes – is evidence enough of the vitality of the intellectual life of the place.

The museum – which contains much pertaining to Ortelius and the *Theatrum*, books, letters, pictures – is for us of the twenty-first century one of humanism's holy places, with its library, fine portraits, refreshing parterred courtyard garden, and superb collection of those instruments of humanism, printing presses, punches, matrices. Yet the *Theatrum* grew, emerged and enjoyed its wide reception during a period of unprecedented agony for the Netherlands, struggling under the yoke of Spain. In the years surrounding the publication of the atlas Antwerp itself was to endure a series of calamities that would bring its Golden Age to a terrible end.

In 1577, seven years after the publication of the *Theatrum*, Ortelius received a letter from his English friend, the sage John Dee: 'I am grieved that your country is so disturbed, nay torn to pieces, that you have hardly any hope of seeing it recover its original greatness and liberty. I advise those who have intercourse with the peaceful Muses, and who possess the excellent monuments of the most noble and useful arts, to seek for themselves and their relatives some temporary place of refuge, against the present raging fury of war.'

No monument of Antwerp's 'most noble and useful arts' is more excellent – or has been more influential – than Ortelius' *Theatrum*. This book considers the unique combination of factors that brought it into being – political, religious, cultural, personal – and also its effect, short-term and long-term, on the public who took it to their minds and hearts. The entire world was the book's subject, but what view of it did the work promote? Mercator congratulated Ortelius on the *Theatrum*'s 'geographical truth'; the Italian Pietro Bizzari believed that as a result of it, all the different countries might eventually lie down together as serenely as they did on its artistically designed pages. What aims for the world did this 'theatre of its countries' have?

Abraham Ortelius *Antwerpianus* – that is the form of his name the editor of the *Theatrum* chose to use. In the sixteenth century a favourite way of honouring a friend was to make a flattering anagram of his name. A French humanist, Nicolas Clément (known as Trellaeus), chopped up ABRAMUS ORTELIUS to make URBIS LAETUS AMOR ('Happy [in his] love for [his] city'). Ortelius (born in Antwerp in 1527, and dying there in 1598) was pleased by this word-play – even though no one knew better than he the difficulties that being an Antwerper could wreak on peace of mind and body, and even though he was twice compelled by events to flee it for a period of time.

CHAPTER TWO

Antwerp in the mid-sixteenth century was the richest city in the world, and still growing in population and wealth. In 1526 (one year before Ortelius' birth) it had had an estimated 55,000 inhabitants; by 1560 they numbered between 85,000 and 100,000. This made it larger by a good margin than any other city in the Netherlands – or for that matter than any other north of Paris. Antwerp, in the province of Brabant, stands on the eastern bank of the Scheldt to which it owes its existence and its success. For this reason it's often known simply as the 'City-on-the-Scheldt'. Everything significant about Antwerp begins with this southernmost of the Great Rivers (the Scheldt, the Waal, the Maas, the Rhine) which have so determined Low Countries history and culture. Even today, their huge estuaries bring a sense of nature's power into one of the world's longest-urbanised landscapes; suddenly the factors behind the commercial, the industrial, the post-industrial become dramatically visible – as low-banked expanses of water open out towards the sea under a vastness of sky.

Three hundred and fifty-five kilometres long, rising in France (as l'Escaut, near St-Quentin in the Artois), the Scheldt is the pre-eminent river of Flanders (western Belgium). From Oudenarde onwards, the High Scheldt (*Boven Schelde*) impresses with its width, particularly after its dramatic eastward turn. It makes many beautiful meanders through wooded countryside rich in tall poplars, and over the centuries has called

Antwerp in Brabant. *This detail from an anonymous painting from 1540, now in the Nationaal Scheepvaartmuseum, Antwerp, gives a good idea of the City-on-the-Scheldt of Ortelius' boyhood and youth.*

forth admiration from painters and poets. The most famous Flemish nationalist poet (who nevertheless wrote in French), Emile Verhaeren (1855–1916) – buried at a commanding spot on the river bank – paid the Scheldt this tribute:

Il n'est qu'un fleuve, un seul,
Qui mêle au déploiement de ses méandres
Mieux que de la grandeur et de la cruauté,
Et celui-là se voue au peuple – et aux cités
Où vit, travaille et se redresse encore, la Flandre!

(There is one, but one river only,
That mingles with display of its meanders
More than mere grandeur and mere force,
A river consecrated to the people and the cities
Where Flanders dwells, works and rises again.)

For a stretch the Scheldt flows due north. Then comes a great bend to the north-east, and it's here on the right bank that the polygon-shaped Brabantine city of Antwerp is situated. The river now, incorporating a lagoon, is wider than at any previous lower point, far too wide for a bridge and substantial left-bank expansion. So it was on the east bank that the huge complex of docks and wharves arose to give Antwerp its international reputation. It owed its growth, and its Golden Age, to the later fifteenth century's 'Great Discoveries'.

The city of Antwerp was the beneficiary first of the extensive Portuguese incursions into Asia following their rounding of Africa in 1487 under Bartholomeu Dias (after his ships sailing south down the African coast had been blown by storms off course), and then of the post-Columbian Spanish colonisation of the New World. In the City-on-the-Scheldt, better than anywhere else, an increasingly productive and technologically accomplished Northern Europe, a Portugal trading in gold, principally from West Africa ('the Gold Coast') and in Indian and East Indies spices, and a Spanish colonial society swollen with wealth and recent property could meet up, doing mutually profitable business.

The Portuguese needed silver to buy from India the spices for which Europe was proving so enthusiastic, and copper to exchange for slaves and ivory from Africa. Both silver and copper came chiefly from Southern Germany, and Antwerp was the port at the most convenient distance from both place of production and place of demand.

This was what first galvanised Antwerp as a commercial centre, but other trades involving other nationalities were also economic stimulants: cloth from England to be 'finished' in Antwerp (the principal means by which the city scored over Bruges, its neighbour and main rival, which had tried to embargo such cloth), Flemish lace, German fustian, South German leather goods, and a whole range of artefacts from Brabant which, from the early fifteenth century onwards, had specialised in such pleasing luxuries as tapestries – all these were sold and bought at the trading-posts of Antwerp.

An average of 2,500 ships a year called at the City-on-the-Scheldt; it handled over 250,000 tonnes of goods. There were many Antwerp merchants who actually owned their own ships. If you walked along the waterfront, you would in no time be hearing spoken Portuguese, Spanish, Dutch, French, English and German – and African and Oriental languages as well. To handle its diversity of craft, Antwerp rapidly transformed itself into the world's most state-of-the-art port. Ships of considerable size could berth without difficulty at ultra-modern quays, efficient new cranes were available, there was even a crane-operators' guild. Beyond the docks stretched a network of small serviceable canals taking boats through the city, with its abundance of warehouses, and so out into the Brabantine countryside – under Antwerp's official jurisdiction and thick with prosperous villages productively engaged in agriculture.

In the wake of so much commercial activity came *money* – money itself as business. With deals of such variety and complexity going on, it was inevitable that bankers would move in on the city – and from an early date they did, mostly from Southern Germany, including, in 1508, the mighty Fuggers, they who in 1520 were to bankroll Netherlands-born Charles V's election as Holy Roman Emperor. As with shipping, so with banking: Antwerp made itself the very pattern of the contemporary; its newly built Bourse or Exchange became almost as potent a symbol of the city as its great sky-piercing church (which we know today as *Onze Lieve Vrouwekathedraal*). Banking and mercantile reforms were established here that were to become common practice everywhere else. It was in Antwerp that the selling of goods by sample acquired proper legal footing; it was from Antwerp (not Florence as generally believed) that double-entry book-keeping was widely adopted.

Sugar-refining was important in city business, as were the trades of silversmiths and goldsmiths. Diamond-cutting, of which Antwerp is still the world centre, was carried on then as now by the Jewish community. Finally – increasing in significance as well as in quantity of enterprises as the century progressed – there was printing. The first press had been established in Antwerp comparatively late, 1481, some time after the more important Italian and German cities and Paris. But within the Netherlands the city soon attained a pre-eminence. Antwerp historian Leon Voet cites that between 1500 and 1540, of the 4,000 books printed in the region, 2,250 emanated from Antwerp; of its 135 printers, 68 were to be found there. For this period we have the names of 271 Antwerp book people, 224 of them printers and publishers, 47 of them booksellers. Put these figures in the context of the city's size, and the outstanding liveliness of all these related activities will be apparent. Among the achievements that gave them their Europe-wide reputation was their production of cartographic works. How could a society so alive with international meetings and negotiations not be interested in maps and information about the various countries that came together so profitably inside its own boundaries? Books on geography, in addition to globes and to maps themselves, were produced and sold in large quantities. The young Ortelius, studying on his own, availed himself of them; they formed the basis of his later library.

The printing business provides an excellent index of Antwerp's cultural health; it shows both its admirable vigour and its outward orientation, and its underlying dilemmas. Antwerp was in a special (some would have said privileged) position, and the very advantages this gave it, the very successes it led to – palpable identity and social cohesion, flourishing trade, enviable fame, over a hundred guilds – were also responsible for the all-too-real threat to its very survival. Survival, that is, on the terms it had come to value above others: as a place of freedom. Freedom (or the feeling of freedom) was a stimulant like no other to productivity and wealth creation. Enterprising and individualistic men – Christophe Plantin would be of their number – settled and set up businesses in the City-on-the-Scheldt because of the appeal of this. The atmosphere was found congenial for both commerce and thought, and printers were soon enterprising and bold enough to take advantage of the seeming intellectual pluralism of the citizenry. Independence of business venture and independence of opinion formed, as they so frequently do, an extremely close but ultimately uneasy partnership. By the time Ortelius' career was properly underway, the earlier years of the century could be looked back on as an era regrettably past.

Something of the remarkable character of Golden Age Antwerp can be seen in two men who held the important civic post of *griffier* (town recorder): Pieter Gillis (1486–1533) and Cornelius (Scribonius) Grapheus (1482–1558).

Pieter Gillis (Petrus Aegidius or Peter Giles in English) makes key appearances in one of the most influential books of the century, written by a friend of his, indeed of both men: Thomas More's *Utopia*, printed in Latin in December 1516, in the Low Countries' then greatest centre of learning, Leuven (Louvain), under the supervision of Desiderius Erasmus (1466–1536), mutual friend of all three of them. It is Pieter whom More sees talking to 'a man well stricken in age, with a black sun-burned face, a long beard, and a cloak cast homely about his shoulders, whom, by his favour and apparel, forthwith I judged to be a mariner'. This is Raphael Hythloday who, after five years of getting to know the island country of Utopia, is an expert on its mores. In the 1518 Basel edition of *Utopia* Ambrosius Holbein (brother of the more famous Hans) supplied a woodcut which charmingly portrays Hythloday, More and Gillis sitting on benches in an urban arboretum engaged in discourse, that essential to any vital civilisation.

Gillis, the dedicatee of More's work, is presented to us as the kind of man the City-on-the-Scheldt not just admired but actually produced:

I, in the meantime (for so my business lay), went straight thence to Antwerp. Whilst I was there abiding ... did visit me one Peter Giles, a citizen of Antwerp; a man there in his country of honest reputation, and also preferred to high promotions, worthy truly of the highest. For it is hard to say whether the young man be in learning or in honesty more excellent. For he is both of wonderful virtuous conditions, and also singularly well-learned, and towards all sorts of people exceeding gentle; but towards his friends so kind-hearted, so loving, so faithful, so trusty, and of so earnest affection, that it were very hard in any

Ambrosius Holbein's frontispiece to the 1518 edition of Utopia. *Later it was felt appropriate as an Antwerper and a humanist that Ortelius should include a map of* Utopia *in the* Parergon. *After all, it was in Antwerp that More, according to his book, encountered Utopia's discoverer, Raphael Hythloday. However, Ortelius somewhat resented the request and his own compliance with it, and felt this map of 'nowhere' was not one of his best.*

place to find a man that with him in all points of friendship may be compared. No man can be more lowly or courteous. No man useth less simulation or dissimulation; in no man is more prudent simplicity. Besides this, he is in his talk and communication so merry and pleasant, yea and that without harm, that, through his gentle entertainment and his sweet and delectable communication, in me was greatly abated and diminished the fervent desire that I had to see my native country, my wife and my children ...

The balanced combination of private virtue and public service and standing was dear to the Antwerper view of things, and was to go on being so. And we shall see that Ortelius, too, was to be praised for Gillis' attributes of gentleness, sociability, good-hearted merriment, assiduous maintenance of friendship, learning and courtesy. He was to be seen as truly such a man's successor.

Cornelius (Scribonius) Grapheus (Cornelis de Schrijver), the other Antwerp *griffier*, also features in the pages of More's book, supplying a verse envoy to the reader:

Wilt thou know what wonders strange be in the land that late was found?
Wilt thou learn thy life to lead by divers ways that godly be?
Wilt thou of virtue and of vice understand the very ground?
Wilt thou see this wretched world, how full it is of vanity?
Then read and mark and bear in mind for thy behoof, as thou may best,
All things that in this present work, that worthy clerk Sir Thomas More,
With wit divine full learnedly unto the world hath plain expressed,
In whom London well glory may, for wisdom and for godly lore.

(1556 translation by Ralph Robinson)

Grapheus was no less exemplary an individual than Gillis – archaeologist, philologist, poet, painter, musician, and close in friendship and spirit to Erasmus. His son, Alexander, asked his intimate friend, Ortelius, to compose a memorial to his father, and this is what he came up with: 'For his loyalty, his erudition, and other qualities of his soul and body, thanks to which he made himself loved by everybody during his life, I, Abraham Ortelius, who when young loved him greatly when he was old, go on revering him now he is dead.'

It's tempting, of course, to trace aspects of Utopia as presented for our admiration, and maybe our emulation, to the Antwerp of Gillis and Grapheus. Perhaps it's safer merely to say that there were undoubted Utopian constituents in the intellectual life of the city. While it would in truth be hard to find in Antwerp that 'contempt for money' which More extols, or all that much interest in shared property or enforced fiscal parity, in the matter of tolerance (approval) of religious diversity – to which More devotes his most impassioned pages (by no means consistent with his own actions when in a position of power) – we could well find that Antwerp had been a model.

> For this is one of the ancientest laws among them, that no man shall be blamed for reasoning in the maintenance of his own religion. For King Utopus, even at the first beginning hearing that the inhabitants of the land were before his coming thither at continual dissension and strife among themselves for their religions ... made a decree that it should be lawful for every man to favour and follow what religion he would, and that he might do the best he could to bring others to his opinion, so that he did it peaceably, gently, quietly and soberly, without hasty and contentious rebuking and inveighing against other. If he could not by faith and gentle speech induce them unto his opinion, yet he should use no kind of violence, and refrain from displeasant and seditious words.

Religious tolerance – if any one subject dominated the lives of Ortelius and his circle, it was this, and the *Theatrum* is, among other things, an expression of its maker's ardent belief in its importance. How else could countries exist in the peaceful juxtaposition that we find on the printed page?

We're fortunate in having pictures of Antwerp throughout the sixteenth century. Portraiture of a city on any regular basis begins when it's well-known, enterprising and moneyed enough to demand it: the kinship here to portraits of people is clear enough. Royalty, nobility, major clerics, the richest and most powerful burghers – they are the usual commissioners of pictures of themselves, or, on account of their importance, the recipients of requests for sittings. Antwerp, by the second decade of the century, wanted and expected to be looked at, to be presented to the outside world, and to itself, from whatever angle would best show off its peculiar merits and outstanding features. And it had enough money to secure engravings and paintings which did precisely this, not omitting all its latest developments and improvements – its super-modern defence system, for instance, replacing medieval walls. Such was the relation of many artists to their native city (or city of long-term residence) that their depictions of it can be seen as a species of *self*-portraiture. But they also displayed that geographical awareness so strong among Antwerpers. The city as disseminating centre of map- and atlas-production is inseparable from the confident ordainer of pictures of itself.

If Antwerp's very existence derives from its position on the right bank of the Scheldt, then it's only logical that these city-portraits would tend to be done from the river's opposite, left bank, mostly from an elevation above it. From here Antwerp could reveal itself most amply, presiding over the all-important docks and ships. City portraitists were expected, just like those whose subjects were human beings, to produce an artefact *gheconterfeyt naer 't leven*, 'counterfeited from life'. Yet problems presented themselves, and were stubborn – how to choose the view of Antwerp most representative of the place's unique quality while including all its salient features. From any one chosen angle these might be far from equally apparent. On the contrary, they might crowd each other out. In a real sense the decisions taken were close kin to a cartographer's: how to achieve inclusiveness with a justice based on objective and accurate knowledge of a place.

What all sixteenth-century *vedute* (views) of Antwerp emphasise is twofold: the city's domination by its lofty cathedral and its determining relation to its busy river. These add up to the most important truth about the place. Today, if you leave the 'roadstead' (river front) and its wharves, descend into the long white-tiled tunnel under the Scheldt, and then ascend on to the raggedly developed west bank, you can have the satisfaction of testing the authenticity of such *vedute* as Melchisedek van Hooren's three of 1557, now to be seen, arranged one on top of the other, in the city's Stedelijk Prentenkabinet. Above everything else towers *Onze Lieve Vrouwekathedraal*. Thomas More's *Utopia* narrator attended 'divine service' here, in 'Our Lady's Church' which he praised as 'the fairest, the most gorgeous and curious church of building in all the city, and also most frequented of people'. Its four-tiered tapering tower, 123 metres in height, was ready by 1518, a mere two years after More had written his encomium

Three views of Antwerp by Melchisedek van Hooren, 1557. Viewed together, they convey the impressiveness of mid-century Antwerp – rich, large, enterprising – and its strong sense of itself.

to it, to stand as the tallest in Europe, the culminating glory of an ambitious edifice begun as far back as 1352.

But it's not only from the left bank of the Scheldt that the cathedral appears so tremendous. From every street in central Antwerp its skyward soaring impresses, causing even the most seasoned tourists to crane necks in wonder and admiration. Walk about in the inner city – through those handsome squares, the Grote Markt, Handschoenmarkt and Groenplaats, civic affluence and self-esteem expressed in all the fine mansions with their gilded rooftop statues and crow-stepped gables; walk round the *artisanat* quarter of Lombardvest and the Vrijdagmarkt or that seedy area of bars and brothels that edges the high burgher fulcrum with surprising intimacy – and you will be conscious all the time of the sheer *might* of the cathedral. In certain weathers, you have the feeling that its tower is 'doing battle' with the clouds – exactly what, centuries later, Spanish poet Federico García Lorca was to observe of New York skyscrapers. In his *Theatrum*, under the heading of Brabant, Ortelius wrote that Antwerp was 'one of the strongest cities in the world, being much beautified by the [spire] of St Mary's (OLV) built an incredible height of white marble'.

But, as in these sixteenth-century *vedute*, the cathedral has to be taken in context with the river if we want to arrive at a realistic and complete picture of the place. The height of the one mustn't be allowed to reduce the width of the other. The Scheldt created *Onze Lieve Vrouwekathedraal*, in that without the economic strength brought by the river and its trade, the community wouldn't have had the riches to create a church so ambitious. During the first two-thirds of Plantin and Ortelius' century, the quays would have been the most likely place in the whole world to meet, as cathedral-reverencing Thomas More did, thanks to Pieter Gillis, a man who 'can tell you of so many strange and unknown peoples and countries', who 'hath sailed indeed, not as the mariner Palinurus, but as the expert and prudent prince Ulysses'. The spirit of Ulysses is constantly present in the great productions that Antwerp has bequeathed posterity. It gave back to the world that came to its waterfront a tribute to its varieties and unity, a representation of these that amounts to a sequence of portraits, and which – matching the great cathedral itself – had no previous equal in scale or intention: Ortelius' *Theatrum* of 1570, which appropriately honours Ulysses in a wholly new and ground-breaking genre, to be imitated everywhere ever since.

CHAPTER THREE

Ortelius was born Abram Ortel on 4 April 1527. His father was Leonard Ortel, a merchant with a good reputation for dealing in antiquities, his mother Anne Harrewayers, who was to assume responsibilities for her husband's business after his premature death. Abram's father's father had left his native German city of Augsburg because of what he'd heard about Antwerp and the opportunities there. He made a wise choice; he did well, as a pharmacist. To express his gratitude he left the city after his death a religious monument, a cross to be placed beside the spot where its criminals were executed. Many a condemned Antwerper had as part of his last sight of this world the statues positioned at the foot of this: the Virgin Mary, John the 'beloved disciple' and, on either side of the cross itself, the two thieves crucified together with Jesus. The Ortels were well-respected in the city, this shrine confirming and preserving the regard.

Posterity has remembered Abram's father for his learning (it was hard, people said, to separate him from his books) and for his religious devotion; he was much given to 'serious meditation on heavenly matters'. Both Leonard and Anne, in common with other members of the family, were Protestant sympathisers. This did not make them particularly unusual among their fellow Antwerpers. As far back as 1518 Erasmus had written to England's Thomas Wolsey about the easy availability in the city of

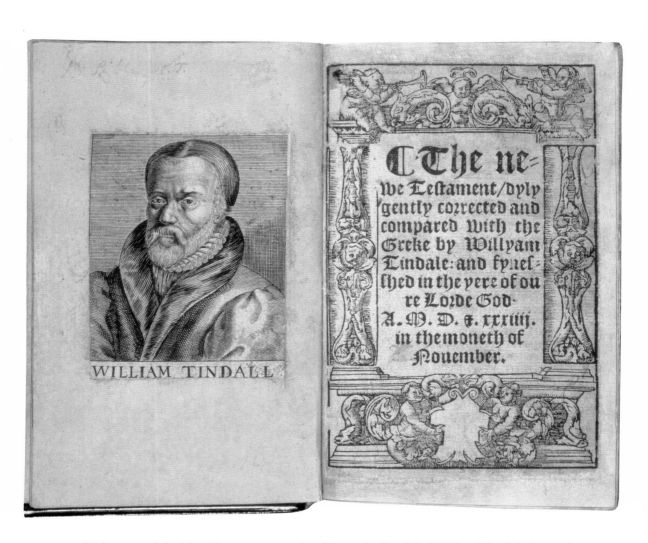

Title pages of the New Testament, translated from the Greek by William Tyndale (revised version), published in Antwerp in November 1534, an enterprise with which Ortelius' father and his cousin were closely involved. The work was admired by Anne Boleyn.

printed copies of Luther's works, and by 1521 the *griffier* Cornelius Grapheus was swapping Lutheran writings with the great painter and proselytising Protestant convert, Albrecht Dürer (one of the artists to mean most to Ortelius himself). Two years later the city saw the publication of the Dutch translation of Luther's *New Testament*, this considerably widening its appeal. Nor were Antwerp's ever-enterprising printers content to leave things there; they produced vanguard works in English: William Tyndale's rendering of the first six books of the Old Testament, and, in 1536, Miles Coverdale's first complete English Bible, works as yet too radical for printing in England itself. With the preparation and financing of the Coverdale translation, a real historical landmark, Leonard Ortel and his brother-in-law, Jacob van Meteren (the second husband of his sister, Odile), were closely engaged. But no matter how wide citizens' sympathy for such activities, this involvement of theirs couldn't be other than risk-running. Antwerp, as a formidable wealth-creator on which Emperor Charles V relied greatly, had been permitted a surprising amount of autonomy, but this could never be taken for granted, nor were Leonard and Jacob so innocent that they did so. The ultimate authority over the whole cosmopolitan and diverse city was the Hapsburg Emperor who ruled (essentially) from Spain: Charles V, for whom Lutheranism – and, for that matter, all other forms of dissent from the established church – were seditious.

Charles had a Netherlander father (Philip the Fair), was Netherlands-born and Netherlands-raised, with Dutch as his first language. He'd been proclaimed ruler of the Hapsburg Netherlands when only fifteen years of age (in 1515), with a grand ceremonious tour afterwards of his territories both north and south of the Great Rivers. Antwerp even had a booklet specially printed for him for this occasion, the *Loeflicken Nyeuwen Sanck* (*New Song of Praise*) including, inter-estingly, a city-map alongside the salutary ode and prayer. Then in 1516 the youth received news of the death of his maternal grandfather, Ferdinand, and in 1517 he left the Low Countries for Spain, leaving his aunt Margaret of Austria as regent. Now he embarked on his successful programme of turning himself into a Spaniard, one who identified with Spanish interests above all others. To complete the end of any intimate relationship to the Netherlands, in 1519 Charles' paternal grandfather, Maximilian, died, and he inherited the German crown as well, being

The Charles V of Titian's great portrait of 1533 would recently have added Italy to his vast dominions (crowned by the Pope in Bologna in 1530) and have just staved off an attack on his eastern flanks by the Ottomans (at Vienna in 1532). Isn't it therefore legitimate to see strain and a longing for another kind of life in the face so individually rendered and, too, a need for affectionate consolation offered him here by his dog?

elected the very next year, with help from the powerful Fugger family, Holy Roman Emperor.

Charles' antagonism to Protestantism dated from Luther's Theses of 1517. In July of 1521 Charles was personally present in Antwerp for the burning of some four hundred books of Lutheran tendency; two further book burnings took place in 1522. Imperial decrees – the hated *placards* or *plakaten* – were pronounced which made heresy a capital offence. Anabaptists tended to be the principal victims here. Persecution was by no means consistent, in fact it was often sporadic – though this didn't necessarily make the social effect of the cruel punishments any the less. Charles had his own reasons for wanting Antwerp amenably disposed, and he censured his aunt Margaret for her high-handed way of dealing with Netherlanders, but nonetheless there could never be any doubting his position as far as those who challenged Catholicism. The question was only how, and to what degree, he was going to manifest his disapproval.

Look at Titian's great 1533 portrait of Charles, now appropriately in the Prado, Madrid, and done after he'd spent almost two years in the Low Countries trying to come to terms with this troublesome part of his huge empire. We see a man at once burdened and determined, thoughtful, lonely, the set of the protruding Hapsburg jaw somehow acknowledging the insolubility of his problems. The gravity of his predicament is wonderfully emphasised by the imploring expression Titian has given to his dog. The dog's head is raised to his master who's holding, almost abstractedly, his somewhat too loose collar. It's hard not see the animal as an analogue of the Netherlands, prepared to be loyal but anxious on its own account, and – though there is no doubt who owns whom – slackly grasped, and with the capacity of breaking free.

However fitful punishment for heretical activities might be, its prospect inevitably inspired fear. In the wake of their involvement with Miles Coverdale's English Bible, Leonard Ortel and Jacob van Meteren judged it best to leave the southern Netherlands for England for a while. In their absence Leonard's house was searched by officers of Charles' Inquisition. Their brief was to look for and seize banned heretical books. Abram saw them enter and hunt about; he was only eight years old.

The episode affected its small boy witness profoundly. It taught him lessons he retained all his life. First, that printed matter could be dangerous as well as instructive and illuminating, indeed often dangerous *because* so instructive and illuminating. He learned that ideas about the meaning of life, about the relationship of human beings to their Creator, could, if not confined to one's self and the ear of God, enmesh one in perilous confusions of loyalties. You couldn't be sure of safety in your own community, or even in your own home. Someone of strongly spiritual temperament who unfailingly saw life in religious terms, Abram Ortelius moved through the years with a highly developed vein of caution – as others were (not always too kindly) to observe. Authority, he knew, could not be trusted; it couldn't be disregarded either. It was quite simply too powerful. Good work and harmonious relationships are hard to sustain when your own person is under threat. So why not safeguard it? The eruption into his home by the Inquisition in 1535 explains a great deal about his later behaviour. What a tremendous relief when the officers had gone away, and the house could be itself again, a familiar tranquil centre of activity!

In 1539 Leonard Ortel, now back in Flanders, died at only thirty-nine years of age. He left behind him not only a wife and son, but two daughters: Anne, to be both her mother's and her brother's devoted companion, and Elizabeth, eventually with her husband, Jacob Cool, and children, to make her home in England. Leonard had not built up his antiquities business in vain; after his death first his wife, then his son, ran it with great efficiency, and both daughters were involved with the (related) map trade.

By the time of Leonard's death Abram's uncle Jacob van Meteren had also returned home. The two men's experience of England communicated itself early to Abram; throughout his life he was to think highly of the country and to have significant relationships there. His sister and brother-in-law's children actually became English; indeed his beloved nephew and heir, Jacob Cool (Jacobus Colius) junior (later officially and appropriately known as 'Ortelianus'), was to be barred from coming to Antwerp to take up his inheritance (hence the presence of so much Ortelius material in England). Two cousins, of the greatest possible importance to Ortelius' life story – Jacob van Meteren's son, Emmanuel (1535–1612), to be for many years Netherlands consul in London, and the humanist, historian and diplomat, Daniel Rogers (1538–1590), who later had himself naturalised – can in effect be thought of as English. During the crisis in Antwerp in 1576 known as the 'Spanish Fury', Ortelius fled the southern Netherlands for refuge in London. The role England plays in his *oeuvre* generally, and in the *Theatrum* particularly, is a strong one, and England for its part was

Tyndale (born 1494) was seized in Antwerp, where he had been active as a biblical scholar, and on 6 October 1536 was put to death by strangling and burning. This illustration of the ghastly event is a woodcut by Fiford Castle included by John Foxe in his 'Book of Martyrs' of 1563.

intellectually receptive of his work. In fact the comparative delay in an English edition of the *Theatrum* can be attributed to the great success of the Latin edition there, with Sir William Cecil (later Lord Burghley), John Dee and Richard Hakluyt among its most articulate admirers.

Their religious inclinations being what they were, Leonard Ortel and Jacob van Meteren had found themselves in England at a particularly propitious time – and it could be said that, with the stay there of these two kinsmen, England itself enters the history of the first atlas, and of atlases generally. In 1533 Henry VIII's Act of Appeals curtailed Rome's ecclesiastical authority; his Act of Supremacy of the following year went further still by abolishing papal jurisdiction and establishing the monarch as supreme head of the Church of England. England's declaration of independence was appealingly consonant with its geographical apartness from mainland Europe. Here was real freedom from imposed foreign power, both papal or imperial, and appreciation of this was clearly stimulating the English into interest in their own country and its individualities, its topography, its natural resources, its long many-stranded past with its legacy of traditions and lore. Ortelius, a passionate historicist from youth onwards, was to have close fruitful contact with many an antiquarian and scholar from England including Richard Mulcaster and William Camden, and the Welshman Humphrey Lhuyd.

The dark side of Henry VIII's new 'Erastian' English state showed in the very year (1535) of the two brothers-in-law's sojourn, in the executions of John Fisher and Thomas More. We can find in this last event a tragic/ironic link to the City-on-the-Scheldt. The great humanist celebrant of the virtues of Antwerp had been put to death for sticking by his beliefs; at the same time he himself had not shown that pluralism he'd praised when there. Perhaps, had they known them, Abram's father and uncle should have pondered lines by Henry VIII's late 'poet laureate', John Skelton:

Though ye suppose all jeopardies are passed
And all is done that ye lookéd for before,
Ware yet, I warn you, of Fortune's double cast,
For one false point she is wont to keep in store,
And under the skin oft festeréd is the sore;
That when ye think all danger for to pass
Ware of the lizard lieth lurking in the grass.

The moral climate into which Ortelius was born. This anonymous pictorial allegory from c.1520 shows a run-down house (the Church) under siege from Protestants and reformers while Pope and bishops try to escape up the roof.

After Leonard's death it was his uncle, Jacob van Meteren, who assumed responsibility for Abram's education. At first this meant exchanging private studies for those conducted by schoolmasters not always congenial to the clever independent boy. But before long he'd adapted himself well enough. Under Jacob van Meteren's guidance Abram's education concentrated on Latin, Greek (in which his father had already given him instruction) and mathematics. Abram took great delight in the 'mathematical sciences', which had a wider, more inclusive meaning then than for later generations. He was a serious boy and he hated above everything else to be parted from his books, a trait obviously inherited from his father and an aversion which remained with him all his life, to be commented on in his late maturity as the one thing which could disturb his otherwise equable temperament. An early deep affection of Abram's was for Emmanuel van Meteren. With this younger cousin he spent much time; it was a friendship the strength of which never diminished, and after Emmanuel's move to England in 1562, it was sustained by regular letter-writing in a warm, colloquial Dutch. There was the most regular contact between Emmanuel's household and Ortelius' (his mother lived to be extremely old, and his sister survived him by two years). There seems to have been nothing of rivalry between the two of them; Emmanuel's father, we are told, never distinguished in affection between the two cousins. Nevertheless, there were ways in which Emmanuel received preferential treatment, and it says a great deal about the natures of both men that this never interfered with their harmonious and mutually giving relationship.

Frans Sweerts of Antwerp, Ortelius' first biographer, wrote of him: 'From his early childhood on, he was of singular promise, great capabilities, and devoid of any conceit ... no vain pleasure, or trifles, or other pastimes (which commonly beset young people) could ever divert him from his other purpose, or alienate his mind from books.' He seems to have been not only industrious and ardent for learning but gentle and sweet-natured, these qualities strengthened no doubt by appreciation of the sufferings his widowed mother had been through; also, one assumes, by his awareness, as an intelligent expanding mind, of the underlying precariousness of both Antwerp's seemingly stable situation and his own family's.

He mustn't appear too austere, however. In portraits of the older Ortelius the conspicuously high-domed cerebral forehead of the writer and cartographer is offset by the sensitive mouth (between moustache and beard) and the bright, kindly, inquisitive eyes. He liked jokes and good humour, it's said, though shunning coarseness or profanity. In other words, he enjoyed the same kind of 'merriment' that More had found in Pieter Gillis. More than anything, from young manhood onwards he exhibited a talent for friendship that amounts to genius. Few anywhere at any time can have known on terms of comparable affection and intimacy so many, variously gifted, interesting (indeed outstanding) individuals. To each friend he himself clearly meant something quite special. As a record of this there's the *Album amicorum* which he started in 1561. In this, following the custom of the times, friends were invited to contribute lines, poems, or even drawings, often taking the form of tributes to the album's owner. Ortelius received praises of a fulsome but patently sincere nature, over and over again. But his personal generosities live on also in his correspondence – both the letters he wrote and the letters he received, later collected by his nephew. They show him knowledgeable about the doings, thoughts and feelings of the many people in his life, almost all of whom were to stress his personal kindness, his capacity for putting himself out on others' behalf.

He was convivial as well as intimate, both in his own home and in other men's, and, though this quality may have grown with age, reputation and wealth (and even expanded to include some attractive touches of the colourful), it's most unlikely that his remarkable capacity for being friendly didn't distinguish him in boyhood and youth also. As a young man, he had an attractive appearance too – tall, slender and fair, with blond hair and a blond beard; his keen eyes were grey.

He always had a lively awareness of money, the circumstances of his young manhood necessitating this – though he was anxious to declare its ultimate unimportance. Exactness over prices and expenditure came naturally to him, a feature, one surmises from references in letters, of Antwerp society, and one that stood him in excellent stead for the business career he would begin at (even for then) a notably early age.

Abram was a voracious, dedicated and retentive reader, and, starting young, a collector of great integrity, and, as will be clear, of influence and repute. A collection was in itself a medium of communication; wisely and imaginatively arranged, it could provide a comprehensive and personal window on to a whole subject, from history, natural history, or the human arts. Ortelius collected prints, paintings, inscriptions and other antiquities, coins – and books. His youthful reading was very much that of the humanist-in-the-making; that is, it reflected the humanists' conviction, supremely expressed in the life and work of Erasmus, that the wisdom of classical Greece and Rome and the teachings of Christianity constituted, when examined, a seamless fabric. '*Saint* Socrates!' Erasmus had famously exclaimed – to emphasise the unbroken line that stretched from Greek philosophers to the Church Fathers. Abram's passion for the classical world (the main testimony to which is that wonderful supplement he provided for the 1579 *Theatrum*, the historical maps of the *Parergon*) began early. It fired his ardent numismatic activities; the devices on the coins represented for him the successive shifts in power and thought within the Roman Empire. It led him too to close looks at surviving ancient monuments, 'reading' them for what they had to say about the civilisation behind them. But his serious antiquarianism was part of a wider curiosity; Abram never passed by an opportunity of reading about contemporary explorations of land and sea. Indeed travel writing of all kinds and provenance absorbed him, and we can find in the text he wrote to accompany the maps of the *Theatrum* and the *Parergon* – and for that matter in his not inconsiderable other publications – rich and ample evidence of his years-long intimacy with Herodotus (c.480–425BC) and Strabo (c.63BC–AD24), with Marco Polo (1254–1324) and Sir John Mandeville (c.1322–1372).

But while all these writers vividly presented the interestingness of our world (and even after the passing of centuries, readers were extremely reluctant to consign their appealing contents to the domain of fantasy: hence the long-persistent belief in Prester John's great Christian kingdom or in the golden cities of Cathay), they were put quite into the shade by accounts by modern travellers of what was being currently found or probed. Here were ungainsayable slices of reality, often unexpected and with obstinate identities, challenging not just earlier geographical suppositions but ideas about human nature – and about Creation itself.

The pace of the opening-up of the world from the late fifteenth century on was unprecedented, extraordinary and felt to be so. Discovery begat discovery (not least out of fear of rivalry and usurpation) – and did so in three directions from Europe: west (the Americas); south (Africa); and east (Arabia, India, the East Indies, though these last were now approached from the south as a consequence of that 1487 rounding of the Cape by Bartholomeu Dias).

A good indication of this pace – and of the public's reception of it – comes from comparing the Behaim globe of 1492 – constructed the very year that Columbus set out westwards in search of Cathay, Japan and the Indies and came to the islands of the Caribbean – and three productions of the following decade: Giovanni Contarini's world map of 1506, and Martin Waldseemüller's world map and globe of 1507. The intellectual backgrounds and attitudes of all three men were not dissimilar, and Martin Behaim (c.1459–1507) and Martin Waldseemüller (1475–1522), immersed in Ptolemy, were both men of international connections nurtured in geographically sophisticated southern Germany. Behaim's globe shows the three-continent world of second-century Ptolemy, though, intimately connected with Portugal as the maker was, it is also palpably the beneficiary of Dias' tremendous discovery. Behaim's Africa does not seal off the Indian Ocean as Ptolemy's does but ends above a generous tract of sea that links the Indian and Atlantic Oceans. To the west of the great landmass of the three joined continents an Atlantic Ocean stretches for approximately a third of the globe's surface area – eventually to encounter China. Fourteen/fifteen years later, and what a different picture!

While his basic geographical sense of the world is essentially Behaim's (i.e. Ptolemaic), Giovanni Contarini not only honours Columbus' discoveries but is able to correct his errors of assumption and deduction. He gives us the 'Columbian' islands of Cuba, Hispaniola and the Leewards, with, to the south of them, a large but vague 'continent' which he calls 'Terra Crucis', and places them all about 3,000 miles *east* of the China coast of which they were at first assumed to be a part. Admittedly Contarini does still think Newfoundland is linked to China; its wooded coasts had been 'newly found' by two sets of voyagers, those under Cabot and those (whom Contarini was informed about) under two Portuguese brothers, Gaspar and Miguel Corte-Real. But by situating this 'land' on a huge eastward sweep of 'China', he puts it in a longitudinal relationship to the Leewards not so very far off the mark (the Leewards lie slightly to the west of Longitude 60, Newfoundland to the east of it). We of today can begin to feel at home here. And then we move on to Waldseemüller.

It's only a year later, but with this map we confront a world recognisably our own. From its handsome upper border the two figures of Ptolemy and

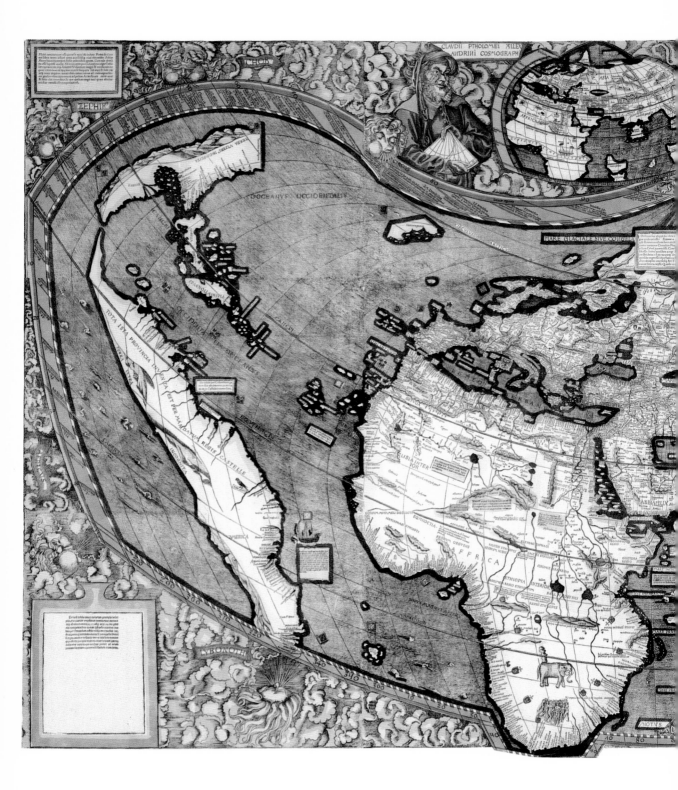

Amerigo Vespucci, each poised before one hemisphere of the Earth, are proudly on display, symbolising what has happened to the planet so recently, its passive transmogrification in the human consciousness. Ptolemy's half is of course the eastern 'Old World', Vespucci's the western 'New World'; Waldseemüller – who had read Columbus' Florentine friend Vespucci with attention and admiration, had corresponded with him and probably met him – had decided that the latter should be named in honour of him, the first man to recognise its continental independence: *America*. And there it is, magnificent in its emptiness in contrast to the busily named lands of the map's centre and on the right – and 90 degrees of longitude distant from China to boot. Its southern part (to knowledge of which Portuguese voyages kept secret from Spain may have contributed) is far bigger than its sliver-like northern (joined to it in the miniature map in the upper border, separated – very narrowly – in the map proper) and endowed with a mountainous western coast. We know at once today what it is that we are looking at; it is the particular not the overall picture that is the problem.

In 1522, five years before Ortelius' birth, the first ever circumnavigation of the world, by Magellan's ship, *Victoria*, was completed. And during the first twenty years of Abram's life, Brazil was explored and colonised, the Spanish crossed the Andes and came to the Inca cities, Jacques Cartier made three voyages to Canada which he claimed for France, the Amazon was traced to its source, Lima, Valparaíso, Santiago and Bogotá were founded, Chile was explored beyond the Atacama desert, mercury was discovered in Peru and silver in Potosí (now in Bolivia) – there was no economic event in those decades more significant than this – and up in the north de Soto followed the Arkansas river. New Guinea was reached; the first accurate map of the Pacific was produced (by Diego Ribera in 1529) and legal definition of the line between Spanish and Portuguese in that

Previous page:

No world map is more historically significant than Martin Waldseemüller's of 1507. Appropriately, the figures of Ptolemy (on the left) and Amerigo Vespucci (on the right) preside not only over the smaller representations of the two hemispheres (the eastern and the western respectively) but over the whole richly delineated and lettered Earth, in which America is named for the first time, and the 'new' continent has recognisable accuracies, such as a mountainous coast of what is now California. Note, however, the narrow strait separating North and South America.

ocean was drawn up; Portuguese sailors and merchants were compelled to go ashore in Japan in 1542. Geography can seem to us the study of a constant, a given; not so for Ortelius and his contemporaries. Far from it. Every year knowledge of the world changed, often dramatically, every year challenging facts surfaced, the fruits of further and bolder contemporary endeavours. The attentive intellect had to fit them into the previously received scheme of things as best it could. This was a further motive for giving oneself to the making and issuing of maps.

Abram never studied cartography or geography academically. Presumably there wasn't enough money for university. It's the case that while Jacob van Meteren treated Abram and his own boy equally as regards affection and attention, Emmanuel was able to study at the prestigious institutions of Tournai and Duffel, while Abram was set to an apprenticeship to an engraver and to hand-work on maps. Not that Emmanuel's earlier career lacked problems. Both youths felt thrust into commercial life with its exacting and sometimes tedious demands when their natural inclinations were for different, more scholarly courses.

But anyway only two universities in the whole of Europe offered cartography as a subject in its own right, Ingolstadt in south Germany and Leuven (Louvain) in the southern Netherlands. In both cases the study had to be contained within the mathematics department (which also, following the practice of the University of Paris, took in astronomy and astrology). In recognition of the insecure place of this comparatively new discipline, the mathematics professors at Ingolstadt and Leuven, respectively Peter Apian (Petrus Apianus 1495–1552) and Regnier Gemma Frisius (1508–1555), men of enormous reputations (when Apian was appointed professor in 1527 it was at a salary six times higher than his predecessor's), wrote books for readers outside academic institutions to encourage them to pursue work on their own. In his biographical essay Frans Sweerts wrote that Abram 'studied and practised [mathematics] without an instructor or teacher, attaining only by his own pains and industry, to the great admiration of others, even to the understanding of the great and deepest mysteries of the same'. Absolutely essential to his self-arranged higher education would have been these books of Apian and Gemma Frisius: Apian's *Cosmographicus liber* (*Cosmographical book*) (first edition 1524), and Gemma Frisius' *De principiis astronomiae et cosmographiae* (*Of the principle of astronomy and cosmography)* (1530) and *Libellus de locorum describendorum ratione (Volume of places described according to a system)* (1533), both actually published in Antwerp itself, more and more *the* European centre for geographical publications, maps included.

Both Apian and Frisius were dedicated scholars of the classical 'father' of geography, Ptolemy, whom Abram proceeded to study also. He himself most probably read Ptolemy in the 1540 edition of Sebastian Münster published in Basel, the *Geographia universalis vetus et nova (Universal geography old and new)*. This added to Ptolemy's presentation of the entire known world, or *oikoumene*, some new maps that caught up with the land and sea discoveries of more recent times. Like many another, the young Abram would have been impressed by the order Ptolemy brought to the complexity of the physical world (which he knew to be spherical) and to the problems posed by its representation on a flat surface. Many of the most vital means for this, which he was himself later to employ in the *Theatrum*, he found – if sometimes in less developed form – in Ptolemy's *Geographia*: lines of latitude and a meridian (longitude), a method of projection, coherent scales, the practice of following a general all-embracing map, that of the *oikoumene*, with a logically arranged break-up into its various parts, a north 'orientation' and a system of co-ordinates. He was himself later to praise all these things in Ptolemy's work.

Peter Apian's *Cosmographicus liber (Cosmographical book)* – reissued by Gemma Frisius in 1529 – was invaluable because it explained basic astronomical and geographical concepts. Readers were shown how to find latitude and longitude, and how to convert the differences between the co-ordinates into reasonably accurate distances. It guided them into the drawing of maps with instruments, and editions of the *liber* would even include *volvelles*, movable appliances made of paper, between their pages. Apian's grounding in Ptolemy was not only responsible for his writing his book in the first place but for his making a significant world map that at once honoured Ptolemy's picture of the *oikoumene* and rectified it. It's a cordiform (heart-shaped) map using Ptolemaic parallels (lines of latitude) and meridians but extending them to the poles, and including (as Ptolemy didn't and couldn't!), if distortedly and elongatedly, the Americas.

Gemma Frisius – as his name tells us – was Frisian, born in Dokkum, Friesland, the northernmost Netherlands province (and home to the language with the closest kin to English). He was educated, however, specialising in medicine, in Leuven where he went on to hold a chair combining medicine with mathematics. Frisius therefore, by origin and experience, was very much a Netherlander, suggesting to his followers that theirs was a culture with the capacity to make a unique contribution to geography and cartography, equalling that of Italians and Germans. Abram would have known about one permanent contribution Gemma Frisius made to practical map-making, for it was pioneered in Antwerp itself: the triangulation method of distance calculation which he arrived at by using the city's lofty ecclesiastical church tower as his first point of reference.

From his early adolescence Abram was himself involved in the practicalities of map-making, if of a less cerebrally taxing nature than Gemma's mathematical experiments. He was engaged in map-colouring, along with his sisters, Elizabeth and Anne, initially under their mother's guidance (she was also carrying on her husband's antiquities business). This work was often assigned to the young, but as the whole map business proliferated, so colouring itself became increasingly professionalised. It could be done 'in house' in the various map-shops, or by specialist practitioners; Anne, Ortelius' sister, was later to undertake colouring for the *Theatrum* and its successors.

Many of the maps on which Abram and his sisters were occupied – printed sheets or, more often, several sheets joined together – would have been glued on to cloth (usually linen) which was then stretched over a wooden frame. The finished article could then be hung up. In a highly map-conscious society like that of the Netherlands (both northern and southern), maps continued for a long time to be the favourite form of wall decoration, almost *de rigueur* in fact for bourgeois households, testifying to their prosperity, to their educational and intellectual levels and aspirations. The hall of Ortelius' own house, when he himself was a famous man, well-off and gregarious, was lavishly covered in maps; almost a century later Vermeer presented the importance of similar hangings for the Dutch people who were his subjects. This fondness for wall-maps positively increased the demand for them in book form, and later for the atlas itself. Ortelius says as much in his own preface to the 1570 *Theatrum* – which as a vehicle for looking at maps he offered as a preferable step forward. Weren't hung maps often extremely cumbersome? They took such a lot of rolling up or unrolling, or folding and unfolding, all of which could decidedly be a nuisance. In addition to which, if glue had been used, they could be only too easily spoilt or torn in the handling. 'Those great and large Geographical maps or charts ... are not so commodious; nor, when anything is peradventure read in them, so easy to be looked upon. And he that will in order hang them all along a wall had need have not only a very large and wide house, but even a Prince's gallery or spacious Theatre.' Ortelius knew what he was talking about.

In the case of manuscript maps of the pre-printing age colour had been assumed to be an intrinsic part of the procedure, and truly it does seem 'natural' to the medium, for aren't land and sea themselves made apprehensible and comprehensible to us through their colours? Today we are unprecedentedly favoured: a satellite-installed AVHRR (Advanced Very High Resolution Radiometer) sensor measuring reflected sunlight can produce images of our planet the colours of which are accurate and wonder-inspiring guides to its surface throughout the seasons. An image taken in late April, for example, shows the rich rolling greens of the great European plain (which includes the British Isles), the raw-meat reds of the arid Iranian uplands, the whites of the permanent Himalayan snows, the deep blue splodges of the east-central African lakes and the harsh yellows shading into greys of the southern Arabian peninsula. The significance of its colours to understanding the organism that is Earth can thus be seen at an awed glance. No wonder then both the makers and the purchasers of maps have always valued colour so highly.

But colour-printing of a quality to match hand-done work wasn't achieved until the early nineteenth century. All coloured maps in sixteenth- and seventeenth-century atlases therefore had been made so by hand. Sellers of books, like Plantin and Ortelius, would (like the model theatre suppliers celebrated by Robert Louis Stevenson in his famous essay on his childhood) offer their wares plain or coloured. In the case of the second, the taste of the buyer could play a part. If someone wanted his own locality to be coloured, say, rose-pink, well, rose-pink this district would be painted. In Italy people had seemed content enough with the uncoloured copper-plate productions with which map-publishers provided them, but in the Netherlands quite the opposite became the case. Well-executed colour-work was a requisite. And there were plenty of opportunities for good colourists to excel: the often ample borders to the maps, the cartouches (or inset areas within a map – the term derives from the word for an 'oval' in Italian heraldry, *cartoccio*) – and all the wind-roses and compass-roses. Personifications and representative figures were features of these last, as were scenes illustrative of life in the places the map depicted. There was scope for imaginative and proficient colouring in all of these.

As there was in the cartographic symbols. Many – for natural features, for towns and important buildings – would be done according to a traditional colour code originating in the physical world itself: blue for rivers, lakes and seas, green for forests and so on. But just as there was room for invention in the devices themselves – finding appropriate symbols to distinguish towns that were administrative centres from ones of lesser rank, or wooded hills from bare peaks – so there was room, too, for fine colour-work with extension of suggestion – or even information. As early as 1500 a great Nuremberg map-maker, Erhard Etzlaub, had recommended the use of colour as a way of indicating the different languages spoken in countries neighbouring his own, a means that would be taken for granted by map-makers today. And if we glance ahead at the *Theatrum* itself, the summation of all these years of Abram's education and training, and look at hand-coloured productions in the first edition of all (in, say, the copy now held in the British Library), we find pages of marvellous artistic beauty, true homage to the wondrous varieties of the natural world. The map of Transylvania (see page 40) is as good an example of it as any. Colour here is not only aesthetically pleasing, it is instructive. Transylvania is a mountainous region generally, but in this cartographic rendering colour gives us a helpful contrast between mountains with good pasturage and wooded slopes, somewhat rougher mountains more densely forest-covered, and the rocky, wild, infertile mountains that comprise the northern Carpathians.

Map-colourists invariably used water-based paints ('washes'). The general replacement in the earlier sixteenth century of woodcut by copper-plate had meant a great improvement in the complexity and the delicacy of the lines on any given map; watercolours, offering opportunities for a subtle range of shades, became an especially suitable medium for filling in the spaces between them.

Designating himself a 'map-colourer' (*afsetter*), Abram Ortel was enrolled in the Guild of St Luke in 1547, when still only nineteen years of age. Guilds were central to Antwerp's social and commercial structure; they safeguarded trades by confining their pursuit to members whom they could also protect against price undercutting and encroachment. Certain

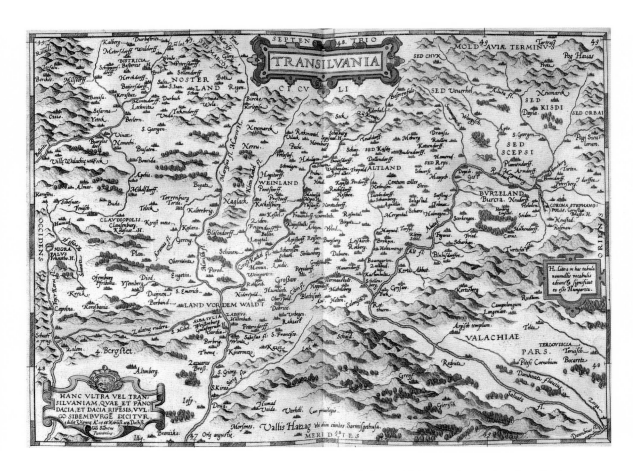

Transylvania: *1570* Theatrum. *A particularly beautiful map drawn by Ortelius'*
Hungarian friend, the 'good and noble' Johannes Sambucus (1531–1584), humanist,
physician, numismatist and great collector, and appointed historiographer to the
emperors Maximilian II and Rudolph II.

professional qualifications were expected of prospective members – for the benefits were large. Entrance fees and subscriptions went towards the assistance to which everyone in the guild was entitled, in sickness and old age, and in looking after dependants. Many guilds had their own (often most impressive) headquarters in which they'd hold social events, every so often on a quite lavish scale. (Look at Antwerp's *Vleeshuis*, built at the beginning of the sixteenth century for the Guild of Butchers; it's resplendent both inside and out with its great brick-lined hall and the vaulted cellars below, both popular venues for public entertainments even today.) Every year the guilds paraded through the city streets in an *ommegang*, a procession with a given theme to test the resourcefulness and ingenuity of the participants. The Flemish were, and perhaps remain, the western world's great masters of the pageant, of carnival *tableaux*.

The Guild of St Luke was one of the most influential of all guilds; its register for masters and apprentices alike had begun almost a century earlier, in 1453. In some ways its prestige and societal impact can be compared with those of the *rederijkers* (rhetoricians) organised in 'chambers' throughout the Netherlands from the fifteenth century onwards, performing plays (increasingly secularised versions of the older 'miracle' plays), organising feasts and other social events and deeply imbued with humanism. The Guild of St Luke admitted a wide variety of callings, wider than most guilds did, but painters, sculptors, engravers and printers formed its backbone. In fact such was the impression made by the first of these categories that it was often known simply as the 'painters' guild'. There was an average of 200–300 members each year. When Abram Ortel became one of these he followed the prevalent custom of latinising his given name – now he was Abramus, or Abrahamus or Abraham, Ortelius.

As a 'map-colourer' he was joining his guild as someone making a key contribution to a major medium of his time and place. As a consequence of his membership he was now in a position to set himself up officially in commerce. This he did, though a young man of only twenty. He was now not just a colourer of maps but a dealer in them, as well as, following his father, in antiquities, coins and pictures. Ortelius was an excellent, a conscientious businessman. In every portrait of him, including the famous posthumous one by Rubens, a distinct canniness emanates from those kindly, grey eyes of his. Appropriately, he was never slow to assess the commercial possibilities of a situation,

*Portrait of Ortelius, generally attributed to Adriaen Thomasz. Key (1570s). It seems
likely – though it can't be proved – that Rubens knew this work and referred to it in
his own famous painting. In the above, Ortelius faces right, as he does not in Filips
Galle's engraving (usually cited as Rubens' principal source), and places his
left hand on a globe.*

and, though a man of honour, was alert to dangers from rivals and energetic in pre-empting them.

The guild was there to assist Ortelius in his new enterprise, and as the popularly styled 'painters' guild', it enabled him also to enter one of the most vital cultural arteries of Antwerp, indeed of the region on which the city drew. Between 1500 and 1600 no fewer than 694 painters were registered in the Antwerp branch, among them men revered to this day, not least for their interest in their surroundings and their artistry in rendering them: Quentin Massys (Matsys, Metsys), Joachim Patenier, Pieter Bruegel the Elder, Cornelis Massys (Matsys, Metsys), Jan Brueghel, Joachim Beuckelaer (who, one's tempted to say, did for fruit and vegetables as laid out in Antwerp markets what Patenier did for rural houses or Bruegel for peasant feasts). These painters didn't just originate in the southern Netherlands, they were quite consciously its portrayers, its recorders, its celebrants.

Ortelius, said Frans Sweerts and others, had catholic taste, both admiring artists of the past (including those of classical antiquity) and doing justice to the eminent of earlier generations to his own, from Hieronymus Bosch (1450–1516) to Lambert Lombard (1505–1566), but this plethora of Antwerp-based men looking at the world around them with such sensibility, intelligence and curiosity must surely have been a tremendous inspiration for him.

The City-on-the-Scheldt was a great centre too for engravers, calligraphers and print-makers. Ortelius was personally to build up a formidable and valuable collection of prints, and his intimate knowledge of the engravers at work in his own community was enormously to his advantage as editor of the *Theatrum* in all its editions. Antwerp was truly blessed with great and energised talents in this field. There was Hieronymus Cock, whose print-publishing business *Aux Quatre Vents* (At the Sign of the Four Winds) enjoyed a wide reputation, issuing work by among others Cock's own brother Matthys, a distinguished illustrator, and Pieter Bruegel (who sent Cock work from his Italian journey). Later on there was Filips (Philippe) Galle (1537–1612), inseparable from the *Theatrum*. Galle, for whom copper-engraving was a major form both as executor and printer, publisher and vendor, had a business of his own, *Witte Lelie* (White Lily). He has a consistent part to play not just in the first atlas but in Ortelius' own story – right through to its end. Christophe Plantin was a mutual friend, and after that great printer's death it was Galle together with Ortelius who valued his stock. Galle was the publisher (rather than printer – who was Plantin himself) of the pocket version of the *Theatrum*, the *Epitome*, and, though inextricably connected through his gifted family with the Protestant faction in Antwerp, was a member of Plantin and Ortelius' religious circle.

If we consult Ortelius' *Album amicorum*, we can find, spanning a considerable period, among other artistic names those of engraver Cornelius Cort (1533–1578), painter and graphics artist Marcus Geeraerts (1520–1590), painter, art historian and tapestry designer Lucas de Heere (1534–1584), Italian painter, graphics artist and architect Pirro Ligorio (1510–1583), the prestigious (and to us today elusive because so much work has been lost) Liège painter, architect and graphics artist Lambert Lombard, the Danish painter and engraver Melchior Lorichs (1527–1583), the art collector and patron (with other avatars besides) Jan Radermacher (1538–1617), and the painters and engravers Joannes Sadeler (1550–1600) and Raphael Sadeler (1560–1628?). It's significant that these men appear in the *Album* alongside so many diplomats, jurists, theologians, historians and philologists. There was clearly no feeling whatever that the visual arts were any less serious occupations than other activities that demanded industry, cerebration and insight; we are also a long way away from the Romantic concept of the artist. The above list has deliberately omitted the greatest painterly name in the *Album*: that of Pieter Bruegel. The mutual regard of these two men has its own special part to play in the progress of Ortelius' career.

Ortelius' fellowship with painters and graphic artists has been stressed because it is absolutely integral to his achievement of the *Theatrum* and its later historical supplement the *Parergon* for two reasons. First, their absorption in their tasks and the solutions they found to problems – how to attain clarity, how to render detail with maximum fidelity and intensity without detracting from the whole picture – was invaluable to him as overseer of a volume which depended, way, way above everything else, on visual material. Secondly, their turning to the world around them, to the town and country at hand for them to study, matched his own evaluation of the importance, spiritual and intellectual as well as empirical, of doing so. His generous and heart-felt words of praise for Bruegel tell us much here: 'I see in his paintings not works of art but works of nature and I call him not the best among painters but *Nature* among painters [my italics]; that's why I judge him worthy of being imitated by all the others.'

The artists themselves must have felt a closeness to the geographers; this is, after all, the period of 'views' (*vedute*) of cities that can act (or very nearly so) as maps, and of maps or town-plans that give us the essence of a place and its interplay of past and present, just as a painting might do, while providing something of the same aesthetic satisfaction. We have glimpsed something of all this already in the portraiture of Antwerp itself.

To think about the artists Ortelius knew and admired is to feel ourselves en route for the *Theatrum*, so coincident are the interests. And it should be said that we are en route also for that great complementary publication of 1572, the *Civitates orbis terrarum* (*The cities of the countries of the world*) of Georg Braun (1541–1622) and Frans Hogenberg (1540–1590) – with the assistance of the remarkable many-talented Joris Hoefnagel (1542–1601) – all good friends of Ortelius who were also inclusions in the *Album amicorum*. This project was to run into six impressive volumes. The city (the microcosm) and the world (the macrocosm) were not only both judged worthy of the same kind of attention; interest in one was seen as a prerequisite for and stimulated interest in the other.

Is there something quintessentially south Netherlands/Flemish about this interest in landscape? The Flemish school was the first for which place – however peripherally in the earlier phases – was a constant, self-renewing source of interest and technical challenge. Italians, the great Venetians and Leonardo among them, were to praise the 'Northerners' for precisely this. Rogier van der Weyden (1399/1400–1464) and Jan van Eyck (active 1422, died 1441) quite logically lead to Joachim Patenier (1485–1524), distinguished from his predecessors by his having landscape as his primary interest. The figures in the Patenier landscape, the incident being depicted there, are essentially justifications for the rendering of the external world. These are all productions of a culture that was to put a unique premium on cartography and make so signal a contribution to it.

If one had to name a turning-point after which a distinctly Flemish approach to place manifests itself and a tradition palpably begins, it would be Rogier van der Weyden's period of study with Robert Campin (1378/9–1444 – often known as the Master of Flémalle) in his Brussels workshop. Here he found a practice he triumphantly continued himself:

that of showing landscape in rich and careful detail from a window, from an upper (second) storey elevation. By doing this the perspective problems posed by landscape depicted from ground level were avoided. Though to be discovered on the edges of the picture, the scenery shown doesn't merely offer a contrast to the interior subject matter of the main body of the painting, it provides an expansion of its intellectual or emotional mood, a conscious amplification of its vision of the world. And in this it compellingly succeeds – to the exasperation of later generations who regret what could have been done on a greater scale with such gifts of observation and representation. The School of Campin's *Virgin with Firescreen* (in the National Gallery, London) provides an excellent instance. Through the window in the top left corner of the painting, we can look down on a town, which can be of no interest to its central figure, the Virgin with the baby on her lap, but is of very great interest to us. Set against gentle hills, the town is definitely in the Netherlands to go by the crow-stepped buildings. We delightedly take in the shop-fronts and the ladder with two men on it propped against a house façade; how easily we could go on to draw a street-plan of this place!

This *thereness* of a town- or country-scape irrespective of the awareness of the central figures in it was taken further by van der Weyden himself and his pupils. In the *Magdalen* the penitent woman certainly can't see the lovely view from the window of winding river and parkland, though we feel in her case that she would appreciate it if she did so. In the superb *Man Reading* (or *St Ivo*) from van der Weyden's workshop the serious dark-haired young man with a scar on his face is absorbed by his reading matter to the point of abstraction, but we have the advantage over him: we see from the open-shuttered window, again in the top left-hand corner, an inviting landscape with water (on which swans are sailing and in which they're reflected), a bridge with people standing on it, and a city with castle and walls. These features seem to be telling us so much: that against the contents of the young man's document (St Ivo is the patron saint of lawyers, and a real young lawyer was chosen as sitter) a major dimension of existence, of the physical world, is asserting itself, possibly as more conducive to realisation of God's greatness than whatever abstruse subject he's pondering. Natural religion versus received, text-imparted religion – perhaps that's too reductive for so intense and moving a work, but it's hard not to see this undeclared conflict as on some level informing it.

From the workshop of Rogier van der Weyden (c.1400–64) comes this fine study of Man Reading (St Ivo) in which the patron saint of lawyers is studying oblivious of the very appealing landscape visible (to us) through the window in the top left corner of the picture.

In Jan van Eyck's creations, it is through his use of light that the importance of the physical world is brought home to us. The very oils he employed for his work were specially prepared by himself with this famous preoccupation of his in mind. They could be put on in transparent layers, and, after these, fine final brushwork could be applied. It is this that's responsible for all the complex and subtle irradiations of sunlight which make his paintings so endlessly rewarding. Van Eyck also rejoiced in mirrors and other reflecting objects (the 'candles' of an overhead candelabra, for example) which can open up any scene on which he is concentrating beyond its immediate self. The most memorable example of this is the celebrated *Arnolfini and His Wife* (1434). Beyond the room in which the couple are standing, with an irresistible little Maltese terrier at their feet, we feel a whole outer world – but of this all we can actually see is a small section of a tallish tree outside the window. It is instead made manifest by the light coming in through the window and by the spherical mirror on the back wall. Jan van Eyck wrote on the picture – putting the words in a conspicuous place, significantly just above the revealing mirror itself – *Johannes de eyck fuit hic* ('Jan van Eyck was here'). No painter before him would have wanted to make this statement, would have felt that his presence in a specific place at a specific time gave his work an invaluable authenticity. But, *mutatis mutandis*, it could have been made by almost every significant Flemish and Dutch painter – and cartographer – in the two centuries ahead, right up to the time of Vermeer of Delft.

Van Eyck's much-praised portrayal of the physical scene in *The Virgin of Chancellor Rollin* (now in the Louvre) and the incomplete *Santa Barbara* (now in Antwerp's Museum voor Schone Kunsten) impresses by its rendering of human movement within it. Surveyed from above (by figures on a parapet) the scene in the first of these is busy with human activity (this is a landscape in which people can *live*). The tower of the church being built by the construction workers in *Santa Barbara* is specific enough, but beyond stretches what would be known as 'world landscape'.

A 'world landscape', seen usually from an eminence, is one that shows a whole range of diverse scenery – say, Alpine peaks and northern European farmland – rarely, if ever, blended in an actual prospect on this planet. We come nearer still than van Eyck when we look at the work of Ortelius' fellow Antwerper and fellow Guild of St Luke member Joachim Patenier. Patenier contexted his people, in no matter what biblical or classical narrative they're

Van Eyck completed only the initial drawing for Santa Barbara *(1437) which in
its scope and variety is, even in its unfinished state, a real milestone in the rendering
of landscape. Here is both movement and permanency, the stillness being embodied
in the main subject, oblivious to her busy surroundings.*

engaged, in a natural world which clearly interested him far more. He revelled in the jagged rocks of his native Meuse valley which he often included. He rendered it at far greater closeness of range than his Flemish predecessors had previously managed, with subtlety and warmth of colour – his celebrated browns for the foreground, a multiplicity of pastoral greens for the middle distance, and for the further distance many various blues. (We can imagine how this must have appealed to 'colourist' Ortelius.) His subject matter – *The Flight into Egypt, The Temptation of St Anthony* – perhaps suggested to him the 'world landscape' with which he became associated. Doesn't a cross-section of the landscapes to be encountered on this planet suggest the universality of the Christian religion (and the opening up and overrunning of the world were always justified by the intention of bringing the Christian religion to all corners of the globe)? It also suggests the world as a place of pilgrimage through the varieties of which we all (to a varying extent) have to pass. But to us who know how geographically minded Antwerp was, we can see the multiform scenery as illustrating the diversity and the ultimate unity of the physical world. There's a definite connection between world-landscape and world maps (Contarini, Waldseemüller). But there's more to Patenier's achievement even than this.

Examine his *Rest in the Flight into Egypt* and we find both immediately surrounding the Virgin and child, and in the right-hand part of the picture generally, a most convincing south Netherlands countryside. Horses graze, men cut corn, and limes and sycamores stand above fields and farmhouses. With Patenier the long line of Low Countries landscape painting which has given western civilisation one of its permanent homes truly begins. The debt to him in, say, Cornelis Massys' *Arrival of the Holy Family in Bethlehem* (1545) is immediately apparent; the scriptural subjects in this last arrive in a Flanders village presented, from only the gentlest of elevations, with the felt thoroughness of first-hand knowledge. And it's there in Pieter Bruegel who indeed took over the 'world-landscape' and employed it to effect even in his great maturity – though he is rightly remembered for other aspects of his art. Among his greater paintings *The Suicide of Saul* (1562), *Tower of Babel* (1563), *Procession to Calvary* (1564), and that superb western icon of humankind's relationship to the seasons, *Hunters in the Snow* (1565), all partake of this genus. In the last-named, however, we can see Bruegel transcending and abandoning it – his hunters leave their heavy footprints on the snow as they pass by an obviously Netherlands hamlet and see below

Antwerper Joachim Patenier (c.1486–1524) is generally acclaimed as the first painter for whom interest in landscape was patently the dominant concern. Here in the Rest in the Flight into Egypt, *for all the dignity of the religious figures, our attention is straightaway held by their context, in particular the very Flemish country scene of the right-hand section. (Patenier, so admired by Dürer, could also achieve convincing fantasy landscapes as in* Charon's Boat.*)*

Pieter Bruegel: The Harvesters. *A tribute to the natural world in both its specific and general aspects. Human beings are bound to Nature and her seasons both in their work (skilled husbandry) and their recreations (enjoyment of a repast taken out of doors).*

them skaters, hockey-players and fishers on frozen and characteristic Netherlands mill-pools.

Now go back and compare the right-hand section of Patenier's *Rest in the Flight into Egypt* with Bruegel's glowing, richly worked *The Harvesters* produced in the same year, 1565, as *Hunters in the Snow*, and a real kinship will be apparent, enough for us to think of them both as of an unambiguously Flemish school. Yet Bruegel's work – taking the Flanders grain-harvest of August–September with all its particularities, the stooks, the scythes, the basket of provisions for the resting workers – also constitutes a touchstone for those qualities Patenier (and his distinguished precursors) were surely striving after. In Bruegel the intense relation, the bond, between Nature and human beings – Nature here in her fullness making demands, humans at work and at play deriving both sustenance and pleasure from her – is inseparable in its immediacy from the painter's imaginative self-installation before an actual corner of the world with an identity all its own. Truly he could have exclaimed, echoing Jan Van Eyck before him: *Pieter Bruegel fuit hic.* Truly Ortelius could have pointed to it, and said 'he is Nature among painters!'

Paradoxically, it is only when artists reveal their appreciation of the particularities, the unique phenomena, of one region, one city, or, even better, of one corner of that region, that city, that they are respecting (and representing) the world as pluralist entity. And the world atlas arrives *after* the 'world landscape' has been largely jettisoned in favour of these fuller and more intimate landscapes.

In this Bruegel masterwork, while fully appreciating its universality of address and its firm place in a wider European culture, one is confronting something that could only have come out of the south Netherlands. The same will be true of the *Theatrum*.

Interest in one's immediate topography – in what Ptolemy, in his seminal distinction in the *Geographia*, termed *chorography*: the (primarily carto-graphic) treatment of the regional, the particular – went hand-in-hand with expanding awareness of the huge extent and variousness of our world, of the hitherto imperfectly understood arrangement of its seas and continents, with all their physical divisions and numerous 'nations' – what Ptolemy called *geography*, the (again mainly cartographic) drawing of or writing about the Earth as an ultimate entity. This relationship tends to the symbiotic – information about the one always renders the other the worthier seeming of attentive study. The landscape round one's own home acquires a new dignity if one appreciates that it is both literally unique and inextricably related to the wider world in climate, geology, vegetation, animal life. If one has observed with care and even reverence one's daily surroundings, one is far better equipped to understand an alien environment. In our own times it can be no accident (though there are other explanations) that ecological Green movements with their accent on respectful local living (Schumacher's famous *Small Is Beautiful* and its progeny) have followed rather than preceded the historically significant – and imaginatively exciting – space probes.

So the 'discovery' of landscape made by the Flemish, which accompanies a great delight in 'chorographical' maps proclaiming the merits of regions and towns, coexists with 'discoveries' of parts of the world whose very existence quite frequently was previously unknown to the men who made them. The scale and pace of so much opening-up of the world must have put severe pressure on the mind, even while it stimulated and thrilled it. Ortelius and his contemporaries had psychically to accommodate ever-expanding knowledge.

The explored and mapped world must be fitted into God's world. Ortelius – like his close friend and colleague, Christophe Plantin – was a man of deep spirituality probably shaped by some interior religious experience in youth. The thinking of these two friends on religious matters, combined with important temperamental and intellectual affinities, led them in the same direction, to that extraordinary Low Countries movement, the Family of Love. The Family was to be crucial to their work.

For Ortelius, in particular, the movement had roots in earlier traditions of which he had himself partaken. It's clear from the books he owned and read and from his letters – particularly those to Ortelianus, which abounded in references to the spiritual life – that Ortelius was steeped in the pietistic, quietist Netherlands religious tradition the roots of which are to be found in the later fourteenth century: in the *Devotio Moderna* (Modern Devotion) movement founded in 1379 by Geert Groote at Deventer in the north-eastern Netherlands. One of its aspirations was a state of being called *dulcedo Dei* ('the sweetness of the delights of the love of Christ'). The movement's influence was far-reaching, not least because of the effect of the extraordinarily popular *Imitation of Christ* (1518) of Thomas à Kempis, its fullest written expression, which itself relates to roughly contemporaneous devotional works such as the *Theologia Germanica*. It was also a major factor in Netherlands social life, through schools. Axiomatic to Groote's beliefs was a reformed system of education more humanistically inclined than the then dominant one. The Brethren of the Common Life, as Groote's followers were called, combined attention to classical language and literature with a somewhat anti-intellectual approach to religion, dismissing the tortuously complicated arguments of Scholasticism. (Erasmus, though no enthusiastic Old Boy, was Brethren-educated.) Common Life schools appealed to a newly prosperous, level-headed and influential middle-class with little time or regard for the rarefied hair-splittings of orthodox theology. A practical outer life and a developed inner one sit well together; the one can safeguard the other, can give it appropriate, even encouraging conditions in which to flourish. Such a cast of mind could well mean that you stayed within the Catholic fold but developed a private spirituality, and this, as we shall see, was the position of many a Family member.

But of course there were those, encouraged by their own devotional habits, who became too dissatisfied with the corruption and negligence of the established Church to want to remain in it. Indeed, from the 1520s for the next four and a half decades the Church signally failed to arouse affection, loyalty or admiration in the greater part of its Antwerpers. In the years of Ortelius' boyhood and youth (the 1530s) the new and magnetising home for seekers was not the Lutheranism interesting so many when Erasmus had known the city and which had attracted Ortelius' own parents, nor Calvinism, whose hour had not yet come; it was the Anabaptist movement. Such was the fervour of those who joined this that though numerically not very strong it was they who, more than any others, were hounded, persecuted and martyred by authority, the sad victims of the monarch whom Plantin was later pleased to praise as 'Catholic in name and deed'. But the dissidents' sufferings added to rather than detracted from their public stature. Who else but these 'enthusiasts' (to use an appropriate term from the next century) had the courage to behave militantly on behalf of their beliefs, to advertise their faith with testimonies, denunciations, even (as in Amsterdam in 1534) with naked protests? Their behaviour was impressive enough for former Lutherans to go over to their ranks.

Anabaptists – as their name proclaims, they held that adult not infant baptism was commanded by the scriptures – had a sizeable, mainly artisan following both in north Germany and in the Netherlands north and south of the Great Rivers. The movement – which had many quite diverse strands – reached a dreadful climacteric in the mid-1530s from which recovery would prove extremely difficult (though made it was). Vicious persecutions and a sense of their own divine inspiration sent droves of the sect to Münster in Westphalia, turning the town into a godly stronghold all set to defy the rest of the world. Münster was nothing less than the New Jerusalem, and this vision of its privileged identity intensified after two Hollanders, Jan Matthijsz. and Jan Beuckelsz. (Jan of Leyden), men of hysteric faith and power lust, assumed control. Soon the community was ruled with a cruel despotism eclipsing that even of established external authority (which proceeded to lay siege to the town), and the more fearsome because the theatre of operations was so intimate, so confined. Baptisms were ruthlessly enforced, wives were compulsorily shared, sexual orgies were pronounced to be the divine will; Jan of Leyden was proclaimed Prophet-King, by now an obscene tyrant, crazed perhaps by what he'd seen his fellows endure in the world outside Münster. Believing himself to be God's vehicle, and possibly God himself, he had any contrary-minded or superfluous people (the ill, the infirm) slaughtered in terrible numbers. The siege of Münster lasted an appalling eighteen months and was to haunt the northern European mind for decades to come, as a warning of what could happen when faith was set free from institutions.

Münster collapsed in the summer of 1535. But the fall-out from the siege was protracted. In the eyes of the world any connection, however tenuous, with the besieged citadel was tainting. For that matter many Anabaptists themselves had shattered nerves and legitimate fears, while a number wanted fully fledged revenge. Factions arose. Two men associated with the Anabaptist crisis who have parts to play in the histories of our atlas-makers are David Joris and Augustijn van Hasselt, of whom for the present only the first engages us.

Some time between 1538 and 1544 – in other words during Ortelius' adolescence – David Joris, a glass-blower of Delft, came to live on the periphery of Antwerp, in Berchem (now a part of the city, with an important train station). He was taking shelter in the household of the Lord of Berchem, and he had need to, as his recent sufferings had been terrible. After a brief experimentation with Lutheranism, he had joined the Anabaptists, and in the wake of Münster had espoused a pacifism which earned him the leadership of a significant section of the movement. His impassioned rejection of revenge, however, didn't make him any more endearing to authority than his blood-demanding rivals. In 1538 his mother had her head cut off, his wife and daughter were taken from him, and twenty-seven of his followers were killed. He himself was compelled to flee. Perhaps it was the grandiloquence of his claims that aroused such antagonism; he had had visions in which the whole world lay at his supporters' feet, and he had no doubt that his own role in history was divinely ordained.

His attitude to his very name illustrates the conception of himself he'd arrived at. He was *David* so couldn't he be the third and last of a great trinity of Davids? There'd been David, king of Israel, composer of the psalms; there'd been Jesus Christ of the Royal House of David; and now there was himself, a craftsman who'd been drawn into radical religion because the established Church in his home town was weak and lacklustre. Did this mean then – his many enemies would demand – that Joris believed himself the equal of Christ, or even His final incarnation? No, of course not, the man from Delft, for all his visions, replied. But he did think he came before men as one who'd completely accomplished that *Imitation of Christ* enjoined of all born after Him, and propounded by Thomas à Kempis. Now, thanks to himself, the age of the Son (the second age of human history) could be declared completed, and the third age, that of the Holy Ghost, could begin (an idea not confined in its appeal to the fifteenth and sixteenth centuries; both Emanuel Swedenborg and his twentieth-century admirer, W. B. Yeats, were much taken by it).

Joris remained with the Lord of Berchem long enough to write a book which became like a Bible for his followers, the Jorisists or Davidists, *T Wonder-Boeck* (printed in 1542 and revised in 1551). This is very much in that northern European tradition of pietistic inward religion. Ortelius owned a copy. Persecution of Anabaptists and other dissidents continuing, Joris was obliged to escape from Antwerp and together with the Lord of Berchem himself and the Lord's brother-in-law took refuge (under an assumed name) in Basel, which had a long tradition of religious tolerance (it had been Erasmus' domicile). Here Joris lived, developing and considerably modifying his ideas, in circumstances of rather considerable luxury until his death in 1555.

For us Joris is important because he had connections with the founder of the Family of Love, who may in fact have originally been a follower of his. Joris was also a forerunner of the movement, who establishes for us in conduct and writings the Family of Love's relationship both to certain earlier Dutch/Low German traditions (adherents of which effected no break with Catholicism) and to Anabaptism. Interestingly, Ortelius didn't care for Joris; he thought him presumptuous to the very point of blasphemy – even though there must have been, judging from our knowledge of his spiritual-literary tastes, much in *TWonder-Boeck* that he admired. In all the religious turmoil of the century many *soi-disant* redeemers and prophets arose, their rhetorical gifts sharpened and their self-criticism and sometimes their very wits blunted by all the opposition and oppression; they grew self-intoxicated, sometimes more than a little cracked, all too ready to throw the judgement and needs of others, along with caution itself, to the winds. Of such company Ortelius was, by training, temperament and education, extremely suspicious – and Joris provides an exemplary instance of this. Reason, proportion, knowledge, the roundness of vision that comes with hard thinking and wide experience – these were Ortelius' guides always.

Early in his life Ortelius himself had an experience of Christ which was to remain with him, strong and lucent, throughout its length. He had taken Christ into himself just as, a century and a half before, Groote's *Devotio Moderna* movement had advised all true believers to do, and only among those who also believed in the supreme importance of this process, of an inner life dwarfing all dogmas and disputes, all hierarchies and rites, would Ortelius feel truly at home spiritually. And such a group Ortelius found: the Family of Love, under the charismatic leadership of Hendrik Niclaes (c.1502–1580) aka HN (or *Homo Novus*, the New Man). In Antwerp this movement flourished particularly well.

A favourite writer of Ortelius – we know from remarks he made and from his library – was Sebastian Franck (1499–1542), whose career is a very paradigm of contemporary shifts in religious thought: German, a Roman Catholic priest who became a Lutheran pastor and ended up as an individualistic sectarian stressing that longing for oneness with God so frequently impeded by doctrines and church obligations – and even by the Scriptures themselves unless read by the light of personal experience. Franck was an enemy of all divisions between believers. In his *Paradoxa* of

1534 he famously wrote: 'As the air filled everything and is not confined to one place, as the light of the sun overflows the whole earth, is not on earth, and yet makes all things of earth verdant, so God dwells in everything and everything dwells in him.' Words that would say much to a young Christian geographer like Ortelius. Franck has roots in those two works which were of such importance to the Antwerper, *The Imitation of Christ* and the *Theologia Germanica*. Says the latter:

> There lives no man on earth who may always have rest and peace without troubles and crosses, with whom things go always according to his will. There is always something to be suffered here, consider it as you will. And as soon as you are free of one adversity, perhaps two others come in its place. Therefore yield yourself willingly to them, and seek only that true peace of the heart, which none can take away from you, that you may overcome all adversity; the peace that breaks through all adversities and crosses, all oppression, suffering, misery, humiliation, and what more there may be of the like, so that a man may be joyful and patient therein, as were the beloved disciples and followers of Christ.

Certainly Netherlanders of the mid-sixteenth century, so many of them wanting more than anything else to lead quiet, useful, contented lives, were to find that as soon as they were free of one adversity, another two, worse and more invasive, would appear. Ortelius hoped that in 'HN' he'd met someone who could conduct him to the *Terra pacis* (Land of Peace), to use the title of one of Hendrik Niclaes' most-read books. Ortelius joined the Family some time towards the end of the 1540s. Christophe Plantin – whose whole debt to the movement was large and intricate – joined the Antwerp branch at more or less the same time, and swiftly became an important official in the Family, responsible for recruitment to its future priesthood after it had triumphantly established itself as a legal, powerful and divinely blessed order.

Hendrik Niclaes, its founder, came from northern Germany (Low German was the language he chose to write in), but he'd lived and worked in the Netherlands, in Amsterdam, for some years, a successful businessman with a wide range of commodities, including cloth and books, as well as of clients and contacts. The idea that his initials HN could also stand for *Homo Novus* (New Man) was very dear to him; thus that contemporary preoccupation with discovery – new worlds, *the* New World – is manifest even in the sobriquet of this energetic if also decidedly tiresome heresiarch.

The Family of Love is absolutely crucial to the history of the atlas. How we see the physical world depends on what we believe it to be, on how we fit it into our vision of existence, into our perception of ourselves and the scheme of our mortal lives. If both Ortelius and Christophe Plantin, the man responsible for roughly half the *Theatrum*'s considerable sales as well as for the paper on which it was printed, and, after 1579, for the printing itself, were both inextricably connected with HN's movement, we are obliged to look at it more closely.

With its accent on spiritual knowledge of Christ, the Family of Love liberated its members from the intellectual constrictions imposed by both the Catholic Church itself and her dogmatic Protestant opponents. Often called a heresy, and later officially branded as one, the Family had among its members people of all persuasions – those who wanted, when all was said and done, to stay inside the established Church, as well as those who'd moved away in their minds too far beyond it for this, in the long run, to be possible. On this subject HN himself, a difficult personality, was not, in fact, consistent. His attitude to Luther was at best ambivalent, his response to the key tenet of Justification by Faith was unequivocally hostile. Nonetheless HN's extensive plans for organisation of his followers and greater systemisation of his beliefs (including later a re-dating of history from his own 'Wonder Year' of 1567!) couldn't be other than antipathetic to the authorities of the Church because, *au fond*, antagonistic to them. His extraordinary *Ordo Sacerdotis* (*Order of the Priesthood*) of the late 1570s, which neither his enemies nor most of his followers, Plantin excepted, would have known about, gives elaborate instructions for the appointment, duties, rites and significance of a priesthood, pointing to some later establishment of the Family as an autonomous confessional and disciplined church. So it's hardly surprising that HN's writings were eventually placed on the Church's index of forbidden books.

Belonging to the Family was something to be kept secret – though perhaps semi-secret was often the best that could be managed, as a letter to Ortelius from his friend the orientalist Guillaume Postel demonstrates. Postel speaks openly of his own knowledge of the movement and fundamental sympathy for it. With so many of its members coming from the educated, professional and commercial class, it was also a network.

'Family' is as apt a name for the movement as any (in Dutch it's also, equally appropriately, called *Huis der Liefde* or House of Love). Links between Familists can't be overstated; this family, like so many blood ones, was at once tight-knit and ramified, contained and intricate, and like so many businesses of the time (conspicuously book-production businesses) revolved round *households* – households in Amsterdam, Emden (in East Friesland) where HN lived many years, in Deventer, Kampen, Antwerp, Paris. Households had secrets as what household hasn't? – how many times daily must the sentence 'Things mustn't go further than these four walls!' be said? – but they were also inclusive entities, uniting rank, age, the sexes. The master, his wife and children and kin, his employees, apprentices and servants could, and did, literally sit round the same table and share conversational topics. The great French Calvinist printer, Robert Estienne (1503–1559) – perhaps Plantin's true predecessor – presided over just such a comprehensive establishment in Paris, and later Geneva (servants and little children would chat there in Latin just like their elders) – and Christophe Plantin's own home in Antwerp, if somewhat grander, was such another household.

There has been much patient uncovering of Family history, outstandingly by British scholar Alastair Hamilton. But a good deal will, probably always, be obscure. So much reliance has to be placed on the – admittedly not insubstantial – documents written by HN himself, or under his guidance, the *Cronica* and the *Acta HN* (both from the 1570s), and highly partisan they are. Though usually accurate enough about date and place, they are so claustrophobically self-justifying, not to say self-extolling, and the vein of paranoia so marked, that the emergence of objective fact is only too often obstructed. Those who upset HN in some way, who failed to come up to his hopes (a sizeable number) or tried to better him at business, turned all too quickly into enemies, into deceitful schemers selfishly pursuing their own ends or enemies eaten up by inexplicable malice towards their one-time mentor and helper. HN at key points in his career put Christophe Plantin into these unenviable categories (and he may not have been entirely guiltless of the charges) while continuing useful relations with him.

By his own account HN had been a phenomenal child. At an age when others are playing or struggling with the rudiments of learning, he was arriving at those core ideas about the Christian religion which led him to found the Family in Amsterdam some thirty years later. At only eight years old he was nagged at by a question his pious father was unable to answer: if Christ's sufferings and death on the Cross were meant to atone for Adam's sin and restore righteousness to our fallen world, how come that humans continued to be sinful, and misery still prevailed? His father decided the best thing to do would be take the boy to a priest, but he chose unwisely. The two friars who saw the child said he'd no right to be thinking about such grown-up matters; he should be beaten instead.

About a year later the small boy, who deep down had been quite undeterred by these unkind snubs, had a wonderful dream. He saw a luminous mountain of amazing beauty which proceeded to engulf him. The mountain, a voice informed him on waking, was the righteousness of Christ, an interpretation confirmed in a dream he had only a few minutes later. This showed him people who refused to accept the truth as just revealed to him transformed into withered trees, mere worm-fodder, or else into horrible menacing animals.

The odd thing about these precocious visions is that the kernel of them remained with HN throughout full and busy mature years of active commercial life to form the very basis of Familism. Christ suffered and died so that we could learn by his example, so that we could carry out that Imitation of Christ recommended in Thomas à Kempis' great book. Says the *Imitation*: 'He to whom all things are one, he who reduces all things to one and sees all things as one, may enjoy a quiet mind and remain peaceful in God. The Kingdom of God is within you, says the Lord ... Learn to despise outward things and to give yourself to things inward, and you shall perceive the Kingdom of God to come in you.'

To take Christ into the self is to let oneself be taken into Christ, an absorption into a mountain of shining loveliness: HN's religion – we can see at once its appeal to Ortelius – is, above all things, *inward*. That's why he was comparatively little concerned with those questions of doctrine and observance tearing Europe apart and aligning leaders and communities against each other. That's why he advised his followers to conform to the established Church of their own society (in some areas of Germany this would be the Lutheran) while cultivating the Christ within. This earned Familists the charge of Nicodemism, of outward practice deliberately concealing beliefs and priorities for safety's sake. We can find eminent Familists who were later convinced Calvinists (the engraver

Filips Galle, for example), some who essentially maintained the faith and attitudes of the earlier Anabaptists, and others, like the later Plantin – and to an increasing extent Ortelius himself – who not only stayed inside the fold of Rome but were eloquent on her behalf.

HN saw himself as a leader and increasingly as much more than this, as the unique revealer of God's truth. He came to expect obedience. The idea of persecuting people for their religious beliefs was genuinely abhorrent to him (that people cared about their faith was, he said, something to rejoice in rather than to punish), and commendably his movement was open to all, to Jews or Mohammedans alongside ordinary Christians. But those who refused what he, HN, had to offer, would incur damnation. That childhood dream of the folk who spurned him becoming desiccated trees or horrendous beasts never quite faded.

People tended to be drawn to the Family out of both worldly and unworldly considerations: no good could come out of strife, the Christian religion was one of peace and love; for it to fuel division and war to the imperilment of a whole continent was a tragic mistake. No book of HN's had greater success than *Terra pacis*, the *Land of Peace*. Undoubtedly this was the destination of every right-minded Christian person. But should the term be taken literally, meaning that the Family must search for some place – beyond the tormented Low Countries – where oneness with God could be safely cultivated? Or was it like the Kingdom of God in Christ's words, only within you?

And if it were the second of these – the more *un*worldly interpretation – then, paradoxically, the (quite sound) *worldly* motive for joining the Family was the more gratified. For what could be more convenient in troubled times – with religion a cause of, and a pretext for, violent conflict – than an extensive web made up of peace-loving households, all in some kind of debt to each other, and all involved in international business? Familists were enabled by membership to cut across frontiers, governments and government agents while on principle not offering them any kind of hostility; on the contrary, here they were leading integrated, sensible, prosperous, enterprising and moral lives, with most satisfactory human, financial and divine securities. Familism joined together a diversity of distinguished men and their families, and conferred on them a sense of unity, of solidarity in fundamentals so badly needed in a tragically riven society like theirs.

A.
Hîc eſt Entroitus Antri
Sibyllæ Cumanæ, quod vulgo
appellatur grotta della
Sibylla.

VERGILIVS VI. Æneid:
EXCISV EVBOICÆ LATVS ĪGĒSRVPIS IN ĀTRVM
QVÒ LATI DVCVNT ADITVS CENTV OSTIA CĒTV
VNDE RVVNT TOTIDĒ VOCES RESPONSA
SIBYLLAE.

B.
Apollinis Templi ab Inco-
lis bꝑ dicuntur eſſe ruinæ

A.
LACVS Agna-
nus piſcibus carens ranis
ac ſerpentibus ſcatens.

B.
Charoneum antrum, ſiue
ſpiraculum, mortiferum ex-
halans ſpiritum, quod vulgo appellatur Grotta de
li cani

C.
Sudatorium S. Germani
vulgo dictum, ſudatorio
ſiue le fumarole
Agnano

C.
Hic olim fuere Triper:
gole, nunc mors nouus, Anno
1538. terremotu congest sus,
omnia tegit.

VERGILIVS VI AENEIDOS
Quam super haud vllæ poterant impune volâtes
Tendere iter pennis, talis sese halitus atris
Faucibus effundens supera ad conuexa ferebat
Vnde locum Graij dixerunt nomine ⸺.
ΛΟΡΝΟΝ.

D.
Pos Chosce montes olim
fuit Capua, nunc patuca ap:
parent Vestigia

A. Ortelius et G. Hoefnaghus hunc
lacum hodie non est Αοϱνоϳ
animaduertentes.

B.

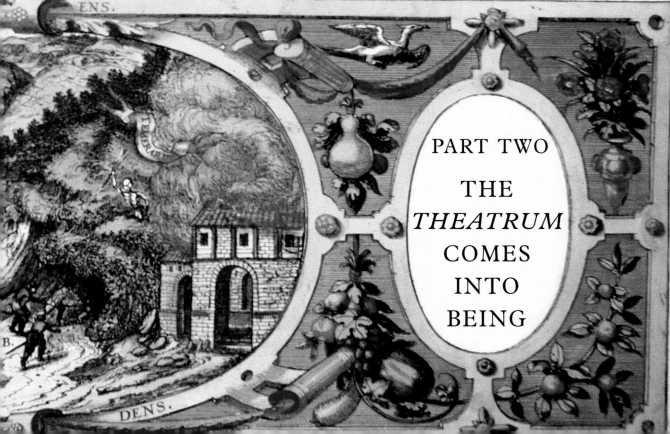

B.

DENS.

PART TWO

THE
THEATRUM
COMES
INTO
BEING

These two charming engravings, published by their friends Braun and Hogenberg,
show Ortelius and Hoefnagel meeting at Lake Agnia, Italy, and impress on us the real
importance of Nature to their sensibilities.

CHAPTER FOUR

In 1603, five years after Ortelius' death, Jacob Cool ('Ortelianus') wrote a letter to one of his uncle's oldest and dearest friends. He wanted Jan Radermacher to help him. What was the *real* truth about the beginnings of the *Theatrum*? Radermacher – Latin poet, art-collector, map-supplier, scholarly businessman and convinced Calvinist – had long been an exile from the southern Netherlands; his religious views had forced him to flee in 1567. He was now living in Middelburg in Holland, getting on in years and declining in health. But as he did his best to answer Ortelianus, co-religionist and well-known to him when younger, he found himself deeply moved by his memories. On Friday 25 July he wrote him a detailed reply. Luckily for posterity Radermacher was not cramped by epistolary pomposity; he was someone with the ability to get in touch with his own past, and to make it vivid for others. Of course he could not be wholly sure of the accuracy of what he wrote – and a fortnight later he sent Ortelianus some necessary amendments. But his first letter remains a major source of information about Ortelius and the first atlas, and is as interesting personally as professionally.

Radermacher begins:

I gladly comply with your request as nothing pleases me more than discharging my duties of affection towards a friend, even after his death. In order to state clearly what first led Ortelius to think of compiling his *Theatrum*, I shall have to narrate how the friendship between him and me started.

At the age of sixteen I lost my father who had destined me for the University. In consequence I was, in 1554, apprenticed to Gillis [Aegidius] Hooftman, the well-known merchant of Antwerp. There I became acquainted with your relative Emmanuel van Meteren, like myself devoted to the study of history, and of the same age as myself, and whom also the drudgery of business precluded from the better arts, the hankering for which we relieved by mutual complaints and discussions on our stealthy studies. In this way we often spoke of Abraham Ortelius, who was a relative of van Meteren and burned with love for study, but who was also hampered by circumstances, having a widowed mother and two young sisters to support. Having a taste for history, and more especially for geography, he endeavoured to gain a livelihood by selling the best maps that he could purchase, after they were mounted on linen by his sisters, and coloured by himself; he exported those made in Belgium even to Italy (which he often explored on such occasions) and importing foreign maps thence and from elsewhere. As for this reason he was frequently absent visiting the Frankfurt fairs, I had no opportunity of making his acquaintance until he was entrusted with the sale of the library of John Rogers ...

In fact Emmanuel van Meteren was not the same age as Radermacher, but roughly three years his senior, and, in 1554 was nineteen years old, and had only recently completed his excellent education. But like so many youths everywhere, Emmanuel and Jan both felt frustrated, finding their milieu uncongenial and unsuitable, and pining for fuller involvement with artistic and intellectual matters. Radermacher's is a convincing and time-transcending sketch of their situation. But what is of particular interest for us now is the view it gives us of Ortelius.

A member of the Guild of St Luke before his twentieth birthday, Ortelius had been enabled by this to begin his commercial life forthwith – helping his mother with his father's business which she'd been trying to run since his death, and setting himself up on his own account as a dealer with a rapidly burgeoning network of contacts (which were later to include Christophe Plantin). But as well as acquiring these professional responsibilities young he acquired personal ones, too. In 1550 his uncle, Emmanuel's father, Jacob van Meteren, died. Abraham thus became, at only twenty-three, the head of the whole family. By the time Radermacher speaks of he'd have been this for almost five years, and his – as everybody agreed – was a dutiful and unselfish nature. But, though they most definitely looked up to him, Emmanuel and Jan – this letter makes quite clear – appreciated that he too was frustrated, much as they were; his keen, already well-stocked mind and constant curiosity were not being given the play they deserved or demanded.

No other document so brings this aspect of the young Ortelius' predicament home to us. Perhaps in other quarters how he comported himself was simply taken as how he really was. This letter of 1603 explains both the comparative tardiness of Ortelius' first achievements and the obvious increase in understanding and resourcefulness which he demonstrated as he moved through his late twenties into his thirties. Ortelius was devoted to his family, of that there is no doubt. His mother and sister Anne made their home with him, for he, like Anne, never married. His sister Elizabeth, Ortelianus' mother, made a comparatively late marriage, to Jacob Cool, and religion compelled her and her family, like Jan Radermacher and so many others, to live away from the south Netherlands, in their case in England, thus paralleling the movement of their relations, the van Meterens. Abraham maintained the closest, warmest connection with the Cools; each side was intimately aware of what was happening to the other. But a fond family doesn't prevent frustration, even if it can alleviate it, and Radermacher's letter surely suggests that it didn't do so in Ortelius' case.

The John Rogers whose library Radermacher cites as the instrument of their coming together was another family connection of Ortelius through Rogers' wife. His story and its bearing on Ortelius' development has a grim but fascinating paradigmatic quality.

John Rogers (1500–1555), born in the (then) village of Deriten near Birmingham, was the first Protestant martyr of England's persecutions under Queen Mary. Ordained Roman Catholic priest, he was appointed in 1534 chaplain to the English merchant-adventurers in Antwerp. Here he came into contact with all the activities surrounding that bringing-out of the first English Bible, with which Ortelius' uncle Jacob van Meteren and his father Leonard were concerned. He was much impressed by what he encountered; he met William Tyndale, and possibly Miles Coverdale too, was converted to Protestantism, and himself worked on the Old Testament and Apocrypha of the Bible, to be put out from Jacob van Meteren's own Antwerp press. Protestantism also led Rogers to forego his priestly vows and marry; his choice of wife, Adriana de Weyden, was conspicuous for her spiritual and intellectual interests, and was related to Ortelius. John and Adriana went to Wittenburg, where they started a large family, to consist eventually of three daughters and eight sons, of whom Daniel (1538–1591), to whom Ortelius was to become extremely close, was the eldest.

After Henry VIII's break with Rome, Rogers felt empowered to return to England and, it has to be said, proceeded to reveal a decided and unattractive opportunism. He was given a living in Essex, made Lecturer in Divinity at St Paul's, and grew close to Thomas Cranmer. It was often later held against him that he refused to use his influence with that archbishop to prevent the burning of a poor Anabaptist woman. Burning, declared Rogers to someone remonstrating with him over this, was a *gentle* punishment for offences like hers. 'Well, perhaps,' came the reply, 'you may yet find that you yourself shall have your hands full of this so gentle fire.' The speaker's sarcasm was to be only too literally vindicated.

Rogers gained quite a reputation for tracking down and denouncing both Anabaptists and continuing Catholics ('papists'), but by the accession of Edward VI his faith seems to have undergone an intensification, approximating to a conversion to Calvinism. He attacked the way monastic appropriations were carried out and refused to wear vestments. Nevertheless in 1552 he took the step of having his wife and children naturalised English. He must have realised, though, the difficulties ahead of an England of Mary Tudor and a Catholic restoration. The very day before the queen's proclamation he preached a sermon emphasising the importance above everything of the gospels themselves, and warning his congregation against popery. Hardly surprising that he received a summons (on 16 August 1553) to appear before Mary's council. As a result he was first put under house arrest, then, in January, removed to Newgate.

Now an inspiriting change came over his personality. In gaol he behaved with exemplary courage and patience and was full of consideration for his fellow prisoners. With a number of these he drew up a 'Confession' of an uncompromising Calvinist nature. The author of many other writings as well, he conducted himself so brilliantly at his trial of January 1555 that his prosecutor was forced to stop his flow of arguments by saying that he refused to dispute any further with a heretic (a term Rogers immediately rejected). As a heretic it was, however, that he was condemned to death. He predicted an imminent restoration of Protestantism in England, and, fortified by this, maintained outward cheerfulness right up to the moment of death itself, which, as the first capital victim of Mary's persecutions, is truly hideous even now to contemplate. His clothes were viciously torn off him so as to rob his last moments of any dignity, and he was burned alive. His conduct at his end so moved the watching crowd that they cheered him continuously, and even little children called out exhortations. Such reactions all indicated the popular loathing of the Marian regime, and gave ample grounds for thinking how right Rogers' prophecy of England's near future would soon turn out to be.

If we reassemble the quartet at the time of the sale of that late learned man's library – Ortelius, in charge of things, Jan Radermacher, Emmanuel van Meteren and John's eldest son Daniel Rogers – and think of them as they were then and as they were to develop in their lives, we must first be struck by what they shared: an ardour for thinking and learning; a serious, reverential attitude towards life; and a strong belief in the spiritual and transforming nature of friendship. Continuing his narrative, Radermacher remembers:

> As this library contained some theological books at that time much sought after on account of their rarity, I went to Ortelius to see these books, of which I bought several which I still preserve as memorials of the beginning of that friendship between us which never after ceased. The warm and lasting character of our friendship appeared wonderful to ourselves, and one day Ortelius declared that to him this mysterious union of our minds, this similarity between our studies, habits and tastes appeared as something supernatural. I congratulated myself on this feeling, considering myself fortunate if I could frame my habits and studies according to his example. We took every opportunity to strengthen our union and this had some unexpected results.

These are beautiful sentiments, and there's beauty in Radermacher's expression of them. We who have the benefit of reading their correspondence, however, know that both Emmanuel and Daniel (Ortelius' own kinsmen) could have written in much the same way. Ortelius' ability to inspire and sustain close and attentive friendship – in no way weakening either his family life or his enjoyment of a wide and stimulating circle of acquaintance – is one of the most remarkable things about him, even in an age in which friends not only valued but gratefully articulated their feelings for each other. And, if we accept, as I believe we must, Radermacher's ensuing explanation of the origins of the *Theatrum*, we can say without distortion that it was the fine fruit of fine friendships. And no one would have known better Ortelius' strength as a friend than the recipient of Radermacher's letter, for Ortelianus was, it would seem, the person for whom Ortelius felt most warmly of all in his later years, with whose fortunes he was most caringly bound up.

Returning to the quartet, we can't but note two other features. Both Daniel Rogers (to be known as *Protestantissimus*) and Emmanuel van Meteren were born into and reared in households of Protestant conversion prepared to uproot themselves for the sake of their faith; Jan Radermacher became a Calvinist and also chose to live outside his native land. But not only were this trio to have hard-line Protestantism in common, they had England as well; two were naturalised Englishmen. Ortelius, the oldest – and this fact may not be without significance – stands alone here. Member of the Family of Love he might be, but he was to stay – and indeed be laid to rest within – the established Roman Church. However, his connection with Calvinists – from 1550 onwards the dominant body among those who opposed the Spanish domination of the Netherlands – was an intimate one. We can adduce many such signatures in his cherished *Album amicorum*. He must, to say the very least, have felt equivocally about the denomination, his admiration and his affection alike for so many of its subscribers being so strong. This adds a dimension to his career which shouldn't be lost sight of. When making prudent adaptations to the uneasy and changeable Antwerp status quo he must have been uncomfortably aware of friends' and relations' predicaments and their concomitant emotions. How keenly he must have longed for HN's *Terra pacis*.

Meeting over the disposal of John Rogers' library, the friends must have spoken of the man's ghastly fate, especially the one who was his son. Like so many stories of the time it is a disturbing compound of time-serving and heroism, of intellectual rigour and politicking, of passionate concern with religious truth and a willingness to inflict suffering on fellow human beings. But perhaps the compound isn't so bewildering. Perhaps we all know that the seemingly conflicting possibilities for all these lie in our psyches, only awaiting a suitable moment for release. Perhaps here also is the key to what made Ortelius so exceptional a human being: the capacity for violence, which acceptance of an all-or-nothing credo can encourage, was not part of his make-up, was a reason for his eschewal of radical commitment. It would come as something of a solution to him, then, to seek solace in an enterprise (from individual maps to the unifying atlas) which throve on and promoted pluralism, which valued the ampler dimension of space over the narrower and more exigent one of time, and which was dedicated to the peaceful imposition of order.

Having quickly become friends, no longer knowing each other only by repute, Ortelius and Radermacher saw a good deal of each other, pooling common interests, for these were years when Ortelius seriously began to build up his great collections. Jan's was an idealistic and scholarly temperament, in harmony with his own: no doubt they spoke a great deal about theology, philosophy and literature. But the merchant for whom Jan was working was no crass philistine, either. On the contrary, from what we know of him, Gillis Hooftman (1521–1581) gives further proof of the close relation between culture and commerce in Antwerp, and in the Low Countries generally.

Writes Radermacher:

My master, though not a man of letters himself, had great esteem for literature, for scholars and for the arts, especially those which could assist his own enterprises, and his liberality enabled me to buy a good many of the books that I coveted and to use them in my leisure hours. He spared no pains to obtain honest profits, and God so greatly prospered his efforts that, among his countrymen, there were few more wealthy than himself, and none, so far as I know, equalled him in mercantile capacities. In nautical experience he surpassed the Antwerp merchants of his time, but yet was friendly to all men, even to the lowest sort. For his nautical observations he wished to possess all necessary instruments but especially hydrographical charts and compasses, which he used in making careful calculations of the changes of the winds, whereby he was often able to foresee the dangers of shipwrecks and deviations from the proper course, and so to gain profits in assurances. He also bought all the geographical maps that could be had for the sake not only of calculating from the distances the freight of merchandise and the dangers they were exposed to. They also enabled him to make calculations about the news that was brought him daily about the wars in Europe and particularly in France.

And as the period was rich in disturbing events, he would buy maps of all the parts of the world that existed. As he didn't tolerate any delay, he would unfold them to examine them during the course of his lunch or his dinner or every time one was discussing places to travel to, or in the middle of conversation with friends or even during the course of personal reflections. And that didn't pass without inconvenience, when the table was laden with food and drink and the maps were too big. And the majority of them were this, better made to decorate the walls than to be handled by individuals.

'The dangers they were exposed to ...', daily news 'about the wars', a period 'rich in disturbing events ...' Radermacher (in Ortelius' *Album amicorum* he wrote of 'this troubled century of ours') is reminding his reader of just how fraught in the Low Countries was the era he's trying to evoke.

The main problem with his letter as a definitive document for the genesis of the *Theatrum* has always been the difficulty of ascribing dates to what it presents. But in the reference to the foreign wars we have an invaluable clue. The writer is remembering himself in apprenticeship which we know, from his later letter of amendment, began in 1554. From 1552 to 1559 the Hapsburg monarchy was engaged in a war against France for which the Netherlands provided the ideal military base, its strategic position causing a Spanish duke to call the region 'the bridle' of France. Begun by Charles V, the war was obsessively continued after his abdication of 1555 by his son Philip II, to the increasing resentment of the Netherlanders themselves who greatly minded having to pay for it. Eventually, after a resounding Spanish victory at St-Quentin in 1557, peace was sued, and the Treaty of Cateau-Cambrésis signed in April 1559. If Radermacher's master was troubled in his commercial life by French wars above all other events in which the period was 'rich', and we stay within the likely term of an apprenticeship, we are surely speaking of the period 1555–1559, or even (before the battle of St-Quentin) 1555–1557,

Antonis Mor's portrait (mid-sixteenth century) of Philip II gives us a convincing image of the young man of principled severity who took over from his father Charles V on his abdication 1555–1556 and dealt with the Netherlands so intransigently.

when Ortelius was between twenty-eight and thirty years of age, and Radermacher between seventeen and nineteen.

The scene Radermacher conveys to us with a born writer's instinctual raciness has the irrefutable quality of felt life. The account of Gillis Hooftman's near-frantic perusal of maps recalls some Netherlands seventeenth-century genre-painting or some even later (eighteenth-century?) British cartoon. We can both see and feel the man's impatience, his itchy eagerness to get hold of the suitable map. Now comes Radermacher's own great moment.

> Myself, I suggested a means of removing in some way this inconvenience. If one reduced to a smaller format all that the maps contained, one could then reassemble them, once they'd been drawn, in a book which could be handled in no matter what place. Hence the task was entrusted to me, and through me to Ortelius of obtaining from Italy – which was then particularly rich in beautiful things – and from France as many maps as could be found printed on one sheet of paper. In this way originated a volume of about thirty maps which is still in the possession of Hooftman's heirs. The use of this collection proved to be very commodious both for my master, on the tables of his office or in his bedroom, and for myself, squeezed as I was in my diminutive office. It gave our friend Abraham the opportunity of taking a decision with useful consequences for those who had a general interest in the topic. He reduced the largest geographical maps of the best-known authors, which rarely had the same format or dimensions as one another, on to single sheets of paper, in a single volume. In the year 1570 he published an ensemble of 52 maps – if I'm not mistaken – each of which bore the name of its author, accompanied by commentaries. As far as I know he had not himself before this edited more than three maps, that of Egypt, that of Asia (begun earlier by Giacomo Gastaldi) and that of the World.

And so we come by way of a seminal, earlier, and more *ad hoc* book of maps to the *Theatrum* itself.

It might be thought this earlier book could be used to settle once and for all the question of the origins of the *Theatrum*, of the existence of an Ortelian *proto-Theatrum*. Nowadays we could analyse paper and typeface

Map of Asia, 1569, by Giacomo Gastaldi (c.1500–65).
Ortelius drew on this as a source for his own.

accurately enough. But though a personal possession of the Hooftman family in 1603, the book is now lost. Yet on 7 January 1604, in his third letter on the subject to Ortelianus, Radermacher wrote:

I have almost forgotten to tell you that recently the Hooftman collection of maps, which served as a model for the *Theatrum* of Ortelius, came into my hands; it is seriously worn by long use and torn. It consists of 38 maps mostly printed at Rome at the presses of Michael Tramezzini, from a large imperial or royal map. Of these maps only eight or nine were edited in Belgium. I would add willingly the names of the regions represented, but I am hampered by lack of time. If you want to know, I will send you them another time. They are all European maps except those of Asia, Africa, Tartary and Egypt and the world map. As Ortelius, in order to understand history, took a passionate and particular interest in history and geography, he procured the best maps that could be had from their place of origin; the greater part of the time they were on plain sheets of paper and he coloured them himself. You must also know this: they surpassed in their elegance all the other maps which were then available to such a degree that people who had seen them just once didn't want to buy any others but those that had personally been coloured by Ortelius.

The question must, of course, be asked: there can be no shirking it. Is Radermacher to be trusted? Could he as an elderly man – though only in his mid-sixties – be allowing sentiment and personal pride to obfuscate the truth? I think this unlikely. His life's record is that of a singularly honourable individual prepared to pursue an independent and demanding course in foreign lands rather than compromise himself in principles and beliefs. The Cool family had done likewise, of course. In writing to Ortelianus, therefore, Radermacher was addressing someone who shared his faith, who was himself estranged by Calvinism from the southern Netherlands. He most certainly wouldn't have wanted to lead astray a man so greatly in sympathy with himself and on such key issues – not even by default. In fact, he is punctilious about admitting what he can't remember clearly, and corrects vaguenesses whenever he can. Over those details where we are ourselves in a position to judge he never seriously errs. Furthermore, Ortelianus being who he was, peculiarly close to and favoured by his uncle, Radermacher would have known he was addressing someone with enough knowledge and memories to refute anything too far from the path of historical accuracy.

Besides, that stamp of reality which his letter possesses is borne out in other facts he gives us about his subject. And, of course, Radermacher was actually to work with Ortelius on the scaled reduction of maps for the *Theatrum*.

Presenting Ortelius the young successful Antwerp businessman, he chooses to stress the importance to him of his visits to Italy (where he bought many maps) and to the Frankfurt Book Fairs (where he did likewise). He was right to make these emphases. During the 1550s Ortelius made four visits to Italy (with a fifth in 1561), and at least four visits (and, more likely than not, quite a number more) to the Book Fairs in Frankfurt. He also went to Paris in 1559 and in 1560 made a tour of France – in the distinguished company of Gerard Mercator and Frans Hogenberg. Italy, Frankfurt and France are all key to the history of the *Theatrum*.

CHAPTER FIVE

Italy was a constant destination for those as soaked in humanism as Ortelius. For however strong and distinguished its Netherlands tradition, it was the southern European country which was its originating home. Italy was also a natural focus of interest for anyone concerned with cartography. During the course of his Italian visits (as Radermacher vouchsafes) Ortelius bought a good many maps, and saw enough of what was happening in the publishing world to influence his ideas about their best presentation.

I see Ortelius' Italian travels as having a similar impact on his life to those made by his friend Pieter Bruegel in 1552/53, shortly after he too had been registered a member of the painters' Guild of St Luke. It was on his Italy-bound journey that Bruegel first turned his attention to the rendering of landscape. He sent the results of this to the Antwerp publisher, Hieronymus Cock, already catering for a growing public taste for Italian subjects. In truth these productions of the young Bruegel show none of the attributes of his great Flemish landscapes, but they do reveal the impact of, first, the drama of the Alps (by which Bruegel was reportedly quite overcome) and then of the light and the varieties of the Italian scene beyond them on a sensibility hitherto fed only by the Netherlands. How many northern Europeans have continued to react as Bruegel and Ortelius did? An awesome roll-call: Goethe, Keats, Shelley, Browning, George Eliot, Ibsen,

D. H. Lawrence, Freud ... Bruegel's response to the River Aniene's splendid, theatrical cascade of water at Tivoli was a fine copper-engraving, the *Prospectus Tiburtinus* – later dated 1555, to be used over a decade and a half hence by Braun and Hogenberg in their *Civitates*. However much we like it, we have to admit it's not a particularly original work; if it were representative of Bruegel, his reputation would be no more than that of many another worthy Guild-member. But what his Italian travels showed him was that he had it in him to be far more than the graphic artist he was in the process of becoming – and in this revelation the great Italian masters past and present played a major part. By applying the lessons of both personal and artistic Italian experience, Bruegel was empowered to move adventurously forward from such a work as the 1552 *Landscape with the Parable of the Sower* (with its wholly conventional upper right-hand section and its already memorably Bruegelesque lower left) and grow towards the vision of the great *pictor* we know.

Italy worked on Ortelius in a comparable fashion. Steeped as he was in classical travelogues, literature and history, Ortelius must have found Italy the realisation of many a mental image and imaginative speculation. His *Parergon* – the historical supplement to the 1579 *Theatrum* and all later editions – is one of the greatest acts of homage to classical culture ever made. But he was also stirred by Italian map-making activities past and present. It had been Italy that had launched the seminal revival of Ptolemy; it had been an Italian (Giovanni Contarini) who'd produced the first world map showing the New World, and an Italian too, Francesco Rosselli (1445–1513), engraver of Contarini's map and himself the 'author' of an oval projection for rendering the round Earth on a flat surface, who is the first professional map-dealer on record, Ortelius and Plantin's professional ancestor. But contemporary Italian achievements were more interesting to him still. For all the long lineage of Italian cartography, the year 1544 saw in a new, infectiously lively phase. Its centres were Venice, long distinguished for maps, and Rome; its leading figures Giacomo (Jacopo) Gastaldi (c.1500–65) and – though he didn't reach the greatest heights of his career until the later 1560s – Antonio Lafreri (1512–77), not a cartographer like his friend Gastaldi but an influentially inventive map-publisher and map-dealer. As Radermacher was specifically to say in his letter to Ortelianus, Gastaldi was directly exemplary to Ortelius – this can be seen in general and in particular terms – while in the case of Lafreri both his achievements and what could be perceived as his weaknesses or limitations galvanised the younger man.

Giacomo Gastaldi was born in Piedmont and trained as an engineer and in this capacity worked for the Venetian Republic. Increasingly, though, he turned his professional attention to cartography. He cuts an unusual and impressive figure in the field because of his purely technical, practical background; of those few others who shared it, Jacob van Deventer, contributor to the *Theatrum*, is possibly the most eminent. Given a 'privilege' (licence) for printing in 1539, he was made Cosmographer to the Republic in the earlier 1540s. Like his mentors and peers Behaim, Rosselli, Waldseemüller, Gemma Frisius, Mercator and Ortelius himself, Gastaldi was a dedicated Ptolemy scholar, and in 1548 made the maps for a brand-new Venetian edition, the first ever with a vernacular Italian text. The first map he actually published (as opposed to executed – he was already the author of one of Germany) had Spain for its subject (1544), a copper-engraving issued on four sheets; it is from this work that the new age of Italian cartography is often dated. It marks also the decisive, indeed permanent move from wood-block to copper for map-engravure. The lines of the maps could now be far more fluid and delicate, and Gastaldi followed 'Spain' with 'Sicily' (which Ortelius was to use as a source in the *Theatrum*).

The great popularity this last enjoyed is an index of one very important aspect of the period's enthusiasm for maps, which has remained a constant constituent in other periods. Of course maps give us a salutary idea of the extent of the world we live in, of the vast context of our own circumscribed lives, but they're also a way of appreciating one's own country/society. A map of one's own region or of one adjacent to it reinforces one's sense of identity; one's immediate context is given the dignity of serious objective treatment. Maybe when less of the world was known, when exploration of it was not so great a preoccupation or going concern as in the sixteenth century, this kind of attention to one's locality was not psychologically needed. But now it was. While every year a new stretch of coast, a hitherto unknown or even unsuspected island or promontory was being announced (and then mapped), the interest in the particularities of areas nearer to hand was increasing. Gastaldi, who made, among much else, a fine map of Italy as a whole and one of his native Piedmont, has a tutelary status here. (Mercator's map of Flanders, it must

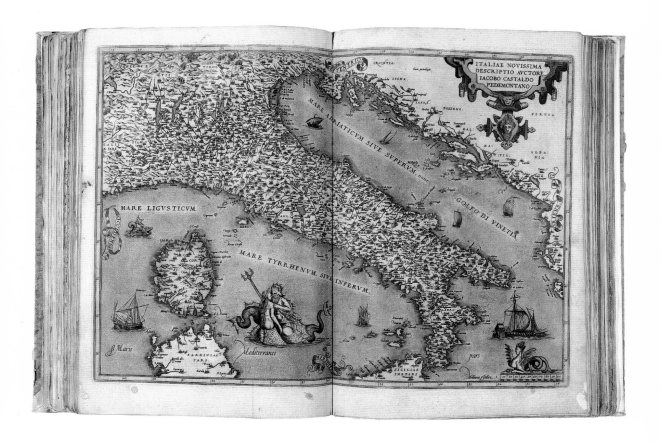

For his map of Italy for the 1570 Theatrum *Ortelius used Gastaldi's, an impressive tribute to the country to whom he, like so many other intellectuals of his day (including geographers and cartographers), owed such an enormous debt. Approvingly he quotes Pliny's words: 'Italy is the nurse and mother of all nations chosen by the providence of God to add lustre to the very heavens themselves…'*

be said, dates from as early as 1540. In that, as in so many other matters, the Flemish geographer was not just abreast but ahead of the Italians, of whose work in general he was often rather less than admiring.)

But it was probably for his coverage of the expanding globe that Ortelius and his fellows were drawn to Gastaldi. His world map, which stands behind Ortelius' own very first publication, appeared in 1546. On it we find the Americas, North, Central and South, in splendidly recognisable form, even allowing for the vagaries of North America's west and north-west coasts, and the absence of a Hudson Bay. Italy, a new world in itself for the responsive young Antwerper, was not least interesting to him because of the comparatively accurate renderings its cartographers offered of the New World, the fourth continent. (The first separately issued map of North America was also Italian, and again from Venice, Bolognino Zaltieri's of 1566.)

Like Ortelius himself, Gastaldi took the liveliest interest in stories of exploration and discovery and was a friend of the author/compiler Giovanni Battista Ramusio (1485–1557), secretary to the Venetian senate, and afterwards holder of a number of important official posts. Gastaldi drew maps for at least two volumes of Ramusio's great treasure-troves *Delle Navigazione e Viaggi* (*Concerning Voyages and Journeys*) of 1550–56. Their subject matter ranges from America's eastern seaboard to Sumatra. Ramusio was personally acquainted with the men making these knowledge-revolutionising expeditions, so that with his books the high seas and the untamed mountains, and the obscurely born, hard-living men who braved them, join up, as they should, with the printer's workshop and the student's reading-room. (Ortelius' own great delight in travel literature, his constancy in keeping up with it, had a marked effect on his own style, as both the Introduction to the *Theatrum* and the commentaries on the map versos show.) The maps Gastaldi executed for Ramusio were trapezoidal and south-orientated; later and more influential ones were rectangular and north-oriented. One map of his, that of Asia Minor, was actually first published in Antwerp, in 1555, by Bruegel's early patron, Hieronymus Cock.

As Radermacher confirms in his memoir-letter, Ortelius was later to bemoan the cumbersomeness of most available maps and Italians were already beginning to appreciate this at the time of Ortelius' visits. Portable maps issued in sheets weren't the answer to the problems, either. They too were unwieldy, and unprotected by binding. The proof of this is that an incalculably enormous number (the overwhelming majority indeed) of single maps, both in manuscript and printed form, have quite simply perished. This fact alone has made the history of cartography difficult to substantiate, so much basic material has been lost to posterity.

So, mindful of all these hardships, the Italians thought: why not offer the public collections of sheet-maps, to be perused in more manageable and durable format in private, even in comfort, away from the wall? A collection would be a practicable and pleasant means of doing justice to a medium which, after all, was intended for the minutest scrutiny.

Unlike Gastaldi, the Burgundy-born Antonio Lafreri didn't operate in Venice (although he obtained much material there), but in Italy's other great map centre, Rome, where he'd moved in 1540. His influence on the course of map-publication was enormous. He was a print-seller and publisher of high reputation; his maps aside, he was famous for issuing reproductions of painters' masterworks. He also put out news-maps which showed where some significant contemporary event – a siege, a battle – had taken place, or even was still raging. (The Italian nobility particularly relished a good battle-map.) Lafreri had both a publisher's and a journalist's eye for what would interest the public.

From about 1550 onwards he began issuing collections of maps bound up together and thus far more suited to private readers. Other booksellers soon emulated him. These assemblages eventually came generically to be known as Lafreri Atlases (whether or not Lafreri himself had played any part in them). 'Atlas' derives here from that Greek mythological figure who appears on the title page of a Lafreri collection of 1570: the Titan who carried the world (or heavens) on his shoulders. This is not the same Atlas whom Mercator honoured in his personal logo, and after whom his own great map-volumes were to be named; that Atlas was a philosophically inclined Mauretanian king, whom the subsequent reading public – perhaps understandably in view of the vivid and apt image conjured up by the other – has preferred to ignore.

These collections of maps are just what that designation suggests – puttings-together, little more. No two Lafreri atlases – and we have about seventy of them – are the same; what was included between the two covers depended entirely on the tastes and interests of the buyer/commissioner, and more often than not these were dictated by familial or commercial

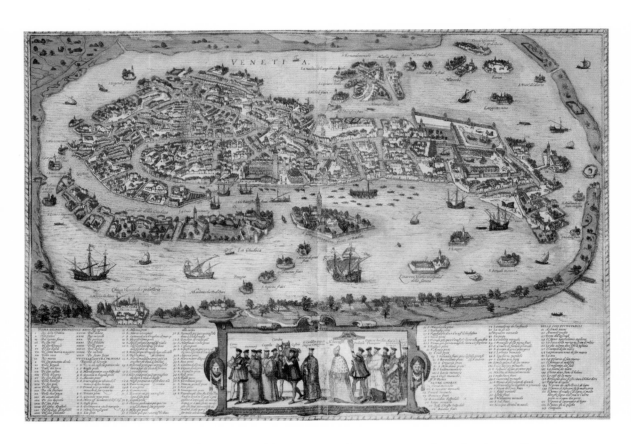

Venice in the 1572 Civitates orbis terrarum *from an engraving of 1565 attributed to Bolognino Zaltieri. This pays homage to Antwerp's great immediate predecessor (the smaller Dieppe excepted) in mercantile, cartographical and typographical domains.*

factors. Small wonder that an early twentieth-century American collector, George Beans, called such compilations IATO – 'Italian, Assembled to Order', a description intended as derogatory. IATO books of maps made no attempt at any kind of balance in their contents or at inner consistency – of scale, nomenclature, symbols – though Lafreri, as his title page announces, does follow the eastwards-moving sequence first established by Ptolemy in his *Geographia*, as indeed Ortelius' *Theatrum* was also to do. Personal preference determined inclusions in the Lafreri school, not the disinterestedness of the real atlas-maker. Not only did the maps differ, sometimes very considerably, in their methodology, they differed also in size. Bound together, they thus had to be trimmed – or enlarged with fancy margins – to make them more easily assemblable.

Why the Italians were inventive and map-minded enough to get as far as the Lafreri atlas but no further is not easy to explain. Was it simply that Italian society was not quite motivated enough? International commerce, so bound up with the Atlantic, increasingly centred on the north-west of the European continent, so there it was that the demand for systemised knowledge of the world would be keenest.

In fact, the Lafreri atlases began to appear just before 1570, but using the term 'Lafreri atlas' more loosely (as indeed it's usually used), Ortelius would undoubtedly have come across them in the Italian visits to which Jan Radermacher refers. One has to ask oneself: can his compilation for Gillis Hooftman come under this heading, especially as it used maps bought in Italy, the majority from Tramezzini? Certainly the maps must have differed considerably from one another, and have had many discrepancies. But from the outset, as Radermacher's letter to Ortelianus makes absolutely plain, the reduction of them to consistent size was integral to the operation. Each map was carefully redrawn with its fellows in mind.

So, at the outset of his cartographic career proper, Ortelius was possessed by the idea of the organic book. He saw this as indissoluble from dissemination of geographical knowledge, as Gastaldi and Lafreri never did. He may have learned from what he saw in Italy, but some of the learning was cautionary. Always he expected, in fact demanded, an intellectual ordering of material. Radermacher's testimony shows that, almost before he knew it himself, Ortelius' mind was guiding him, by its own instinctual inclination, towards the logic and inclusiveness of the *Theatrum*. And the outcome of his thirty-map work for Hooftman was that he started, virtually as soon as he'd completed it, to apply himself to just those systemising processes of which his atlas would be the handsome summation.

Twice a year a book fair was held at Frankfurt; this was the major international meeting point for all connected with the writing, designing, printing, publishing and selling of books – just as it is, only annually, nowadays. We know of at least four visits Ortelius paid to the Fair in the 1550s, but general accounts of the man suggest he was a regular attender. We remember Radermacher's words: 'While dividing with his mother the care of the family, he visited the Frankfurt fairs where besides transacting the necessary business, he conversed with scholars and neglected no opportunity to promote studies.'

If Radermacher's portrait is accepted and we think of Ortelius in these years as often regretting he couldn't lead a fuller intellectual life, then we see how the Frankfurt Fair was a great opportunity for him, compensatory for that university milieu he had never had. The Book Fair partook of a stimulating conversazione, like Plato's School of Athens (as shown in the Raphael *stanze*), or Aristotle's Lyceum, or the great *Mouseion* (Museum) in Ptolemy's city of Alexandria – to all of which Ortelius' own household was, in later years, to be compared.

To Frankfurt went writers to meet – or to find – publishers, Eastern European men of letters, particularly from Poland and Hungary, for whom the city on the Main was a convenient place of rendezvous, and a fair cross-section of western and southern Europe's book world. As we have seen from his knowledgeable handling of John Rogers' library, Ortelius was well-informed about many different kinds of books, and shrewd about their value. But he elected quite early to specialise in geographical works, geography and history being the two disciplines most deeply congenial to his mind. And when he started his search for maps suitable for a properly organised, *un*Lafreri-like volume, Frankfurt was the obvious place to go.

Frankfurt had been a thriving centre for trade fairs in medieval times, boosted by the city becoming (in 1356) the elective capital of the German kings. The Book Fair as such only got going after the 1445 Gutenberg breakthrough. Very soon it became a cultural as well as a commercial occasion – just as, since its reinstitution in 1949 as a beacon for a needy post-war world, it consciously and deliberately is today. Erasmus himself

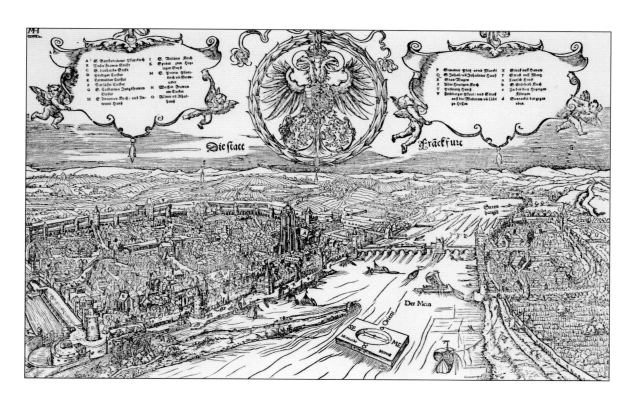

This woodcut by Conrad Faber (1552) appears in the 1572 Civitates orbis terrarum.
*The book fairs at Frankfurt, a city famous in the mid-century for organised commerce
and liberalism of thought, were unsurpassed and therefore indispensable as focuses for
the book trade. Ortelius and Mercator first met at Frankfurt; Plantin valued its fairs
so greatly that he kept a warehouse there for his goods and employed a regular agent.*

made use of it, urging his publisher to work flat out so books could be ready in time, and Luther, at the height of the bitterest controversy, was granted permission by city authorities to offer his works there. In the charged climate of the mid-sixteenth century this spirit of liberty made the Fair especially attractive to men such as Ortelius and Christophe Plantin (who went every year from 1557 and employed a regular agent for it) who throve, personally, intellectually and commercially, in so ecumenical an atmosphere. Sadly this spirit was not to survive into the next century – and showed grave signs of diminution even before the 1600s opened.

Visiting Frankfurt, however rewarding when you got there, was by no means a trouble-free procedure. The roads could be very dangerous, requiring circumvention, and, thirty years later, Plantin's agent was actually to be kidnapped *en route*. Nevertheless Netherlanders judged the Fair absolutely pivotal to their enterprises, and formed an easily recognisable body there.

It was at a Frankfurt Book Fair of 1554 that Ortelius met Gerard Mercator. They had friends and associates in common, notably the bookselling Birckmann family of Cologne who introduced the two. This encounter between a man of twenty-seven – who had as yet produced no work of his own – and a celebrated scholar of forty-two, globe-maker, cartographer and writer of Europe-wide reputation, had inestimable consequence for our entire Western civilisation. The two men – soon to become dear friends – met in the year (as we shall see) of one of the older's most considerable and durable triumphs. Ortelius undoubtedly knew and admired Mercator's work before their meeting. The eminent geographer would have been a natural magnet for him. The swiftness with which the friendship developed, establishing itself as a firm feature in both their lives, tells us that Ortelius communicated with those older than himself as easily as with those younger (van Meteren, Radermacher and, later, Ortelianus). What, we may ask, was the appeal of Ortelius for Mercator? Letters, entries in the *Album amicorum*, indeed the history of their whole discourse suggest real warmth on the latter's part. One assumes that Ortelius had an immediately palpable integrity, an unusual capacity for enthusiasm, a liveliness of mind and a readiness of appreciation that called out to something in Mercator's rare and sensitive nature. He must also have been extremely charming.

Ortelius was to speak of Mercator as the 'Ptolemy of our century'.

Paradoxically Ortelius' *Theatrum*, his claim on posterity, is seen by us as the first true specimen of a genus that history has named for Mercator's great work. So, as we envisage them in conversation in Frankfurt for the very first time, this is the point at which to say that to compare Mercator and Ortelius is in truth not to compare like with like.

No doubt their personalities were mutually sympathetic, with a (very fruitful) coincidence of both interests and moral values – but this does not mean that either their temperaments or abilities were akin, and it's important for this not to be assumed as the case. Ortelius is often referred to as a geographer – Johannes Sambucus (1531–1584), his Hungarian humanist, numismatist friend and contributor to the *Theatrum*, is the first person on record to call him a 'cosmographer' (the then current equivalent of our term). But it's debatable whether he's really entitled to these designations. Yes, Ortelius, as an ardent young man, acquainted himself with the latest developments in the subjects in which he was interested, but that doesn't mean that, for all his knowledge and understanding, he could have made original 'hard' contributions to them himself (any more than Vasari or van Mander could have painted works ranking them with the Italian or Flemish masters they so intelligently appreciated). Ortelius' contribution was to the dissemination and imaginative arrangement of geographical information – and to their wider recognition as essentials for a forward-looking and vigorous society. When the appropriate allowances have been made, Ortelius is closer akin to his neighbour a few streets away from his home, Christophe Plantin, printer, publisher, book-businessman, than to Mercator. Hence the emphases of this book.

It's obvious from all the entries in the *Album amicorum* as well as from Radermacher that, even as a young *commerçant* in his mid-twenties, Ortelius had qualities distinguishing him from his fellows, just as Plantin showed himself early to be no ordinary man of the book trade but an outstanding individual of remarkable energies, ideas and inner religious awareness. Ortelius' was a creative spirit; he transfigured all in which he engaged with the intense light of his own personal beliefs and enthusiasms. He was an original personality too, very much his own man, but without being any kind of original thinker. (How he would have disclaimed any notion that he was.) He was constantly alert to what was going on in geographical science and theological/philosophical ideas, but was no scientist or philosopher himself. Mercator, in contrast, was pre-eminently these.

Ortelius was to become the most inspired and resourceful of sixteenth-century editors, matching his friend Plantin's publishing genius. He was a communicator whose imagination, insights and vigilant good sense enabled him to appreciate where his society had vacuums to be filled, hunger to be assuaged. Mercator, however, was battling with problems which he came to believe could be solved only by himself, and one of these solutions (his Projection) was radically to change global communication. Ortelius' legacy, on the other hand, will be seen to have been primarily to the human imagination, to, quite literally, the *Weltanschauung* of the ordinary person.

It is of this that the present book is a celebration and analysis; its justification is the *Theatrum*'s career as informative and affective artefact. If we wish to bestow the term 'genius' on Ortelius, it would be for his ability to conceive such an artefact, and bring it, in all its diverse parts, to fruition. But Mercator, in contrast, was a *mind*, and all his works are attempts to give out what that mind had, often with great labour and wrestling, thought out and investigated.

Just as we tend to see Ortelius as Rubens posthumously depicted him, a man of almost daunting gravitas, so Gerard Mercator most often appears as Frans Hogenberg, a good friend, depicted him: a man of sixty-two, of seasoned face and long grey beard, his right hand holding his compasses, his left hand resting on one of his globes, and an expression in his eyes that suggests that the gaining of his knowledge has, of necessity, all but suspended him from the stuff of daily life. The Mercator whom Ortelius encountered at Frankfurt was indeed already a man of stupendous learning and intellectual achievement, but far from being detached from the world, he was a family man with six children, the support of whom could be a severe strain on his resources; he was involved in a number of complex projects involving regular movement between Duisburg (his German home) and Leuven (where he worked at the University) and was someone who – to a far greater degree than either Plantin or Ortelius – had actually been imperilled by the religious preoccupations so important to him. Information about him comes not only from letters, documents and his own writings, but from a biography, *Vita Mercatoris*, published only a year after his death by his Duisburg friend and neighbour, Walter Ghim (one-time mayor of that town), a work written out of heart-felt admiration for its subject.

Frans Hogenberg's portrait (1574) of his friend, Gerard Mercator (1512–1594), at the age of sixty-two. The artist has managed to convey Mercator's spirituality as well as his intellectual strength and geographer's wisdom.

CHAPTER
SIX

Mercator was born on 5 March 1512 in Rupelmonde, a largely undistinguished village on the right bank of the Scheldt, situated where it's joined, in pleasant water-meadow countryside, by the little river Rupel. A few miles away is the market town of St Niklaas, nowadays itself somewhat prosaic and undistinguished, except for its immense, handsomely flanked square, the Grote Markt, the largest in all Belgium, and, nowadays, for the Mercator Museum, with its exhibitions, library and opportunities for study. In the long village street of Rupelmonde one has only to confront the drab little house of dark brick, set among modest neighbours, which, as a plaque announces, was the great geographer's birthplace, to appreciate that unlike Ortelius, born into a highly esteemed and prosperous Antwerp family, Gerard Kremer (only called Mercator after he'd been enrolled in the University of Louvain in August 1530) came into the world in humble circumstances. The Kremers (Cremers) were of German origin, from Gangelt on the other side of the border from Limburg, and indeed Germany was to play almost as important a part in Mercator's story as his native southern Netherlands.

Gerard, the seventh and last child of his parents, Hubertus and Emerentia, was born when they were staying with Hubert's brother (or possibly his uncle), Ghisbrecht (Gisbert), a priest acting as chaplain to the hospital at Rupelmonde. His part in Gerard's life is analogous to Jacob van

Meteren's in Ortelius', for he it was who taught the boy the elements of Latin and who made the all-important choice over his education. The boy's parents found it impossible to make ends meet from the small-holding they ran, and returned to Gangelt but without success. They then came back to Rupelmonde even poorer than before. Hubert took up making shoes, supplying Ghisbrecht's hospital, but when Gerard was only twelve, his father died, prematurely worn out; his wife's death followed only a couple of years later. The upbringing of the children now fell to Ghisbrecht, and the decision he made about Gerard's education in 1527 had enormous consequence. Gerard had been attending school in Rupelmonde; now he was sent to a boarding school in 'sHertogenbosch of the Brethren of the Common Life, a school for the propagation of that *Devotio Moderna* of Geert Groote, whose quietist, pietistic teachings, as we've seen, influenced generations of Netherlanders, including Ghisbrecht himself. In fact, the school at 'sHertogenbosch was a particularly famous one, Erasmus himself having studied there half a century before (though it got little thanks from him; he'd loathed the place). So we can see a striking and significant concurrence in religious influences and thinking between Mercator and Ortelius, one which furthermore would have facilitated their discourse with Plantin, for all his so different provenance.

On 30 August 1530 Mercator enrolled as a poor student at the University of Leuven (Louvain), an institution to be central to his life. Leuven, which has only precariously survived the cruel wars of the centuries, is a major player in the history of the atlas, with its university founded in 1425, its stupendous Town Hall graced with elaborate stone tracery, its massively buttressed cathedral, and beyond these the sequestered peace of the Groot Begijnhof, a community within a community, originally for poor women and now for students, Mercator's successors. Mercator took his degree in philosophy (this comprised logic, physics, metaphysics and ethics). His choice of discipline should never be forgotten when appraising Mercator's career, with its impressive practical fruits. Everything he undertook was contexted in his mind by the significance of its place in God's world.

Indeed, after obtaining his Master of Arts in 1532 he passed through a spiritual crisis of tremendous and at times corrosive intensity, a period of his life about which Ghim in his *Vita* has nothing to say. Both his philosophical studies and those newer academic activities which were interesting him and which (Ingolstadt excepted) Leuven was alone in developing, gave him great mental anguish when he tried to review them against the ideal devotional life. That transition from classical to Christian ideas about the universe so essential to humanism, and which Erasmus for one had seen as seamless, was problematic for Mercator. Could Aristotle be so easily reconciled with the Christianity of the Testament? Or did such reconciliation diminish the significance of the Incarnation itself? Could the scrutiny, measurement and representation of the physical world not be in some way in conflict with the acceptance of revealed truth recommended in the Gospels and by the Church Fathers? Mercator decided to take himself to Antwerp and consult the eminent humanist geographer, astronomer and thinker, Franciscus Monachus. Monachus was a globe-maker of distinction, one of the first to enter into collaboration with a commercial publisher (Roeland Bollaert). He was also the author of the first printed map to show the Straits of Magellan.

Over a period of time this eminent man convinced the brilliant student that scientific probing of both the Earth and the heavens, far from being some atheistic impertinence, was in itself an act of worship. The findings that came from it only added to the glory of God and heightened Christian rejoicing in it.

Mercator would appear to have been both consoled and heartened by Monachus. He returned to Leuven in 1534. With Monachus and Gemma Frisius, whom he now got to know, he embarked on profound study of mathematics, astronomy and cosmography. Through these mentors – Gemma Frisius immediately appreciated the exceptional quality of Mercator's mind – he also learned instrument-making, at which he became one of the foremost practitioners of the age. In 1536, the year of his marriage to Barbara Schellekens, his terrifying doubts assuaged, and both his faith and his sense of personal vocation strengthened, he assisted Gemma Frisius with the first of his two globes. And the assistance he gave is of a most interesting nature – and makes us see how later there could be such common ground for him and Ortelius to tread.

Mercator had already been studying engraving (on brass and on copper) just as the young Ortelius would be apprenticed to do not many years hence. In the process he became convinced that the italic hand had far greater clarity and cleanness than the Gothic, that it was, naturally enough, considering its place of origin, far more suitable for the rendering of Latin, the contemporary *lingua franca*, than any other. More particularly, and from his own point of view, even more importantly, it made for easily legible and grateful-to-the-eye lettering on maps and globes and any other scientific documents or instruments. Humanists had long been disposed in the italic hand's favour, Erasmus having recommended it in a Latin dialogue of 1528, but it had been employed only rarely, and the Low Countries had never taken it up. Mercator – who wrote a treatise on italic calligraphy in 1540 – changed all that. Thanks to Mercator who, the most modest of men, nevertheless realised that his *Literarum latinarum* was 'a very important writing book', the names of places on those maps in which the Low Countries excelled over all other societies during the sixteenth and seventeenth centuries are given us in beautiful and immediately intelligible letters.

Mercator did the lettering for the first of Gemma Frisius' two globes, the 1536 terrestrial, the first instance both of the use of the italic in the Netherlands and of the name 'Gerardus Mercator Rupelmundanus' on a scientific instrument. But for the second globe, the celestial, his name appears not just as a letterer, an embellisher, but as a professional collaborator. With this his career as a cosmographer begins.

His marriage was to bring him six children between 1537 and 1542, the eldest being the geographically gifted Arnold. While his children, three boys, three girls, brought him much joy, they were also to cause him heartbreak, for from 1567 he lost them one by one, with the exception of the penultimate, his son, Rumold, who, himself distinguished in cartography, survived him and edited the great *Atlas* to completion. So, like Ortelius, Mercator had familial and professional responsibilities early. The second of Gemma Frisius' globes launched him as an independent producer of maps and instruments. That very year he issued a map of the Holy Land, greeted with enthusiasm as a real improvement on any previous one, even that of Jacob Ziegler whose work he drew on and acknowledged. And the year following, 1538, he produced his first world map, the *Orbis Imago*.

By now Mercator was applying his mind to that problem with which his name has since been indelibly linked: how to convey our spherical world on a flat sheet of paper. (It's a problem obviously with no possible complete solution; one can merely have more or less satisfactory methods of presentation.) For the *Orbis Imago* Mercator's projection was that cordiform (heart-shaped) one pioneered by Oronce Fine (Finé) in his maps of 1519 (single heart) and 1531 (double heart). Mercator in his world map assigns one heart to the northern hemisphere, one heart to the southern. If the one is mounted (in the mind or in reality) on the back of the other something not unlike a globe results. At the dip between the two 'lobes' of the heart Mercator has situated the polar regions.

His map paid particular attention to the Americas, in fact is of historical importance in that it differentiates between a South America and a North America (and doesn't connect the latter with Asia, as Monachus' map had done). It was extremely successful, enjoying no fewer than three Italian editions, and has a parental relation to later mid-century essays in the medium, including Gastaldi's and Ortelius'. Its good reception inspired him to apply himself to two major projects, the one a map of Flanders, which came out two years afterwards and was widely bought (especially in Italy and the Low Countries), and the other a map of Europe, which was fourteen years in the making. Indeed, it was not ready until the year of his meeting with Ortelius in Frankfurt. Both maps are outstanding landmarks in cartographic history.

Today appropriately housed in the Plantin-Moretus Museum (Mercator was later to enter into business arrangements with Plantin to their mutual advantage), the map of Flanders is at once very beautiful and very precise; the two attributes complement each other and have given the work its reputation. North-oriented and engraved on copper-plate, it features about a thousand places, all named in neat italic. Towns are marked by a bell-tower – appropriately, since Mercator utilised Gemma Frisius' triangulation method of ascertaining distance, established, it'll be recalled, by the ascent of Flanders and Brabant church towers. Bigger towns are denoted by clusters of houses encircling these belfries. Woods, rivers, hills, meres, the waves of the sea itself are all finely done (look at the course of the Scheldt, or the forest south of Aalst or the more scattered woods in the vicinity of Lille) and the whole is magnificently bordered, top and bottom. The design is of medallions containing the names of the leading Flemish noble families, right and left the margin is graced with the coats-of-arms of Flemish cities and the heraldic banners of Flemish seignories. All these details show that Mercator, like his younger friend-to-be, had a lively awareness of the historical past, and of the cultural loyalties and emotional tensions of the present. There are, unusually for Mercator,

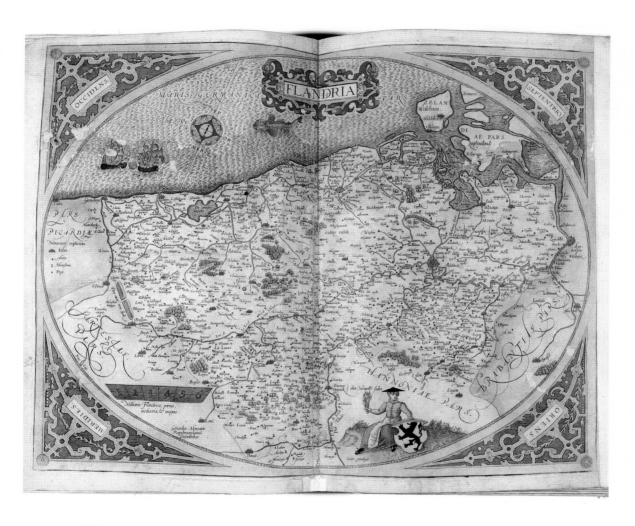

Flanders. *This beautiful map is Gerard Mercator's own, drawn and engraved by him. The text reads as a litany of loved names and admirable attributes, natural and human.*

no latitudinal or longitudinal parallels, yet accuracy is of the map's very essence. Much studied – not least because it was for a long time lost and when found in the 1870s was thought a suitable rallying icon for Flemish nationalism – the map has an overall discrepancy between its distances and the real ones of only 3.4 per cent, while the relationship of place to place has admirable geographical truth.

No doubt it's significant that Mercator chose to follow a world map with one of his own native province, and then to move out from that into the larger subject, into the continent of which Flanders was a politically strategic and cartographically conscious part: Europe itself. For almost a decade and a half he worked at what had formed the major part of Ptolemy's *oikoumene* and redressed the *Geographia*'s imbalances through a wholly modern system of meridians (longitudes). This is partly what caused him to take the time he did (though his Mediterranean remains wider than in reality, if less so than the Alexandrian's). Yet, despite this distortion, this map, on a huge scale, and as beautiful a piece of work as that of Flanders, constituted a nonpareil of geographical research and knowledge, and was greeted as such. It brought him fame, and Walter Ghim, never reluctant to extol his friend and neighbour, said that it 'attracted more praise from scholars everywhere than any similar geographic work which has ever been brought out'. Plantin was to do very well with sales of this work.

In the years between the Flanders and Europe maps, Mercator was intimately involved with his own University of Leuven and fellow academics there, and continued to make globes. Globes were by no means made redundant by either world maps or atlases. They had their own validity, their own unique truth. The later sixteenth century/early seventeenth century was a great period for globe-production. The world's roundness still exercised a power over the contemporary psyche that subsequent centuries, with their systematic mastery of the whole sphere from pole to pole, have proceeded to reduce – until our own era of space travel and satellites, when it has acquired fresh significance. Mercator's globe of 1541 was a major contribution to the form.

This new globe was of the greatest importance for mariners. The lines proceeding from its 'wind-roses' were those following the direction of the constant compass (i.e. loxodromes or rhumb lines), a great advantage for the plotting of navigational routes, which would be further aided (the globe being always awkward to carry about) by the projection system

Mercator himself finally arrived at for his great world map of 1569. The 1541 globe also provided information about the night sky useful for any voyager. We know what Mercator's working methods were for making globes (how they evoke the patience, the dedication of the man!): the placing of engraved gores (segments like the scored 'quarters' of orange peel) over a carefully fashioned spherical body consisting of paste covering plaster covering cloth covering specially pressed strips of wood.

So Ortelius at the Frankfurt Fair was in dialogue with a man of enormous repute and attainment, whose career had been exemplary, not to say enviable. But in reality it could also act as a fearsome warning, and this was only reinforced by Mercator's distinction and excellent moral character. Why, after all, was he not living in a Flemish society, despite his close working connection to Leuven University? Why was he living away, in a German community, in Duisburg (then only a small town of some 3,000 inhabitants and not the present big industrial member of the Ruhrgebiet)?

Ten years before his meeting with Ortelius, in 1544, Mercator's name had featured sinisterly on a list, and sinister too had been the consequences of this. Mercator had gone back to Rupelmonde to discuss family financial business with his uncle Ghisbrecht. He was therefore out of Leuven when the Attorney General of Brabant arrived in that city to arrest forty-three people. Their crime? 'Luthery' – which, as we've seen, was another name in the eyes of authority for intended sedition against Charles V and his regent. Mercator was alleged to have written letters to friars in Mechelen, something never authenticated and doubtless trumped up; his being out of town was held to be highly suspicious in itself, proof of guilt. On 15 February he was arrested as a 'fugitive from justice' in the village of his birth.

Today an appealing walk away from Rupelmonde's square takes you to an old mill and mill-stream, and at their back a tower; this is the keep of the old castle of the Counts of Flanders. It was here that Mercator was imprisoned, long months from February to September. During that time of uncertainty and dread an agent was sent to Mechelen in search of the letters Mercator was supposed to have written, but none was found. The University of Leuven, appreciative of Mercator's immeasurable moral and intellectual worth, protested his innocence and implored his release.

This eventually was granted. After seven months one of the foremost thinkers and scientists in the entire Hapsburg domains was free again.

Whether or not he'd had Lutheran sympathies (in fact these were a feature, in Flanders and Brabant, of an earlier period than the 1540s) Mercator now began to realise that for someone who believed as he did in the free range of intellect and spirit, the Spanish Netherlands was no place to be. Eight years later, after dealings with the city's Duke William, he and his family moved, as did a number of other like-minded Netherlanders, to Duisburg.

Of the people accused together with Mercator, one man was punished by having his head cut off, two were burned at the stake, and the two others – both women – were buried alive. If Mercator ever confided in his friends Ortelius and Plantin what he'd been through they must have listened with horror, certainly, but also with complete comprehension. These things did happen, and in their own country.

CHAPTER SEVEN

In 1558 Ortelius, now thirty-one, bought from Christophe Plantin a number of books, including six copies of Erasmus' *Colloquies*, in Dutch and French, and van Staden's map of America. In return he supplied him with several other maps, including two copies of Mercator's *Europe*. Not long afterwards Ortelius purchased several more maps from Plantin, who was then conducting business in a house in central Antwerp's Kammenstraat called *Gulden Eenhoorn* (The Golden Unicorn) – its name would be changed to *Gulden Passer* (The Golden Compasses).

These are the first recorded dealings between Ortelius and Plantin, but it's hard to believe, their shared interests being what they were – from the Guild of St Luke to the Family of Love, from books to engravings and maps – that they hadn't met well before this. They became firm friends, their social circles overlapped, and, to a significant extent, their fortunes also. From 1564 Ortelius' name occurs quite regularly in Plantin's ledgers, providing him with maps he himself had coloured. In the mid-1560s Plantin, who'd been selling maps and globes for a decade at least, obtained a monopoly for the sale of all maps. He was to supply Ortelius with all the paper for the *Theatrum*, was responsible for the sale of more copies of that work than anybody else (probably for half of all those sold anywhere) and in 1579 became the book's printer as well. There's more to the close connection between the two men even than these facts. Plantin, through force of expertise, industry and vision,

4.

IMPRESSIO LIBRORVM.

Potest vt vna vox capi aure plurima: Linunt ita vna scripta mille paginas.

Ioan. Stradanus inuent. Ioan. Galle excud.

Though this print by Filips Galle (after Johannes Stradanus) is from c.1550 (the year that Plantin became a citizen of Antwerp), it gives a good idea of the atmosphere prevailing in the printer's later and far larger establishment. By 1561 Plantin had four presses in use, a number rarely surpassed. Pressmen worked in pairs. Plantin became one of Antwerp's biggest employers. The workforce (dealings with whom were carefully documented) was not nearly as peaceful as the ambience of today's Plantin-Moretus House (or even this print) would suggest. The men who worked for Plantin were a tough lot, if also industrious and often highly skilled, and always potentially unruly; disputes and even fights could and did break out.

had created the greatest printer/publishing concern not only in Antwerp, not only in the Netherlands, but, during his heyday, in all Europe. His success permeated the success of others; the provenance of Antwerp was an insurance for authors desirous of being known elsewhere, like Ortelius or Mercator. Furthermore Plantin's career – its ups and downs, its inconsistencies and highlights – has a meaningful similarity to Ortelius' own. Now that we can see Ortelius moving in the direction of his *Theatrum*, something more needs to be said about his great friend Plantin.

On 21 March 1550 Plantin, a Frenchman by birth, swore the oath which made him a citizen of Antwerp. No one can have been prouder to have been made this than he. He'd moved to the City-on-the-Scheldt with his wife and small daughter probably only the year before; certainly he'd been a resident for no more than two years. The man whose patrician-aspected mansion on the Vrijdagmarkt would become a magnet for Antwerp's visitors, rivalled only by the house of Peter Paul Rubens (intimate friend of his own grandson), called himself on this important occasion merely 'Christophe Plantin, son of Jean, of Tours, bookbinder'.

And even this doesn't tell us as much as we now want to know, and the description 'bookbinder' may well have been a blind. Some of Christophe Plantin's descendants, reluctant to believe their illustrious family had only humdrum forebears, indulged in high-flying speculations about his origins, smothering the few certain facts with snobbish fantasies. In truth we can't be sure either exactly where their ancestor was born, or when. But it seems likely that 'of Tours' was correct enough, counting the village of Saint-Avertin as part of the city. As for the year of birth it's now generally assumed he was born in 1520, this being consistent with what he gave out about himself for the greater part of his life. In his last five years, however, he changed his mind and gave himself an extra eleven years, while if we go by his tombstone his birth-year was 1514.

Plantin's father, who was indeed called Jean, was a long way from being, as was later claimed, a military man of noble blood: he was in service. Plantin's mother died in the plague which hit the locality in the 1520s. Jean fled the stricken area with little Christophe and obtained a post in Lyons as footman to 'canon obedentiary' Antoine Porret. Living in this churchman's household were five nephews of his, all of whom he was bringing up, one, Pierre (surname Porret) the son of his brother, the other four (surname Puppier) the sons of his sister. A close friendship developed, from the very first, between Pierre Porret and Christophe, one which lasted all their lives. 'We were brought up together from our earliest childhood,' Pierre was to write, going on to refer to their 'brotherliness' and 'great friendship'. And truly Pierre showed himself brother and friend to Christophe by providing shelter in his Paris home for him and his family when they were in real danger. He allowed his household to be used as one centre of Plantin's diversified business.

It is to Pierre Porret that we are indebted for the most valuable material about Plantin's earlier years. In 1567, when Plantin was in danger for his life, Porret wrote his 'brother' a letter which reads like a potted biography of him, clearly intended for the recipient to show if he felt the need arose.

Porret relates how, at the end of some years of service in the canon's household, Jean Plantin, with Christophe, accompanied a Puppier nephew, another Pierre, to the universities of Orléans and Paris, Jean and Pierre returning to Lyons in 1537, and Christophe being left behind in Paris. Why? The abandonment of him has never adequately been explained (and Plantin never seems to have held it against his father). A seventeen-year-old alone in Europe's metropolis, with only a little money from his father, and that intended to pay for his studies! – it's a strange situation, and anyway what *were* these studies? Plantin in mature life was adamant about his lack of academic education, a deficiency he tried to remedy with the publication of learned books. According to Pierre Porret the plan was for father and son to meet up later in Toulouse where Jean was to go with another nephew of his master's. But in the event Jean went to Toulouse without Christophe.

Considering the distinction of his later chosen career, it seems to me probable that Christophe, young though he then was, had already interested himself in book-production and its current state. Lyons, after all, was second only to Paris as an independent centre of French printing and publishing, just as it was of finance. Celebrated, like Frankfurt, for its great trade fairs, Lyons had an internationalist culture attracting humanists in general and printers in particular and leading to the establishment of a strong Protestant constituent; in all this it reminds us of nowhere more than Antwerp. Lyons had entered the sixteenth century with about forty flourishing presses, and among those that prospered later was one which employed François Rabelais as an editor, indication enough of the quality of the city's intellectual life (*Gargantua* was launched with great success there). In the years of his pre-eminence Plantin would arrange for Lyons booksellers, such as Clement Baldin, to have their books bound in Antwerp. Lyons should be accorded a proper place in Plantin's pedigree.

After trying to fend for himself in Paris, Christophe Plantin took action on his own account, going to Caen in Normandy. It isn't surprising that his choice lighted on the book business there. Caen was the seat of a major university founded in 1432, and now a centre of Protestantism. Here Plantin entered the service of bookseller and bookbinder Robert Macé (1503–1563).

He acquired real and lasting expertise in both sides of Macé's business. At bookbinding he truly excelled; his Antwerp career began with him practising this craft, and he went on doing so even after he'd officially discontinued it in favour of other activities. He was proud enough of his own skill to give Ortelius, in the later 1560s, a present of a book bound by himself.

In Caen Plantin met the girl who was to be his wife: Jeanne Rivière was a maid in the Macé establishment from the Norman countryside. Christophe married her in 1546, and their first child, a daughter Margareta was born the following year. Margareta was to play a prominent part in her father's printing and publishing firm and to marry a distinguished humanist scholar and aide to her father, Frans Raphelengius (1539–1597).

Then Christophe Plantin made another major decision – this time to leave Caen. Writes Pierre Porret to him in that letter of 1567: 'Then you brought your family to this city of Paris, where we were constantly in each other's company.'

This (second) stay in Paris is vital to our understanding of Plantin's whole subsequent life (and therefore by extension of Ortelius'). The key to its conundrums and tensions is surely here. But that key, though at times we may feel we've got very close to it, finally eludes us; the necessary hard objective evidence is wanting.

Paris, though soon to be overtaken by Antwerp, had long been Europe's greatest centre of printers/publishers. During his reign (1515–1547) François I took a strong personal interest in printing and not for wholly altruistic reasons either. He realised the public power of the printed document. He was on terms of real friendship with his 'Printer to the King for Hebrew, Greek and Latin', Robert Estienne, a man of the greatest learning and judgement who, together with Venice's Aldus Manutius, should be seen as Plantin's true ancestor. He must have heard a good deal about him.

And what he heard would have made him understand that the situation of independent-minded printers in Paris, indeed in all France, was a seriously deteriorating one. After François' death in 1547 (when Plantin was living in Paris) Estienne felt only too vulnerable, and in 1550 left for Calvinist Geneva.

In this climate Plantin's mind examined religion. All believers had to decide about the relative importance of outward observance (the sacraments, the rites, public professions of belief in cardinal dogma) and inward knowledge of God and Jesus Christ. The first seemed essential for the binding together of society, for the maintenance of a God-fearing nation; but the second addressed the individual's soul. By temperament, and maybe also by private intimations, Plantin already inclined to an emphasis on personal religious experience. In the times he was living in, however, whether in France or, as was soon afterwards his home, within the Holy Roman Empire, the personal all too swiftly became the political – no matter how accommodating the individual intended to be (or to seem) to the ruling powers. Any turning away from authority and orthodoxy would be looked at suspiciously, be thought to smack of subversion.

Plantin's ideas on religion – which were those also of his wife, Jeanne – were developed and sustained by the people he met through his 'brother' Pierre Porret. Pierre, now practising in Paris as an apothecary, was one of a circle of friends strongly involved with the Family of Love.

It's hard to make out whether or not HN actually met Plantin in Paris during his and Jeanne's stay there with Pierre Porret. But beyond doubt it was at this period that the young couple's lives became bound up with prosperous influential Paris Familists – and therefore linked up with Hendrik Niclaes himself. This connection was to be the foundation of Plantin's Antwerp publishing business, and therefore logically leads to his creative friendship with Ortelius.

A theory has been put forward (by scholar Eugénie Droz) that Plantin, during his stay with Pierre, worked for a printer (in fact a Calvinist), Jacques Bogart, whose house, Saint-Christophe, was a clandestine meeting-place for Family members. HN, knowing of the young printer's good work here, invited him to Antwerp to continue it. Which he did. His description of himself to the city authorities as 'bookbinder' was therefore a screen for secret organised printing activities.

While holes have been picked in Droz's arguments, which certainly require ampler confirmation, I believe there's truth in them. We know that Plantin achieved spectacular success early, we know that he had friends of influence and substance in Paris, and that he encountered Netherlanders in their company, we know that he joined, and was to become important in, the Family of Love. We do not know, on the other hand, what his working life was during his stay with Pierre Porret. Is it really likely that a man as energetic and determined as Plantin didn't seek out interesting and fruitful business opportunities for himself at this time? Droz's interpretation of the 'missing' year(s) also highlights a key quality of Plantin sometimes downplayed: his love of risk-taking – which strangely coexisted with a desire to be comfortable and affluent. He responded to, even courted, the challenge of the difficult and dangerous. Droz's ideas are also consistent with a persistent ambiguity about Plantin's attitude to Protestant persuasions, including Calvinism itself (an ambiguity Ortelius almost certainly shared), which all his later fervent professions of Catholic devotion shouldn't keep us from appreciating. Plantin was by no means as constant in his opposition to the New Religion as sometimes claimed.

'And,' continues Pierre in his letter of 1567, 'in the year 1548 or 1549, you went to Antwerp where you are still.'

Recognition of a change for the worse in the French political climate? (The new king Henri II was intolerant of heresy, exercising special vigilance against printers.) Hopes of an inspiring and useful Low Countries association of intellectuals and businessmen (even though the political atmosphere in which they lived was if anything more fraught than in Paris)? Involvement with a strong religious fraternity which offered material rewards? Which was the dominant factor we cannot now say, but certainly Christophe and Jeanne were impelled northwards, to the banks of the river Scheldt, towards one of the most illustrious careers of the century, of which participation in the first atlas was to be a spectacular high point.

For all that he suffered there Plantin always felt bound to the city; it was to Antwerp itself rather than to the Netherlands as a whole that he was to feel loyal. About the relationship between Christophe and Jeanne one can only make surmises, aided by the legacy of hearsay. Their marriage was a lasting one; they were to have together six (possibly seven) children. Jeanne was extremely practical, skilled (all agreed) in every aspect of housekeeping and a good manager economically; she seems to have been devoted to both husband and children, was kind and unselfish, and – most importantly – she shared Christophe's religious views. His 'brother' Porret, who took her in when the crises came, was clearly very fond of her.

But a sadness hangs over the image of her that posterity has been left. Her husband became a 'great man', but only in her loyalty to him was she a great man's wife. She didn't care for 'finery', we're told, she could neither read nor write and yet she was pivotally part of the leading publishing house of her continent and century. She had next to nothing in common with the many eminent and brilliant intellectuals who were Plantin's regular guests, men like Justus Lipsius (that close friend and admirer of Ortelius) who, while respecting her housewifery, judged her ignorant. One imagines her, if always busy, as often extremely lonely. This comes out in the marvellous portrait of her by Peter Paul Rubens, done over thirty years after her death at the request of that great painter's friend, Jeanne's grandson, Balthasar I Moretus, from contemporary likenesses. Her eyes with their oblique gaze are joyless; there's a sourness about her tightly pursed mouth.

Rubens shows Christophe Plantin too as melancholic (see page 112); he suggests a life almost too beset by responsibilities and anxieties, and this tallies with the mass of his correspondence, with its heartfelt reiterations of racking money worries, apprehensions of political instability with personal repercussions, and health problems consequent on business ones. But he also had, according to Rubens, immense inward reserves, great trust in his own intellectual powers. This inner confidence is fittingly symbolised by the position of his hands – the left holding a well-bound book (the binding of his own making perhaps), the right the pair of compasses that he had made the universally respected symbol of his mighty enterprise, his mature lifetime's achievement: the printing/publishing house known as *De Gulden Passer* (The Golden Compasses).

Plantin began his life in Antwerp by working at the skills he'd acquired in Robert Macé's Caen ménage: bookbinding and bookselling, especially the former. He soon showed himself an outstanding bookbinder. Samples of his exquisite work on morocco are on view in his Vrijdagmarkt house to this day. His productions attracted much attention particularly from businessmen looking in on his premises on their way to or back from the Bourse, and from scholars. His premises were in Lombardvest, in that quarter of the city most favoured by printers and binders. Not that he practised bookbinding only; he also, said his grandson Balthasar I Moretus,

Rubens carried out the commission by Balthasar I Moretus for a portrait of his Plantin grandmother (born Jeanne Rivière) between 1630 and 1636. It's hard not to see sadness in her severe aging face.

This portrait of Christophe Plantin was commissioned by his grandson Balthasar I Moretus from his old friend of his schooldays onwards, Peter Paul Rubens (1577–1640), who executed it from contemporary likenesses some time between 1613 and 1616. Note the Golden Compasses, which gave their name to his whole enterprise, in the printer's right hand.

'[made] small chests and boxes, which he covered with leather and gilded, or wondrously inlaid with small pieces of leather of different colours. No one equalled him in the making of such caskets, neither in Antwerp nor in the Netherlands. Thus he soon won fame with Mercury and the Muses ... The scholars bought elegantly bound books, the merchants caskets or other precious things that he made himself or had sent from France.'

Among those impressed by this newcomer from France was the town *griffier,* Alexander (Scribonius) Grapheus, son of Cornelius Grapheus of More's *Utopia.* He was a man of great prominence in the Antwerp community, not only on account of his distinguished father, but because he himself was learned, an admired jurist, a man of taste and serious friendships. There's no doubt that he was familiar with those circles in Paris that Plantin himself had frequented. So – had the two of them indeed met there? The questions multiply. Was Grapheus in fact a sympathiser with the ideals of the Family of Love, or even an associate member? Was he part of the design that brought Christophe Plantin out of Paris and into the City-on-the-Scheldt? It is, of course, perfectly possible that the quality of Plantin's work was so outstanding that a connoisseur such as Grapheus, like many another Antwerp dignitary, would have been drawn to him anyway. At any rate it didn't take long for the young foreigner to obtain a major and surely coveted commission: to bind all the *griffier's* books. The style of his work had, we're told, a curious quality that appealed to Grapheus.

Grapheus' friendship with Plantin was to be a very strong one; many letters between them have survived. He was a friend of Ortelius also, featuring in his *Album amicorum.* Grapheus' growing respect for Plantin's capabilities, character and business acumen resulted in his lending him enough money for him to start a proper shop. Plantin never ceased to be grateful. In a letter to him (in Latin) of 1574 Plantin speaks of the 'debt I owe to your sincerity and generosity of spirit to me at that time when I first came into these regions'. As Grapheus was, after all, *griffier* of the city, it seems probable that the speed with which Plantin became an Antwerp citizen – and was thus enabled to join the appropriate and necessary guild – owes a good deal to him.

But his kindness to Plantin appears different if Grapheus did have connections, even an affiliation with HN's Family of Love. A piece of invaluable evidence (though from a later date) has come to light, and Ortelius is involved. Thanking Ortelius for sending him a copy of his

Synonymia geographica (1578), Grapheus wrote the author a poem containing a figure of speech popular with, and possibly peculiar to, the movement: 'Hercules at the crossroads', a reference to the Greek hero's having to choose between two women, Virtue or Pleasure. Family members used the expression as a synonym for Free Will in which they, in complete and all-important distinction to Lutherans or Calvinists, believed. Grapheus, man of the world as well as man of letters, would hardly have employed the Masonic-like phrase innocently. It is a provable fact that Plantin was swiftly accepted socially (and legally) by Antwerp society; we are in no doubt that he joined the Familist circles there not long after his arrival, becoming before very long an 'officer' in it. It therefore seems more than likely that Grapheus played an insider part here.

Once he was a registered citizen of Antwerp, Plantin was eligible for membership of a guild. He joined the Guild of St Luke later that year (1550). Ortelius was, of course, already a member of this.

When registering himself for the guild, Plantin interestingly did not this time put down 'bookbinder', nor 'casket-maker', which would also have been accurate enough. Expressing his intention rather than his (overt) current occupation, he called himself 'printer'.

The next decade of his life was amply to vindicate him here, and later history more amply still. By the time he died Plantin had been responsible for the publication of 2,450 works, an average of 55 per annum, good figures even today; the sixteen presses he had in 1575 constituted a record not broken until the nineteenth century.

Plantin taught himself Dutch. Henceforth, as an Antwerp citizen, he would use the Dutch form of his surname, Plantijn, as well as the French. Dutch was obviously necessary for him as an Antwerp businessman; in 1552, thanks to the loan from Alexander Grapheus, he opened his first shop, in Twaalfmaandenstraat, just off the Meir, then, as now, Antwerp's principal commercial street. And he would have dealt with his many customers, as he'd have been expected to, in their own language which, however, he always spoke with a French accent.

While working in the shop he must have kept a constant eye on the city's many thriving printing works – though if Eugénie Droz is right, he was also himself busy printing clandestine religious books. In either case he most definitely hadn't styled himself 'printer' for nothing; he knew his own immense capacities, not least for unstinting work and for razor-sharp

Christophe Plantin lived some years in the street (Twaalfmaandenstraat) that ran (runs) from the Exchange (Bourse/Beurs) shown here to the Meir, still Antwerp's principal commercial artery. The building was the heart of Antwerp in its capacity as a world financial centre; it was burned down in 1868, and its nineteenth-century replacement has been restored, its walls displaying a vast map of the world.

assessment of business potential, and had clearly determined that it should be as a printer (which then meant 'publisher' also, and usually bookseller as well) that he would make his fame – and his money. What is more, he persuaded others of this, through (one conjectures) his strength of personality.

In 1555 a crucial and curious episode took place. By this time Charles V, prior to his official abdication, had made over the Netherlands to his son. Philip had not yet arrived there from Spain, however; his secretary in Antwerp was Gabriel de Çayas, with whom, following an unmistakable and surely not innocent pattern, Plantin had already become friendly. (De Çayas would remain a recurrent figure in the dramas of his career; the Frenchman wrote him many fervent letters assuring him of his political loyalty and religious orthodoxy at times when both – with some justification – were in doubt.) The royal secretary wished to send the Queen, Philip's wife, a jewel, which was to be set inside a particularly beautiful casket. Who better to make such a casket than Plantin?

After he'd been working on it for some days, Plantin was ordered to bring the completed object round in person to de Çayas' house in the evening. A messenger would take it to Spain early the next morning. Darkness had fallen by the time its maker finally set out for his destination. Somewhere between the Bourse and the Meir, Plantin was set on by a group of drunken merry-makers returning from a party. They were looking for a zither-player with whom they had a bone to pick, and thought the casket Plantin was holding was a zither-case. Aggressive as well as drunk, they chased Plantin, and when they'd caught up with him, one of them thrust a dagger into him, stuck it in so deep in fact that it was hard to pull out. Plantin comported himself with real bravery, and, realising they'd made a bad mistake and panicking, the men dispersed. The casket-maker was left to stagger home bleeding. Two eminent medical men were called round to his house, but they were far from confident that the victim of this attack would recover. One of these physicians was Joannes Goropius Becanus (1518–1572), who was also a philologist of standing, a member of the Family of Love, and, later, one of the Golden Compasses' major authors.

Plantin did get better, of course, though even in later life his wound sometimes gave him pain. He refers to it in the verses he wrote. Very soon, however, he appreciated that what had happened to him necessitated a change of occupation; bookbinding (his principal trade, whatever other ones he also practised) required too much bending over and moving about, too much physical exertion, to be good for him now. He would become what his registration in the Guild of St Luke had proclaimed him to be and what he in secret maybe already was: a printer.

So far the story must be in essence true; it can be corroborated. It's what happened next that is in doubt. The account by Plantin's grandson – reliable up to this point – has been found on examination so full of inconsistencies, so lacking in substantiating evidence that to set it aside altogether is probably the wisest course. Balthasar I Moretus says that Plantin recognised his attackers, and afterwards made them pay up for what they had done. Another version is that the drunken revellers themselves made him a cash offer so he would keep quiet about the whole sorry business, general knowledge of which could do their own reputations no good; this offer Plantin accepted. With the compensation money, however obtained, Plantin was able to set himself up as a printer (though without totally stopping bookbinding; there's fine work by him dating from the 1560s). And certainly in the first half of 1555 Plantin obtained an official permit to bring out two books, having already been legally registered as a printer by the Council of Brabant. These are the forerunners to one of the very greatest 'lists' in the whole history of publishing; Plantin's great Antwerp career had now begun.

Leon Voet, formerly director of the Plantin-Moretus Museum, says, in his authoritative, fascinatingly comprehensive and empathetic work on Plantin and his achievements, *The Golden Compasses* (1969) – explaining his conclusions with wholly convincing detail – that no paying up by a handful of revellers, however handsome the amount, could possibly have been enough on its own for the establishment of the business that Plantin started. Such an operation requires a workplace and its costly maintenance and the payment of employees, as well as a certain outlay of cash to get things going before books can generate any income themselves. Capital has to have come also from another quarter altogether – though Plantin was to refer throughout his life to the incident and injury as *the* turning-point in his career. Leon Voet directs us back to HN, and the Family of Love, and indeed we have the Niclaes-dictated *Cronica* and *Acta HN* as further confirmation. Niclaes was now actively seeking a printer for his writings, most particularly for what became the bible of his movement, *Den Spegel der gerechticheit* (*The Glass of Righteousness*). Who would be a more appropriate printer than

Plantin with his links to the well-off and well-connected in Paris? How could they fail to come up with the requisite cash for the launching of a press that would promote them? Niclaes himself would bear the costs of his great book, and of further works as well.

And this is (more or less) what happened. And in it all Joannes Goropius Becanus, leading physician, Familist, as well as married connection of a rich and powerful family, must surely have had some part to play. Maybe he was able officially to diagnose the wounds so that the cross-over from binder and casket-maker to printer/publisher could be publicly made easier.

Eugénie Droz's hypothesis would have us rephrase the above to say that it was now that HN and his fellows decided that Christophe Plantin would no longer be a clandestine printer/publisher but an open one (though still undertaking work best kept from the authorities). In Antwerp, of course, there's no doubt at all that Niclaes and Plantin had a lot to do with one another. Niclaes' son François had married into a prominent business family of the city; Niclaes was frequently there, and Plantin was a friend of the family as well. And if Plantin soon became an Elder of the Family, he would have been in regular contact with HN, being of the 'Order of the Countenance of Peace and Perfection' and therefore helping to select men to be the movement's *de facto* priests, expected regularly to hear confession and to play roles in the great future.

Relations between HN and Plantin were not smooth, but then HN's prickly, suspicion-ridden personality impeded his dealings with almost everybody. Reading between the lines of his *Cronica* and *Acta*, despite the accumulated grievances and misinterpretations, the two of them maintained – until their break, itself brought about largely by external factors – a mutually useful continuity of dialogue.

HN was too often a tedious monomaniac. But without him and the Family, Plantin could never have got going, and Ortelius would not have been fortified in the views of life that enabled him to make the *Theatrum* a correlative for them. Eventually Plantin's own critical judgement, personal good sense and business acumen took over, and – while his religious faith never waned – he would begin, along with many others, to weary of HN's over-reaching self-evaluation, which increasingly put himself, and himself alone, as the sole dispenser of Christ. Yet without this impossible man, this inspired if inflated writer, neither the Golden Compasses nor Ortelius'

Theatrum orbis terrarum would have taken the forms that have made them so precious to posterity.

The first two books that the newly licensed Plantin brought out in 1555 were the bilingual Italian/French *La Institutione di una fanciulla nata nobilmente/l'Institution d'une fille de noble maison* (*The upbringing of a young girl of good family*) and a selection from the writings of Seneca translated from Latin into Spanish, *Flores de L. Anneo Seneca* (*Flowers of L. Anneo Seneca*). Plantin was printer as well as publisher for the first of these but not the second. Both set the tone of the house he intended to build up and reflect strong currents in the thinking of the age. *La Institutione* was the work of a Venetian humanist temporarily resident in Antwerp, Jean Michel Bruto, and shows that the education of women was taken seriously by the Antwerp intelligentsia. The second book points to one of the presiding spirits of sixteenth-century culture, Seneca (the Younger c.4BC–c.AD65), a figure as important to its philosophy as Ptolemy to its geography and astronomy. Montaigne, whose *Essays* are contemporaneous with the *Theatrum*, spoke of himself as ceaselessly drawing from the springs of Seneca's mind. It was Seneca, the author of essays, tracts, treatises (the *Consolationes* or *Consolations*) and reflective letters, the man involved in public life but with a preference for the quieter one of contemplation, who was so widely admired; the reputation of his dramas, which had such impact on Elizabethan England, was a separate matter. The Stoicism Seneca articulated, if not conducive to private mysticism in the way of HN's Familism, must nonetheless have not been so dissimilar in appeal. Like the Family, Seneca emphasised constancy, tranquillity, forbearance, resignation, the belief that happiness could only come after acceptance of the pain inherent in the natural order, and yet – over and above that, for all the murky political arena in which Seneca himself had played – came the desire for peace, the natural and ultimate home of the human spirit. Stoicism itself, Seneca declared in a letter, called 'all mankind to live in harmony'.

Following these first two books, Plantin published (the major condition of his business existence) Niclaes' *Glass of Righteousness*, a religious work in a line of descent from the *Theologia Germanica*, and, if Droz is to be believed – secretly, with a deceptive printers' mark suggesting Lyons as provenance – *Le baston de la foy chrestienne* (*The struggle of the Christian faith*) by Guy de Brès, a Calvinist.

The Death of Seneca *by Peter Paul Rubens. Now appropriately hanging in the Justus Lipsius Room in the Plantin-Moretus House in Antwerp, this painting (1613–1616) epitomises the Stoic ideals to which the Plantin household, Justus Lipsius himself (1547–1606) and Ortelius largely subscribed, even if they chose not altogether to live them out.*

Plantin at this time was still in Twaalfmaandenstraat, the street where that unfortunate – but also fortunate – accident of his had occurred. He applied himself to his new business with extraordinary energy. Success bred success. Figures speak for themselves. The press put out 10 books in 1555, 12 in 1556, 21 in 1557, 23 in 1558 ... by which time he made a change of premises. He went back to the very heartland of the printing trade in Antwerp, to Kammenstraat, near Ortelius' home, and now Abraham and he were the best of friends.

CHAPTER EIGHT

About a year after his first recorded transactions with Plantin, and at a time of his life when his friendship was Mercator was at once firm and still developing (they would go together the following year to France, the tour a milestone in the history of geography), Ortelius wrote his cousin Emmanuel van Meteren a letter. It's dated Monday 3 July 1559:

The Prince of Piedmont was married yesterday amidst great rejoicings. But there was sadness also, as twelve royal counsellors were imprisoned for the sake of religion ... In Spain the solemnity *della sancta Inquisitione* was held last Trinity Sunday (21 May) and about 30 persons (doctors, noblemen, savants) who had been imprisoned for their religious opinions, were led to Valladolid and given as much time for conversion as a candle would take to burn down. Seventeen repented; they forfeit all their property, and have to bear a mark for the rest of their life etc. One of them, a Marquis, has lost his whole marquisate, is no longer allowed to ride on horseback, or to wear silk or velvet, or be served out of silver. Fifteen persevered till the moment that preparations were made for burning them alive, when they recanted, and as a reward, were first strangled before being burnt. Only Dr Casallo remained firm, and after having stood on a scaffold, bound to a stake, from 5 a.m. till 6 p.m. with his tongue pierced with an iron, was burnt alive.

Ortelius' letters are full of discussion of the affairs of the day. He was well-informed about politics, though often not as much as he would have liked. His keen mind was forever anxious to probe, to get to the truth of things. While he was usually careful not to appear too partisan (spies and informers were a constant danger, and after the accession of Philip II the dangers multiplied), we can in his letters to intimates tell where his sympathies lie. He is committed to tolerance, out of moral principle and out of realistic pragmatism. When tolerance is withheld, denied, then Ortelius is opposed to the persecutors and feels pity for the victims. As here.

See how Ortelius follows the announcement of a royal wedding with news of savage repression for religious independence; note how he makes a brief excursion into the 'Roman' vernacular Italian when speaking of that most hated of the Church's institutions; appreciate the wry presentation of the authorities' 'clemency' – which doesn't extend to significant reduction of their punishment. In his epistolary narrative Dr Casallo stands out in all his tragic dignity.

The doctor was burned alive in Valladolid, in his own Spain. In the Spanish Netherlands the situation was gravely deteriorating; Philip's intransigence, his determination to impose his will on a society he knew to be religiously diverse, infuriated his northern subjects. Their resistance was galvanised by two ever-intensifying factors: Calvinism, which in the later 1550s took hold of a far wider cross-section of Low Countries society than ever Anabaptism or Lutheranism had been able to do, and the charismatic personality of William of Orange (William the Silent).

Calvinist congregations (consistories) were set up in Antwerp, with aid from German and Walloon organisations. In 1561 the well-known Calvinist preacher in Valenciennes, Guy de Brès, published his *Confessio Belgica*, very soon recognised as an authoritative statement of the Calvinist position and translated into the vernacular the following year. As for the Prince of Orange, though himself Catholic – and loyal to Spain, he would proclaim, merely anxious to defend his fellow Netherlanders from any injustice meted out to them – in 1561 he married Anna of Saxony, whose uncle was a leading German Lutheran prince. His marriage significantly increased his popularity. Philip could not but be afraid of William's remarkable ability to harness the forces of Calvinism, while himself remaining visibly inside the 'universal' Church.

★

Portrait by Antonis Mor of William the Silent (1533–1584), Prince of Orange, at the age of twenty-two, when he became the influential Stadholder of Holland, Zeeland and Utrecht.

In 1559 Ortelius took advantage of the peace between France and the Hapsburgs, and went to Paris. As a great reader of travel literature he would have noted the impact of the genre on the presentation of other disciplines, in particular natural history (a subject with obvious kinship to geography). The travels of Pierre Belon (1517–1564) had prompted him to publish in Paris work on marine animals and birds from 1553 on. Belon brought plants from Greece, Asia Minor, Egypt and Arabia to his native country, and founded botanical gardens.

The following year Ortelius went again to France, this time on a more general tour, in the company of Gerard Mercator, Frans Hogenberg and Filips Galle. Frans Hogenberg (c.1540–1590), from the nearby archepiscopal city of Mechelen, and himself the son of a (Munich-born) engraver, was to be a very close friend and valued publishing associate of Ortelius. As a painter, graphic artist and engraver of enormous distinction, posterity is incalculably indebted to him for his vivid visual depictions of current events – including the most violent of them all, the Spanish Fury of 1576. His own interest in geography is shown by the fact that two of his closest friends were the nephews of Gemma Frisius, the brothers Ferdinand and Ambrosius Arsenius, who, when they moved to Cologne in the year of the *Theatrum*'s publication, were to join him as assistants in his workshop there. (Ortelius, in the edition of 1595, the last of his lifetime, added the brothers' names to Hogenberg's in his grateful introductory acknowledgements.) In Cologne Hogenberg, with theo-logian and cathedral dean, Georg Braun, would begin editing and engraving work on the *Theatrum*'s first child, the magnificent *Civitates*, which brings city after city alive to us in map-like bird's-eye views, and the first volume of which appeared in 1572, the last (*Theatri praecipiarum totius mundi urbium liber sextus*) as late as 1618 (still under Braun's editorial aegis). The printer of the *Civitates* was the fourth man on this stimulating holiday, Filips Galle, himself an eminent engraver and graphic artist, writer, archaeologist and a Calvinist. In addition to his work for Braun and Hogenberg, Galle proposed and prepared the *Epitome*, the first and extremely successful pocket edition of Ortelius' *Theatrum*. A great deal can be traced back to this French tour, and all of it commanding respect.

The friends took themselves to Poitiers (thirty-eight years later to be included in Volume V of the *Civitates* with an illustration from 1576 by a mutual friend of this eminent quartet, Joris Hoefnagel). Here they visited the celebrated *Pierre Levée,* a rock, supposedly of druidical association, standing on four legs of stone and, even then, a tourist attraction. You were meant to carve your name on it and, as three of the group were professionally trained engravers – and Mercator a highly experienced one by dint of his own work – how could they resist? So we find 'Gerard Merc[at]or', 'Philippus Gallaeus', 'Abrahamus Ortelius' and 'Franc. Hogenberg', all dated 1560.

The inscriptions were intended as a sealing symbol of their friendship. And the stone's druidical connections would have fascinated Ortelius; his correspondence with Welsh antiquarian Humphrey Lhuyd shows the pull of the subject on his imagination – and the only essay the *Theatrum* was to include was Lhuyd's on druids and the isle of Anglesey. But in fact the adjective 'druidical' wouldn't be too inapposite to Mercator (thought by some suspicious minds to practise 'white magic' – there was after all his friendship with the sage John Dee) or to Ortelius (also a friend of Dee's) with their stores of learning, including hermetic arcana, their association with circles of *illuminati* and their pervasive desire for intellectual mastery over vast areas of time and space. The carved stone could well act as a logo for the *Theatrum* itself: Ortelius editing it, Hogenberg, as Ortelius' profuse thanks reveal, responsible for all the careful engraving of the maps; Galle also contributing engravings and later initiating a cheaper, more popular edition of the work – and Mercator, the greatest name in his field, supplying major maps, either directly or as their principal source, and, in 1573, writing a laudatory preface which undoubtedly, with his unique authority, did incalculable good to both the atlas' reputation and sales.

But did Mercator, in addition to these, contribute the controlling idea itself? According to Mercator's biographer Walter Ghim, it was on this visit to France that Mercator said how in need society was of a proper systematic book of maps covering the whole world, in other words of an atlas precisely as we understand the term, and as Ortelius realised it in 1570 – and Mercator himself (its initial volume) in 1585.

For conversation between these friends not to have considered the furthest-ranging and farthest-reaching ways of publishing maps is most improbable. We know that Mercator was highly critical of cavalier Italian methods of presentation (though Lafreri issued work by him), and as Ortelius had had experience of Italian cartographers and publishers, it's

In 1560 a distinguished group of friends, travelling together, visited the famous rock supported by four stones at Poitiers: Gerard Mercator, Filips Galle, Abraham Ortelius and Frans Hogenberg. Following tourist practice they all engraved their names on the rock face.

inconceivable that their deficiencies – and how to issue work free of, and superior to them – were not discussed. And if Mercator had arrived in his mind at his own greatly more sophisticated concept of an atlas, would he – could he – have refrained from telling his travel companions about it?

Assuming he did, where does this leave Ortelius?

There has, I think, been a tendency to see the matter in too absolute terms. It surely is something that can't be 'settled' once and for all. It seems to me, for reasons already given, that we are justified in taking Radermacher as a reliable source of information. That means that, by the time of the French tour, Ortelius had already completed his proto-atlas for Hooftman and was now busy looking out for maps to include, reduced, in a new more ambitious kind of compilation logically proceeding from it. I am not saying here – *contre* Ghim – that it was Ortelius who suggested to Mercator the idea of an atlas, rather that during their talks and travels the two friends would have appreciated that they had all this while been pursuing the same mental course, and had arrived at the same exciting point of departure for a radically new and greatly needed project. The exterior facts of their dealings *vis-à-vis* the *Theatrum* would indicate this – the strong presence of Mercator in its pages, his solicited written blessing on the book and statements about its likely and deserved longevity, the obvious respect in which he himself held Ortelius, the cordiality that prevailed between the two of them, and the admiration that Ortelius never ceased to articulate for Mercator both man and cosmologist.

Mercator did not start work on his own atlas until twenty years after this visit to France in Ortelius' company, a fact itself worthy of thought. Walter Ghim, whose personal admiration for Mercator knew no limits, says that his friend delayed publication out of affection for the younger Ortelius. There's probably an element of truth in this – though we have to add that the length of time of his delay stretches credulity. Such truth as we can arrive at about to whom we should accord the idea of the modern atlas – and when this idea was mooted – seems to me best approached by consideration of the essential differences between Mercator and Ortelius already adumbrated. Mercator approached his great work as a cosmographer in every respect of that calling: scientific, humanist, cartographic, religious. His *Atlas* could not possibly have been contained in a single volume of 53 sheets. His furrow-ploughing originality as a geographer, together with his passionately religious vision, made him want his great work to be nothing less than a reflection of his own apprehension of the workings of God's universe. Ortelius – the connoisseur of books, maps and travels – was animated by something very different, but which Mercator intensely valued: the desire of a gifted communicator to create the means by which a larger section of the educated public could have the whole world brought home to them, using the insights and achievements of the most respect-worthy intellects of the day. Behind this was the desire of an honourable, serious and devout man for peace. Peace, he felt, could be encouraged and promoted by a conscientiously edited book of maps with informed commentaries.

So when one contemplates the historical fates of the two atlases, Ortelius' and Mercator's, it's impossible not to feel that a kind of justice has been done by posterity. Ortelius' was to quicken the world's attention to its own amazing varieties and unity, set in train geographical and ethnic awarenesses merely dormant before. Its place in history is entirely secure, its influence incalculable. But Mercator's, when finally published, replaced it, teaching lessons which, in their detail and accuracy and relationship to astronomical and metaphysical dimensions, were absent from the earlier work. And so it is his work which has given the genre its name. Which is to say nothing that diminishes the earlier achievement of the younger man.

The celebrated cartographic historian R. A. Skelton wrote in his foreword to the 1964 facsimile edition (Amsterdam) of the *Theatrum* that 'the time required for compilation, drawing and engraving of the maps and for preparation of the texts suggests that Ortelius can hardly have set about his task [the editing of the *Theatrum*] much later than 1560 [in other words coincident with or shortly after his trip to France]; it appears probable that the work gathered momentum and that from about 1565 it was being intensively pushed forward.'

Searching out the best maps of any given region, reading round, especially inside his own ever-growing personal library, a later lodestar for so many – these did not preclude but rather encouraged Ortelius' own ventures into map-making. In the earlier 1560s he produced three maps of his own. For all his reservations about the genre these were wall-maps. In 1564, fittingly for the inauguration of a cartographic career, came his map of the world. Ortelius took Gastaldi as his principal model here, paying scrupulous attention to the coasts and lands of the New World. Inspired by Gastaldi, too, were the illustrations that accompanied it, taken from Ramusio's books of

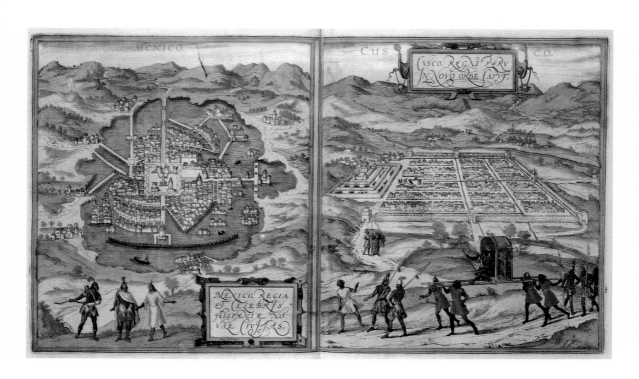

Mexico and Cuzco stand side by side in the 1572 Civitates *in woodcuts by Antoine du Pinet of 1564 (in the case of Cuzco based on a plan in Ramusio's* Navigationi, *1556). Neither picture evidences what most readers would have known: the appalling slaughter and destruction the Spanish conquistadors had wrought on both Aztec Mexico and Inca Peru.*

travels: the view of Cuzco, the old capital of Peru, and the map (after Cortés) of Mexico City show the importance of the Americas for both map-maker and map-users (while the wealth of Europe and its commercial relationship to elsewhere was apostrophised by a table of all the products imported to the newfound continent). But whereas Gastaldi used an oval projection, Ortelius, like Mercator in his *Orbis Imago*, employed the cordiform. This had a hermetic significance for Ortelius and other Familists. The heart (*cor*) represents the harmony of all things, *concordia omnium rerum*, the acrostic initials of which are COR. So the very projection, determining our reception of the world, is itself irenicist (peace-promoting).

But Gastaldi's wasn't the only mind behind Ortelius' first work. He paid tribute to Gemma Frisius who had given cordiform his particular blessing, and to Cologne map-maker Caspar Vopelius (1511–1561), author himself of a Frisius-indebted world map. Ortelius took the greatest pains both to scrutinise other men's efforts and to check these wherever and whenever possible. What he produced is a thoroughly professional and thought-out concentration of the best that had recently been done, in both printed and manuscript form.

This map, which was in eight sheets, was published by Gerard de Jode – *apud Gerardum de Jode* reads the imprint. He was a print-maker and print-seller who'd joined the Guild of St Luke in exactly the same year as Ortelius, 1547, and who had regular commercial dealings with Plantin. He lived and worked near the Bourse. He had a personal stand at the Frankfurt Book Fair, and in 1555 had issued a world map of his own. The considerable amount they had in common presumably led Ortelius to solicit de Jode as publisher of his new world map, and de Jode for his part reduced it for use in his own atlas later. But the relationship between the two men seems – unusually for Ortelius – to have been an unhappy one. Details, explanations are elusive. Maybe Ortelius found something predatory or underhand in de Jode's attitude to him. At any rate the next two maps he made do not have de Jode's imprint.

These, both from 1565, were a map of Egypt, taken from both ancient and modern sources, and one of the Holy Land. For the Egyptian map Ortelius' Italian connections were again useful, for he consulted the famous Scipio Fabius, professor of medicine at Bologna, and dedicated it to him. The map of the Holy Land is now lost, but it was very successful. Christophe Plantin sold many copies.

CHAPTER NINE

Bruegel's *Dulle Griet* (see pages 134/5) hangs today in Antwerp's Mayer van den Bergh Museum, a fine mercantile house on Lange Gasthuisstraat, on view in which is a splendid private collection of paintings and *objets d'art* willed to the city. As soon as one enters Room 9 and confronts the famous picture, what impresses is its fierce compound of reds and oranges. *Dulle Griet*'s tyrannically governing element is fire: this is a view of hell. In fact, Bruegel – already the creator of *Flemish Proverbs* (1559), a visual realisation of some hundred of them – was inspired here by a Flemish saying, 'Dulle Griet could plunder at the mouth of hell and remain unscathed'. In all directions fires are burning, the whole sky is alight, in a lurid red punctuated by gusts of black smoke, while in the foreground of this bespoiled 'world landscape' we see not just one large hellish mouth (or anus) but several, all of them spawning hideous and malevolent humanoids. Against such beings and their gratuitously evil tricks how can that crowd of panicking or struggling (and obviously Flemish) women hope to prevail?

Far, far taller than any of these beset and innocent unfortunates is Dulle Griet herself, with her loping but determined walk and her loopy but determined face, her right hand holding a pike, to ram into whosoever might accost her, her left clutching a heavy assortment of panniers and bags all stuffed with booty. Not even the largest, the most unmistakable of the mouths of hell, past which she will soon be striding, can detain, or even distress her. Insensitive, very nearly insensible, but possessed by unadulterated greed, it is she and she only in this appalling scene who can dominate it, who can triumph. Bruegel, one feels, has stared into some possible landscape of the near future, one immanent in the present scene around him, and asked himself: 'Who will be its most natural inhabitant?' In light of the troubles so soon to come, *Dulle Griet* seems quite uncannily prescient.

We are in a very different world, and a far more hopeful one in *The Sermon of John the Baptist*, painted in 1566 (four years before the publication of the *Theatrum*) after Bruegel had completed several major works depicting biblical scenes in faithfully represented Flemish settings. This work could also be so described, but attention to it shows that the painter is wanting, through the New Testament story, to show us a truth about contemporary life in the southern Netherlands of urgent, topical importance. In a wood within sight of a river and a city (these last perhaps belonging more to 'world landscape' than to Antwerp and the Scheldt) a large and variegated crowd – including in its press a mother with her baby, a young dandy, a very old bearded man and a swooning young half-wit – are attending a meeting addressed by the vigorous, austere and manly person of John the Baptist. So charismatic a figure is he that a fair number of people have climbed trees (clinging to a trunk, seating themselves in an ample fork between branches) so as not to miss a word he might be saying. But John, for his part, is gesturing towards another figure, one at the edge of the crowd, and though in fact somewhat taller than those immediately round him, not the object of anybody's direct attentions. We of course (unlike the members of this crowd) know who he is: he shines out in gentleness and tranquillity of bearing; he is Jesus.

Nobody at the time could have failed to see in the painting the 'hedge preachings' that suddenly, it seemed (though antecedents for them can be found), became a feature of life in Antwerp and of most other cities in the southern Netherlands (and, as time went on, beyond, in Holland and Zeeland also) during the summer of 1566.

As Bruegel shows us, the audiences for these open-air conventicles were socially varied and often of considerable size; one held just outside the mighty city walls of Ypres boasted 25,000 people. The meetings were peaceful, the crowd self-controlled and protected by armed guards; the sermon over, as in biblical times, the people would often troop off after the

preacher(s), sometimes, as in Ypres, back into the city itself, singing hymns and generally moving those who saw them with their combination of devotion and restraint. (All this too is implicit on Bruegel's beautiful canvas.)

If we compare these 'hedge preachings' with the religious meetings of three decades earlier, when it was Anabaptism that met the spiritual and emotional needs of discontents, what a difference we find. The sermonisers were of the New Religion, Calvinism, far more formidable intellectually and therefore appealing to a far wider cross-section of society, including some of its most educated and professionally significant members. We have already noted the favourable response to Calvinism of those close (one might say closest) to Ortelius, but the roll call of Antwerpers attracted to and eventually embracing it is long and impressive, and we may add to it here the names of Frans Raphelengius, Plantin's son-in-law and distinguished orientalist, Filips Galle, Pieter Heyns, educationalist and poet, Augustijn van Hesselt, printer (and also prominent Familist), and Joris Hoefnagel, artist and writer. All also dear to Ortelius and connected with the *Theatrum*, they reveal the address of Calvinism to the learned, and humanist, mind. Humanists, it would now appear, by no means always wanted to emulate their chief mentor, Erasmus, and stay, however critically, within the Catholic fold.

The old idea, later encouraged by themselves and their spokesmen, and by subsequent historians, too, that Plantin and Ortelius were somehow inherently opposed to Calvinism doesn't stand the test of prolonged thought and analysis. If only because of their relationships to men and women of the New Religion, whom they respected and who were the closest of colleagues on important enterprises, they must have felt not just the New Religion's undeniable power but its claims to righteousness also. Furthermore, they must have recognised in it (and found not altogether

Previous page:
Pieter Bruegel: Dulle Griet *('Mad Meg'). 'Mad Meg pillaging at the mouth of hell,' commented Bruegel's first major critic and biographer Karel van Mander in 1604, evoking the Flemish proverb. Here, derived from the painter's (vindicated) apprehensions of Antwerp's possible fate, is a world in which morality and reason have capitulated to greed and bloodlust. Interpretations of this painting have been many, and have tended to centre of late on the rapacious capitalism of Antwerp as well as on its fealty to Spain. Seen today in Antwerp's exquisite Museum Mayer van den Bergh it can still terrify in all its lurid flame colours.*

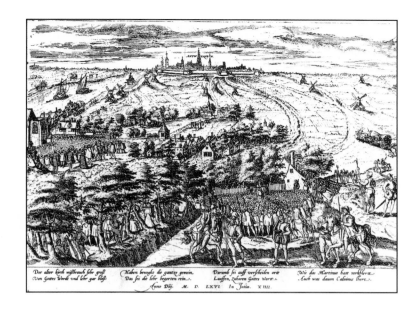

The 'Wonder Year' of 1566 saw a summer of hedge preaching, Protestant enthusiasts addressing and enrapturing large crowds of people outside the towns of the southern Netherlands, as seen in this engraving. Pieter Bruegel transformed the 'hedge preachings' into major art in his Sermon of John the Baptist from 1566, the painting recalling chapters of the New Testament as indeed the Flanders and Brabant scenes themselves must have done.

alien to their thinking) what made it so alarming to the authorities: its profound kinship with separatist sentiment, with the desire (now far stronger in the southern Netherlands than was often later to be conceded) to be rid of Spain and all the restrictions it chose to impose on so highly developed and successful a society as theirs.

Admittedly at this stage many of those (most notably William of Orange himself) causing the most bother to authority professed themselves basically loyal to the Spanish, or, if pressed, to Spain's king Philip; their quarrel was with those who carried out repressions in his name. This was, of course, disingenuous, as those who propounded it knew perfectly well, especially as Philip II was personally the main architect of what gave them such distress: the absolute refusal to countenance religious diversity, to accept the already lively worship outside the ordinance of the Catholic Church.

Philip's rigidity in the matter of Low Countries religion increasingly appeared (what it surely was) wilful blindness, an unimaginative and in the longer run quite intolerable determination to see his northern domains only in the narrowest Spanish terms. Again and again Philip spurned advice proffered by wiser and more sensitive quarters. No dismissive gesture of his was so bitterly resented as his snub to the Council of States, the various regional governments in the Netherlands, in October 1565. The council had urged him to scale back the anti-heresy laws in the Netherlands, the loathed *placards*, and to reduce also his zeal for persecuting those who offended against them. In a letter to Brussels from his hunting lodge at Segovia, Philip had dismissed the request outright. More than any one factor, it was this snub that spurred the Netherlands into the activities and protests of what became known – because of the surge of indigenous faith and self-confidence that took place within it – as the 'Wonder Year' of 1566.

Now pamphlets against Spain proliferated, popular feeling was aroused and strong, Protestants who'd hitherto been playing a waiting game came out into the open, especially among the aristocrats of the northern Netherlands. In December 1565 such men had formed themselves into a league, the League of Compromise – the Compromise being essentially a demand for religious pluralism – and in spring 1566 they had presented a petition to Philip's regent in the Netherlands, Margaret of Parma. The Inquisition, the body that enforced the anti-heresy laws, had to be abolished. As before, for all their numerical strength (over four hundred, half of whom had signed the petition) the protesters had been anxious to

Margaret of Parma (1522–1586). The illegitimate half-sister of Philip II, she was Regent of the Netherlands in the turbulent period 1559–1567, determined to see the region loyal to the Catholic Church. However, she was appalled by the brutal methods of her brother's appointee, the Duke of Alva.

establish credibility as loyal subjects of Philip II. That was dubious enough in itself, but in truth the petition was not quite as its authors claimed, since its wording contained more than a hint of armed insurrection to come if the demands were not agreed to. So perforce, and with a bad grace, Margaret had accepted it. The petitioners were at first dismissed with a contemptuous phrase; they were *un tas de gueux*, a 'heap of beggars'. But *Gueux*, 'beggars' – or better 'supplicants' – was quickly converted by themselves and their supporters as a sobriquet to be proud of (just as the epithets 'Christian' and 'Quaker' changed from insults by others into self-compliments). *Gueux* became indeed another name for freedom-fighters, and as such has survived into historical lore. (Over a century later English children were to remember this nickname for the independent-minded Dutch when they sang – at the time of the accession of William to the British throne: 'Hark hark the dogs do bark,/ The beggars are coming to town;/ Some in rags, some in tags,/ And one in a velvet gown.')

Philip had had very good reason, obviously enough, for being afraid of religious freedom. Now, as a result of the *Gueux*, Calvinists who'd fled the Low Countries felt they could return. Now they could organise tighter and more articulate consistories, with paramilitary groups formed to protect their own conventicles. Strengthened by experiences gained abroad, they preached convincing sermons to populaces who'd fervently hated the Inquisition and still resented or despised, or both, a Spanish-controlled Church. By summer the woods and fields outside towns and cities were the sites for successful meetings where what perhaps had up till then been inclinations only were drawn forth from people, and orchestrated into a symphony of belief and confidence. As in some Gospel scene, as indeed in Bruegel's masterpiece from the 'Wonder Year', the very trees would be climbed by those who felt ardently enough that the time had now come round to assert not just religious tolerance or freedom but a (*the*) New Religion.

To return to the Bruegel painting, it is to Christ himself, there in the flock of folk modest but lucent, that the preacher, the Preparer of the Way, is pointing. That strikes at the very heart of the protests against the established Church – that it was forgetting Christ Himself, but that He still lived, He could be encountered afresh, outside its purlieus, and be rallied round.

What was it like listening to these 'hedge preachers'? Clearly they were found inspiring; they seemed full of a learning, shown especially in explanations of the scriptures, and a moral conviction for the most part lamentably missing in the Catholic priesthood whose general apathy they lost no opportunity of pointing out. Apathy combined with privilege and automatic and misused authority could not fail to be resented; the 'hedge preachers' stoked the fires of contempt and anger that had indeed been many years in the building. Philip II was surely justified in realising that to allow these zealots too much scope was a very dangerous policy. Bruegel had rightly painted John the Baptist as one of the Calvinist sermonisers, for they were harkened to as if they indeed shared his peculiar divine blessing.

The 'Wonder Year' of 1566, when this blessing was to animate so many into physical action, was also the year when there was finally ready the magnificent building which now stands between cathedral and waterfront, and which has long been as cherished a landmark as either of these and which injects into the Antwerp atmosphere a third quality – civic pride complementing commerce and religion. This is the *Stadhuis*, town hall, designed by Cornelis Floris, its impressive façade, culminating in a handsome gable and a somewhat Chinese-style roof, asserting and generating a confidence in the prevailing culture emphasised by the crowning statues of Justice and Wisdom. With an irony not lost on citizens, this superb edifice was to burn (though not to its complete destruction) in the literal fires of the Fury.

What would have happened had Philip acted differently from how he did in the August of 1566, if he hadn't deliberately vaunted his indifference to Netherlanders' feelings and had chosen, if only superficially, to curb his taste for demonstrations of his – and Spain's – power? Given the whole summer of 'hedge preaching', things would surely have erupted sooner or later – and with violence; feelings were too fervent, too vehement. But Philip's policy could hardly have been more provocative; he declared that he wanted public shows of Catholic devotion, even at the cost of enforced humiliation, and as a result he invited hostile counter-demonstrations. So on the tenth of the month the Netherlands exploded by way of reaction – into the *Beeldenstorm* or Iconoclastic Fury.

It began in Steenvoorde or, to be more precise, just outside the walls of that Flanders town (now in France), as the result of a stirring sermon by one Sebastian Matte, back from exile in England. Fired by his words, twenty men proceeded to break into a monastery church and set about them, wreaking destruction. This was the first manifestation of a seizure of society, a chain-like outbreak of unleashed resentment expressed in the

Nach wenigß Predication
Die Câluinsche Religion

Das bildent sturmen siengen an
Das nicht ein bilde dauon bleib ston

Kap Monstrantz kilch, auch die olear
Vnd woß sonst dort vor handen war

Zerbrochen all in kurtzer stunde
Gleich gar vil leuten das ist kundt.

Anno Dñj M. D. LXVI XX Augusti

Wrote Ortelius: 'Wherever these iconoclasts, armed with sticks, axes and burning torches, ran from one church to another, everybody fled, though they sometimes were only six or eight in number … all the churches looked as if the devil had been at work there for some hundred years.'

smashing of images and the wrecking or stealing of church treasures that spread westwards and knew, while it was in progress, no kind of restraint. Rather it was characterised by orgiastic relish and savagery. No church in any neighbourhood once entered by the iconoclasts stood the remotest chance of being spared their vehemence. On they went, and on. After a week there seemed no stopping the 'storm'.

It was inevitable that sooner or later it would reach and take over Antwerp as not only the largest, the most important city of the southern Netherlands, but also the one in which the Calvinists had been able to build up a considerable strength and a sense of identity. The 18th of August was the first Sunday after Ascension. So, as per Philip's demands, Antwerpers were made to endure an *Ommegang* (ritual procession) during which they were forced to bend the knee when the priests passed along with effigies of the Virgin Mary. It was an extremely mistaken reading by authority of the public's mood, already darkly shaped by what had been happening in neighbouring Flanders in the previous few days.

Ortelius himself, in a long letter to Emmanuel van Meteren, has left a vivid account of what followed (dated Tuesday 27 August 1566):

In my last letter I told you of my journey to Brussels which was delayed by what happened the night before; namely, on the 20th inst., between 5 and 6 p.m., when the priests were entering the Church of Our Lady (*Onze Lieve Vrouwekathedraal*) for service, a tumult arose between some mischievous boys and the woman who sat before the image of the Blessed Virgin Mary in front of Our Lady's chapel to receive offerings; the boys began to jest at Our Lady which made the woman angry, who began to speak on behalf of Our Lady, and when this was of no avail, threw water upon them, and the noise increased so much that the priests left the church fearing some riot. Round these rogues a crowd began to collect, it being rumoured through the town that the priests had been driven out of the church. Thereupon the Margrave appeared with the magistracy who ordered the people to leave the church, saying that no service would be held; and some of the people leaving, they closed three of the doors, the magistracy quitting through the fourth; leaving perhaps fifty persons inside. Before they could depart, the crowd outside had increased so much that this door could not be shut, and the people began to sing Dutch Psalms in three or four places, in front of the choir, of the pulpit etc. After a little while (between 6 and 7 o'clock) twenty or thirty perhaps of those inside (for most of them remained spectators only) commenced a furious attack on the images and paintings. In about an hour's time the same happened in all the churches, convents etc in the town, and before 1 a.m. all the sculpture and ornaments in the churches had been completely destroyed. It is a marvel that no one prevented it, as everybody was awake with guns in hand, and lights were burning outside the buildings. Wherever these iconoclasts, armed with sticks, axes and burning torches, ran from one church to another, everybody fled, though they sometimes were only six or eight in number.

Next day all the churches looked as if the devil had been at work there for some hundred years. [*Des anderen dachs heeftet in alle kercken gesien ofter de duijuel sommyge hondert iaren huijs gehouden hadde* – reads the Dutch for this vividly descriptive sentence.] The town began to clear away the ruins and to cut down all that was damaged. They saved only three or four of the best paintings in Our Lady's Church from these iconoclasts by bravely crying *Vivent les gueux*. Further, every kind of sculpture, at the corners of streets, above the gates of large houses, was thrown down by the inhabitants or proprietors themselves, who wished to give no occasion to the iconoclasts to climb upon their houses. On the 22nd, before noon, Herman[nus] Moded [the leading Calvinist preacher in the city] ascended the pulpit in Our Lady's Church to protest that nothing of all this had happened through his or their Consistories' advice, requesting that all things stolen or taken away should be given up to the Magistrate (for much was stolen by wretches of both sexes who carried away from the churches whatever they could get hold of). He did not then preach, but in the afternoon he again ascended the pulpit and preached an ordinary sermon.

The same iconoclasm took place in all villages, churches and monasteries round the town within a distance of two or three miles. At Mechelen etc it was done by the magistracy themselves. At 'sHertogenbosch it happened in the same way as here. All churches have since been closed, and the Catholics forbidden to preach; only in St George's Church the magistracy appointed him who had been formerly at Kiel. The Calvinists preach with consent and in great numbers in the New Town where they will probably remain till the States or the Prince [William of Orange] order otherwise. The latter has arrived here again. The *Gueux* and the Council at Brussels are of one accord in many matters; the Prince of Orange is head of the *Gueux*. Two *Gueux* (M. de Toulouse and M. de Ham) have been sent to preserve the reformed churches. From Spain we have heard that the queen was delivered on the 10th inst. of a daughter.

This is a most revealing document, about the state of things in Antwerp and Brabant generally, but equally about Ortelius himself. In it is nascent his whole subsequent stance. Significantly, considering the dramatic nature of the scenes he not undramatically describes, he is more than a little detached from the conflict of beliefs and values he's so recently witnessed. It seems not unfanciful to ascribe this to his Familism, which united what was common to the different Christian persuasions while standing aloof from any overt fracas between them. His account of Iconoclasts (predominantly Calvinist) versus Catholics might surely have been made by a comparative foreigner to the society of which he's a lifelong member. And, as he did not share the convictions of the former and probably disdained the idleness, timeservingness and conservatism of many priests of the latter, perhaps this is how he indeed felt; spiritually his real home was the House of Love. And we can find vindication of this view of him in a letter he again wrote to Emmanuel just over a year later; he sees the time he's living through as a sick patient:

[who] will soon be entirely prostrate, being threatened with so many and various illnesses, as the Catholic evil, the Gueux fever, and the Huguenot dysentery, mixed with other vexations of black horsemen and soldiers. All of which will hurt him with so many paroxysms, that there is no hope of curing all of them with any physic, but rather that the one will be trampled under foot by the other, so that finally, when we might expect him to be cured, he will be so weak and exhausted as to be unable to stir, and will therefore suffer all that might be inflicted on him and choose that as good which luck may give him. I expect that every one, after having done what he can in the way of robbing and murdering, will be so tired as to wish for the peace which he had formerly but did not value.

Common to both letters, that of August 1566 and that of September 1567, is a hatred of disorder, of any wanton release of destructive forces. Ortelius doesn't say that he thinks the Iconoclasts or the New Religion they (principally) represent are wrong, either morally or doctrinally, and for the eminent Herman Moded he would appear to have had a certain respect. But any orgy of breaking up and pulling down is anathema to him; the emotions it releases are abhorrent to him, and no course of action that encourages them can he really approve of. There is, I believe, something else too: as a collector, with a partiality for prints and paintings, as a dealer in books and curios, as a map-colourist and map-maker, as an amateur of archaeology, Ortelius clearly had a heightened feeling for the visual, the tangible: the image, the icon. Therefore image-breaking – no matter what opinion he actually held of the institution under attack – would be repellent to him; it affronts the respect he felt towards human creativity, a central article of his faith if ever there was one. And that is why he would never have been able to move away from the established Church into the New Religion, even if history had proceeded otherwise from how it did in the south Netherlands. This is not to say that there wasn't a very good measure of ambivalence in his attitude to contemporary events and alignments. This ambivalence was to be sublimated in the *Theatrum*, where in the peaceful rendering of countries, one next to another, painful divisions could be overcome, indeed made to appear of secondary significance to the glorious whole to which they all contributed.

CHAPTER
TEN

P lantin's experience of the 1560s was far more fraught, far more
tempestuous than Ortelius'. There was remarkable accord between
the two men, from religion to the niceties of business, but at times
following them to the convergence of their careers in the *Theatrum* is like
tracing the courses of two very different rivers: the one (Ortelius) – whatever
the dramas on its banks – flows straight and steadily, the other (Plantin)
passes through gorges and rapids, and yet after all these vicissitudes, emerges
deep and impressive enough to attract a remarkable diversity of craft, and to
unite with the other one in a great forward-moving current.

Already, before the decade opened, Plantin had chosen the logo and
motto which were ever afterwards to be associated with his enterprises. In
1557, after experimenting with two other devices, he came up with that of
a pair of compasses and the slogan LABORE ET CONSTANTIA (THROUGH
WORK AND CONSTANCY). The fixed point of the compass stood for
constancy (to God, morality, virtue), the moving point for work, hard
unstinting work such as Plantin was singularly capable of, without which
no good task could be realised. It was in 1561 that Plantin changed the
name of his Kammenstraat establishment to *De Gulden Passer* (The
Golden Compasses), a suitable name for a business to deal virtually on a
daily basis with globes, maps and geographical works, and to be involved
with the first atlas.

In the decade now ahead of him Plantin would consolidate his successes as printer/publisher, but he would also find himself in trouble with the government, in fear for his life, enmeshed in legal and financial difficulties – and despite (and sometimes because of) all these tribulations, arise, at whatever cost to nerves and health, the most respected printer in all Europe (that is to say, the entire world). The dangers Plantin ran were all in the cause of success: his was never by choice the martyr's path. The curiously inter-threaded pursuit of financial triumph, admiration from the eminent, independence from irksome authority and personal spiritual fulfilment is nowhere more fully shown than in his adherence to the Family, in which he was so important an officer. HN was aware of the complexities of Plantin's character, that there was a side of him with a penchant for intrigue. HN's *Cronica* gives a vivid impression (perhaps too vivid for fairness) of Plantin's craftiness. Yet he realised he couldn't do without him.

In 1562 three of Plantin's apprentices took advantage of his absence in Paris (where he kept up with his old circle) to print a 'suspicious booklet', the Calvinist tract *Briefve instruction pour prier* (*Brief instruction on prayer*). This came to the notice of Philip II's regent in Brussels, Margaret of Parma, who made inquiries and summonses, and an alarming sequence of events followed: Plantin taking protracted refuge in his 'brother' Porret's house in Paris, the search of his own house in Antwerp by government officers; the displeasure of the regent herself; the arrest of his apprentices and their being sentenced in court to the galleys (they were in fact never sent there); the confiscation of his Antwerp effects and their public sale (as it happens, in the Vrijdagmarkt itself, where his later handsome house is on view to this day), not to mention the various troubles swirling round the heresiarch HN. Yet the strange upshot of all these trials was that Plantin, after some skilful and murky manoeuvring, ended up forming a new *compagnie* (company), called after the house the *Gulden Passer*, with four other men, well-connected and rich Antwerpers all of them, as his backers. One of them was that eminent physician and philologist, Goropius Becanus, who'd come to his rescue so constructively after the malicious wounding. Clearly the network of the Family of Love was at work again. Before long, as HN rather exasperatedly and enviously recorded, Plantin had 'sixteen presses, bookshops, and a quantity of agents in other countries' and 'a far greater international repute than any other printer in Antwerp'.

★

The iconoclasm of August 1566 had shaken both the society that had produced it and the authorities who had been trying for so long to impose their will on it. (After August the outbreak had ceased in the southern Netherlands but continued north of the Great Rivers, convulsing the northernmost province of Friesland.) In Antwerp the immediate effects of the riots, their repercussions in late August/early September, promised well. Margaret of Parma begrudgingly agreed in an 'Accord' that (as in Germany) Protestant worship should take place where it was already doing so. And on 2 September, William of Orange came over to Antwerp to negotiate an agreement even more welcome than this; that Protestants, both Lutheran and Calvinist, should be allowed to build churches of their own inside the city. Was this religious peace at last? Many thought so; William of Orange began to travel the country trying to persuade city councils to make tolerance a legal fact of life. But, tragically, by the end of the year it was already clear that this social peace was not going to last.

For one thing, the violent disruptions had worried not only the regent and the government but powerful magnates fearing a wider anarchy. They were far from certain they really wanted a pluralist southern Netherlands. For another, what freedoms had (limitedly) prevailed were not backed up by proper legislation, and tended to favour, above any other faction, the Calvinists, the largest, the best organised, and – most important – the richest. By winter, Margaret of Parma was revoking the accords she'd so reluctantly consented to. The new year opened to tension, protests, punishments. Army contingents were sent in by order of the regent. 'I have resolved not to go to Antwerp,' one of Ortelius' German friends wrote to him from Cassel in February, 'especially not during the present state of things.' 1567 was, in all truth, a sad and depleting year for Antwerpers, and for Plantin it was worse than that. In March a Calvinist attempt to seize power in the city failed, not least because the Catholics co-opted the Lutherans to make common cause against them; there'd never been a satisfactory alliance between the two Protestant groups. An armed band of militarily woefully inexperienced men led by Calvinist de Toulouze was surprised and slaughtered just outside the city at Oosterweel.

These were seen not just as set-backs but as telling indications of the insuperability of government forces. Depression took hold of the whole society, both north and south (but especially south) of the Great Rivers. Many of those who, only a matter of months before, in the 'Wonder Year' of 1566, had felt themselves receptacles, willing vessels inspired by the hedge preachers for the Reformed religion and its wider transmission, now slunk back into the Catholic fold; others who were convinced of the righteousness of their position and their beliefs judged it high time to leave the Low Countries. There were thousands of Protestants who left their homes and joined or formed colonies abroad, particularly in England and Germany. They had a role to play in the building up of Dutch Protestant strength. Emmanuel van Meteren kept away from the land of his birth, a naturalised Englishman now, as did Daniel Rogers; the Cools (Ortelius' sister Elizabeth and her husband) were in London too.

As always these expatriates for reasons of conscience never ceased to follow and feel for events in their own country: exile constitutes a double loneliness, as the century now past has illustrated only too amply. A Flemish physician, fellow humanist, and friend to van Meteren, Johannes (John) Thorius or Bellanus, wrote to him from England on Sunday 18 May 1567 (thanking him, one assumes for some act of generosity): 'How can I return all these kindnesses? ... Every day we hear the saddest news about our fatherland; nay, the whole Christian world is broken to pieces, shaken to its foundation, and threatens to fall into utter ruin.'

One who left Antwerp never to live there again was Ortelius' beloved Jan Radermacher, who, now a declared Calvinist, departed for London and stayed there till 1580. He had been enthusiastically helping Ortelius with the collection and reduction of maps suitable for that exciting and venturesome book which was to succeed the volume for Gillis Hooftman. There were so many problems that he could help his older friend and mentor to sort out, projection, scale, the measuring systems to be used ... But it wasn't safe for him to stay in his native city and bestow his help directly.

No doubt that the irenicist vision controlling the *Theatrum*, placing the world's countries in harmonious relationship, was animated, propelled forth by the unrest, repressions and consequent diaspora in the Netherlands, all of which were to get worse. Ortelius greatly missed Radermacher who, for his part, was sad he couldn't assist the *Theatrum* in its growth towards completion. In tones of utter certainty he insisted in his letter as an elderly man to Ortelianus that Ortelius had been hard at work on his project all during this stressful time, even though many didn't know what this project was. He was too cautious, Radermacher said, to want to speak about his work much, and besides 'he required many years for the engraving and

Lucas van Valckenborch (c.1535–1597) was an eminent genre painter whose friendship Ortelius enjoyed (though Lucas, like his brother, Marten, was obliged to flee Antwerp for religious reasons). Here, in his Country Feast *(1576), Valckenborch honours Ortelius by including him, together with himself, among the revellers at a 'kermess' or country fair.*

drawing of so many maps'. And, he might have added, as no one would have known better than himself, the climate for these complex operations was spiritually uncongenial. In his later letter, however, Radermacher cast a backward and loving glance to those days of cooperation with the older friend so dear to him, which history had broken off:

> In the execution of this plan Ortelius consulted me first as to the art of drawing lines as first done, I believe, in the form as it were of an heart, by Orontius Finaeus [Oronce Finé], and afterwards about reducing larger maps to the size of his volume. In the same way he consulted his other friends and especially the celebrated geographer Gerard Mercator, only seeking intercourse with those by whose learning and skill he hoped to improve himself. Kind he was indeed to everyone but familiar only with men of merit, though he was not always thinking of his own benefit, but would often be useful to others ... I will not speak of the great benefits that he bestowed on engravers, printers, booksellers etc by the publication of his works.

Ortelius did, however, apply himself to a successor to his three previous maps on which he now had built a reputation. Asia was its subject; in format another wall-map, a large one, and again with Gastaldi as the principal influence. The Piedmontese cartographer had published his own *Asia* in Venice in 1559–1561. But now, once again, Ortelius showed his inherent intellectual integrity because this was no mere addendum to maps of Asia but, thanks to conscientious and zealous research, it marked an advance on all previous work – above all in his mapping of Japan, a country in which the *Theatrum* too was to excel (though there are obvious errors in the 1570 edition).

Asia was sold through Christophe Plantin's *compagnie* and with great success; the ledger records attest to this. And it brought Ortelius praise from a man whose opinion was greatly to be esteemed, Guillaume Postel (1510–1581), professor of Greek, Hebrew and Arabic at the College de France, a philosopher in his own right, passionately interested in cartography – and in religion to the point of paranoid mania.

On 24 April 1567, only a fortnight after a letter thanking Ortelius for the map of Asia and intelligently concerned with geographical matters, Postel wrote to him. How were things in Antwerp? And in Valenciennes, so

*Cordiform projection. The world in heart-shape by Orontius (Oronce Finé)
from a coloured woodcut of 1536. This had great influence on geographers
including Peter Apian and Mercator.*

important a Calvinist stronghold? Had Ortelius actually received that first letter of his, 'as he thinks that by Divine Providence he the writer occupies such a position that it could not be advantageous to the Common Weal if any fragment or any letter of his should be lost'. This letter was, however, to cause both Ortelius and Plantin, to whom he showed it, anxiety, because the writer signalled his knowledge of the Family of Love.

Plantin himself was caught up in a new difficulty with terrifying possibilities; 1567 was already proving that 'Year of the Great Fear' which he was to label it.

Yet the crisis for Plantin, the loneliness of Ortelius, the isolation of Mercator, the worried exile of Radermacher and van Meteren, were to have apotheoses. Plantin's greatest success was still ahead of him, Mercator was to arrive at his long-sought projection before the decade had finished, and, the year following, Ortelius was able to publish what was by now well underway, and was continuing to progress against a background of hardship and despair.

In July 1567, the *compagnie* founded after Plantin's prolonged and to this day somewhat mysterious absence from Antwerp was dissolved, despite all its indisputable successes. Its directors had no real choice. Events throughout the year had turned in favour of the Spanish monarchy/regency with infinitely more resources and disciplined soldiers behind them than Calvinist separatists. Resistance had grown dispirited; William of Orange had taken himself temporarily to Germany. Of Plantin's fellow directors three at least were Calvinists, and the Familist Goropius Becanus was most probably a sympathiser. Plantin never broke with these men; in fact he was to go on doing business with and borrowing money from them. Nor was his position after the dissolution of the company unmanageably difficult for he had capital at his back and superb printing equipment. What was difficult was the political atmosphere in which he was now forced to operate, and when news came of the imminent arrival in the southern Netherlands of the Duke of Alva – he entered Brussels in August, determined to chastise and subdue the entire region, southern and northern, on behalf of Philip – he knew full well he had every cause for personal alarm.

From the end of 1566 he had been supplying material and equipment to a fellow Familist and former employee, the printer Augustijn van Hasselt, who had gone to set up a business in the south Holland town of Vianen, in the fiefdom of van Brederode, the leading 'Beggar', and a centre of both

Calvinism and anti-Spanish activity. Hasselt himself was a protégé of HN – who, ever Nicodemist, ever anxious to do nothing that would get adverse attention drawn to himself (with his long-term plans) – thought Plantin had been very mistaken in getting himself so involved. Plantin himself was to think this. Why, given the deteriorating situation in the Netherlands with every sign of a restoration of Spanish authority, had Plantin quite deliberately and knowingly acted as he had?

Leon Voet, in his *The Golden Compasses*, offers as explanation the pressure put on Plantin by his Calvinist partners (before the dissolution of the *compagnie*). But Voet, normally at pains to present Plantin as a man of honour and honesty (as indeed he basically was) and also as essentially anti-Calvinist and, his strong Familism notwithstanding, a sincere Catholic, is just a little perplexed by this key episode in his subject's life (vindicated, as he superbly shows, by what came out of it). He writes, conceding certain qualities in his subject he has been a little reluctant to admit to before: 'Plantin cannot be called a commercial adventurer. He lacked the ruthless, self-assured effrontery of such types. But he did possess their reckless spirit. His dare-devil gambling with fate carried him to the highest point of fame and prestige that a printer has ever reached – and soured his old age with racking financial worries.' Even so, he prefers to exculpate him from the Vianen matter, attributable to 'Calvinist... culprits'.

But is his behaviour here so alien to the man as we perceive him throughout his extraordinary career? And anyway, does it compromise his honour? We must remember – even bearing in mind the fervent, often frantic professions of Catholic orthodoxy and devotion that Plantin was to make so regularly in 1567 and 1568 – that, in common with many Familists, not least Ortelius himself, he was above all else a pluralist in matters of faith. With growing intensity he was, like Ortelius again, to stress the essential private nature of religious experience. For many, he said, and he implied that he himself was of the number, church, denomination and creed were comparatively unimportant; they were needed principally as structures to help people less sure in their faith than himself. Knowing that so many in the Netherlands inclined, for a mixture of political and psycho-cultural reasons, towards Calvinism, he was prepared to do business with them, in both the figurative and the literal sense of that phrase. There seems to me morally sound reasons why he would be prepared to support a Calvinist publishing house operating from a predominantly Calvinist region. If we have to censure him for anything, it is for the craven, beseeching, sucking-up manner of those letters with which he bombarded such prominent Spaniards as de Çayas, the dignitary who had commissioned the jewel-box from him all those years ago and was now back in Spain.

Yet good came out of it, including – by extension – the *Theatrum*.

Long before the Duke of Alva made his fear-inducing arrival in the southern Netherlands, Plantin had persuaded van Hasselt to write a letter. This stated that Plantin had played no part in van Hasselt's going up to Vianen to start a press. The Vianen printer himself took refuge in Germany. So assiduously did Plantin cover up his tracks that much of this tense episode has been clarified by an expert, Dr Bouchery, only in the twentieth century. Bouchery uncovered what Plantin had during those months most dreaded to hear: that officialdom *did* know something of his clandestine activities. Plantin, who knew how his duplicity could be interpreted, also elicited the alliance from a powerful Cardinal, the Archbishop of Mechelen, de Granvelle, who was also of great assistance, and patronage, to another man of political ambiguity, Pieter Bruegel. Nevertheless, by day and night Plantin suffered acute terror that his head might be in danger – for assisting in the dissemination of anti-Catholic material, for conniving at sedition against the Spanish crown. It brought him, one infers from letters, close to nervous collapse. It should also be emphasised that Plantin was a devoted family man. His eldest daughter Margareta was already married to the brilliant orientalist Frans Raphelengius, whose linguistic skills made him an invaluable proof-reader for Plantin's firm. The couple lived with Christophe and Jeanne Plantin. Martina, the second daughter who had been born in 1550, was to marry (in 1570) Jan Moretus (1543–1610), who carried forward his father-in-law's work, reputation and family. There were three other daughters, and one, Henrica, was still only a very young child, probably no more than five years old. And it was in the troubled 'Wonder Year' of 1566 that at last Plantin had a son – Christophe, named for himself – who would not live many months after his fourth birthday. Plantin felt desolate at the little boy's death, and it's not hard to appreciate that his grief must have undercut his response to all the other happenings of the times.

The Netherlands after the arrival of the Duke of Alva in the August of 1567 was a far worse place to be living and working in than under the regency of Margaret of Parma, whatever her reluctance to grant its inhabitants the freedom they deserved and demanded. The Duke of Alva,

LE DUC D. ALBE.

The Duke of Alva, Ferdinand Alvarez de Toledo (1508–1582), as history – the subsequent century – saw him. A brilliant tactician even in youth (he was a general by the age of twenty-six), he was sent by Philip II to the Netherlands in 1567 to deal with their revolt, deliberately pursuing policies of savage repression and the instilling of general fear. His 'Bloody Council' was responsible for a vast exodus from the Low Countries, particularly to England.

though sixty years old, was an obvious choice; he had been consistent in his opinion, expressed repeatedly to Philip, that this bothersome part of the Empire should be treated with the maximum severity. There were two reasons for this: the first, that a people recoiling under harsh treatment and filled with fear that more would follow, would cause little trouble; the second, that Spain's army – the duke brought 10,000 men, not all of them Spanish, but from other parts of the Hapsburg Empire – was in imminent danger of being overstretched. With the Netherlands crushed and submissive as a result of immediate action, the army could move on elsewhere – provided, of course, that garrisons were set up in all significant towns as a regular reminder of Spain's power.

Margaret of Parma was horrified by what one might term the Duke's principled cruelty (officially sanctioned from Madrid). Alva's was no spontaneous release of authority's anger but intellectually planned methods of emasculating a whole population through terror and suffering. No one could feel safe. Arrests, executions for heresy and treason, reprisals for renegade actions *pour encourager les autres*, were commonplace. A *Conseil des Troubles* (Council of Troubles) was set up to look into dissidence and putative insurrection and then see to the punishment of offenders (often by death). Margaret was personally distressed by first the summary arrest and then, ten months afterwards, the public beheading of two of the Netherlands' most prominent and widely respected nobles, the Counts of Egmont and Horn (loyal to the Catholic Church but found, even more importantly, wanting in loyalty to Spain). It's one of the imaginatively seminal events of these terrible years – the two counts having their heads cut off in the magnificent civic setting of Brussels' Grand Place with the public standing by, weeping at the official crime they were witnessing.

Margaret resigned in protest; by December 1567 she'd left for Spain. The Duke of Alva was now the royally appointed governor-general of the Netherlands, and his gubernatorial career proved to be entirely consonant with the whole brutal assertion of his martial arrival.

It was a dreadful time to be maintaining a balanced working and personal life and Plantin, in spite of his specific worries about the Calvinist press, cannot have been the only one to think of 1567 as a 'Year of Great Fear'. Alva, in addition to his military probes of the entire Netherlands region, exercised special zeal in putting down the *haute bourgeoisie* of which Antwerp was a prominent bastion, judging them, correctly, to be in their prosperity and education enemies of Spain in their hearts (and maybe in the disposal of their purses also). Plantin was terrified of what might happen to him and his family. He had offers then as later from elsewhere – Paris and Frankfurt begged so distinguished a man to come away from Antwerp, to transfer his business – but he did not. Many took the opposite decision: the exodus of dissenters began on a new scale, and included many of Plantin and Ortelius' most cherished friends.

But a solution to Plantin's fraught predicament was imminent, indeed had already been conceived, and it was to have the most beneficial effect on the fortunes of the *Theatrum*. All that was needed was its shaping (or re-shaping), its bringing forward for attention in the right quarters. It would be a project that, most welcomely, harnessed his own well-known, indeed indisputable, printing and publishing capabilities to Catholic devotion – and even reverence for the Spanish monarchy. What a mercy that something which seemed like a godsend was in fact not only to hand but had already been discussed.

This was a Polyglot Bible. Back in the second decade of the century such an enterprise had been launched from Alcalá in Spain with the blessing of the renowned cardinal Ximenes. Plantin's original plan was to reissue this six-volume affair, with appropriate scholarly amendments reflecting the contemporary advance in oriental and biblical studies, acknowledged now in Catholic circles (e.g., with qualifications, by the Council of Trent) as in Protestant, as indispensable to an informed religion. Even in the spring of 1566, before all the troubles, Plantin had had a specimen page prepared. Now, in changed circumstances, he saw that this could restore his reputation and earn an income for his press. De Çayas saw, and in letters developed with him, the preferable possibility of a new multi-lingual Bible, a radically re-thought undertaking replacing the Alcalá edition. This was judged more likely to be found pleasing to Philip. And so, against a decidedly palpable and worrying background of real fear of investigation for treason and heresy; of uncomfortable ponderings on what he knew himself to have, of his own volition, done; of a second alarm caused by his publication of a Calvinistic New Testament (admittedly re-edited by a French Catholic priest); and, in the outside world, throughout the Netherlands, of the draconian measures of the Duke of Alva – against all this the Polyglot Bible (*Biblia Polyglotta* or *Biblia Regia*, the *Royal Bible*) got slowly underway. It received the support, intellectual and financial, of Philip II – though to Plantin's vexation and outspoken complaints the money was often slow, and erratic, in coming. (It has to be said that in spite of being a rather practised and accomplished sycophant – who carefully made and then corrected drafts of his letters of flattery and appeal to the great – Plantin was quite forthright even to a monarch when it came to the all-important subject of payment.)

The first volume of the Bible came out in March 1568, the fifth and last, devoted to the New Testament, in 1571: a mammoth publishing venture indeed. It is in five languages: Hebrew, Chaldean (or Aramaic), Greek, Latin and Syriac. On view nowadays in Plantin's Vrijdagmarkt house (the Plantin-Moretus Museum), it is an arresting and aesthetically pleasing triumph of the typographer and book designer's art, a tactile correlative of what it embodied, a faith with roots in the far past, in ancient civilisations, and yet reaching out to a diversity of cultures in the actual world. Though it certainly was to have critics, there is no doubt that it brought about the desired restoration of the house of Plantin's reputation and fortunes.

The achievement of the *Biblia Polyglotta* is one directly comparable with the *Theatrum*, for which Plantin was to sell Ortelius paper only eighteen months after publication of the Bible's first volume. It is comparable in ambition, in determination to match the subject matter with sophistication of book-production and in internationalism of address – confirming, surely, my view of a profound pluralism at the heart of Plantin's mind and endeavours. Nor is the Bible the only testimony from this new, almost Phoenix-like stage of his career to Plantin's unrivalled ability to match belief with fine format, superlative printing and sound publishing judgement about numbers of copies, distribution and sales. Roughly contemporaneous with it are a Hebrew Bible for sale in the Jewish diaspora of North Africa; a *Psalterium* and an *Antiphonium* printed in corresponding black and red (for Antwerp up to the disturbances of the mid-sixties was a great centre of musical activity, thanks above all to the genius of Tielman Susato, composer/compiler – a distinguished name to this day – whose publishing ventures Plantin was shrewd enough to take over); a book of French dialogues for Dutch speakers; the first-ever Dutch *Thesaurus* (dictionary) with explanations in Latin, French and Dutch, making use of Plantin's own experiences of learning the language of Antwerp; a comprehensive herbal by the eminent botanist Rembert Dodoens (Dodonaeus), physician at the courts of first Maximilian II then Rudolph II; and an index of different typefaces. All these works involve almost virtuoso printing techniques, for the reproduction of illustrations and diagrams, for the setting out of musical notations, for the juxtaposition of contrasting types including those in (not-so-common) non-western alphabets. In addition, all, to use that term of praise of Petro Bizzari's, cited at the very beginning of this book, could be called 'world-machines', devices for bringing harmony into the (often warring) parts of a great whole – and so form a company the *Theatrum* could itself proudly join. With a list such as this, Plantin's printing-house seems the most fitting place from which to put out Ortelius' atlas, as it did from 1579 onwards.

To assist Plantin with work on the *Biblia Polyglotta* Philip sent over his chaplain, Benito Arias Montano (Arias Montanus – the name celebrates his native mountain village in Extremadura – 1527–1598). A famed biblical scholar, who had indeed actually studied in Alcalá, he had played a prominent part at the Council of Trent. His arrival in Antwerp was not exactly propitious. The ship in which he left northern Spain was caught in an appalling storm and wrecked on the Irish coast, so Arias Montanus had to travel all the way across Ireland and then the whole breadth of Wales and England in order to get to Antwerp at all – where he found that Plantin had given up on him and taken himself off to Paris. However, once the two men had met up, the rapport was remarkable. Plantin's letters – particularly those addressed to anyone with anything to do with the Spanish court – are apt to be fawning and flowery, but in this case there's no mistaking the genuine emotion – not just liking but also warmth, intellectual accord, unequivocal admiration, and an affinity both felt almost as soon as they came together. Arias Montanus – whose sage, thoughtful, lofty-spirited (and somehow very Spanish) face was wonderfully rendered (again from contemporary likeness and oral memories) by Rubens, and glowingly hangs today in the Plantin-Moretus Museum – lived in Antwerp for four years, working at all sections of the Bible, for, impressively, he knew all its languages. He averaged, so Leon Voet estimates, eleven hours a day – and yet was able to draw on Antwerpers of great learning and great capacity for hard work, not least Margareta Plantin's husband, Frans Raphelengius, whose zeal and knowledge won heart-felt praise from the Spanish prelate.

Benito Arias Montano is a perplexing figure, whose influence on all who came into contact with him – and he was a priest with considerable authority and access to the ears of the mighty – was beneficent. Whatever his official positions, his was no conventional Tridentine viewpoint on

Knowing the immensely important place Benito Arias Montano held in Christophe Plantin's life, as in Ortelius', Balthasar I Moretus requested this portrait of him from Rubens between 1630 and 1636. Though dressed as a Knight of St James at the Spanish Court, he suggests here the intelligent independence of mind and relentless capacity for intellectual work for which his friends so admired him.

religious subjects; on the contrary, he seems to have been more than usually receptive to differing shades of opinion, and certainly was aware – and perhaps a good deal more than aware – of the Family of Love, unexpected in a royal chaplain to the court of Philip II. Alastair Hamilton in his study of the Familists presents Arias Montanus' progress during his Antwerp years as one from a hard-line position to a much more inclusive attitude to religion, politics and culture, all as a result of sustained contact with the distinguished Netherlanders who formed the Plantin circle. On his arrival he staunchly believed that Catholicism as the one true faith must be maintained, even if by force, in the Low Countries, and gave his approval to the Duke of Alva's regime and campaign. However, he became disgusted by the cruelty with which Alva discharged his mission – after all, forgiveness and mercy were virtues enjoined of Christians. Arias Montanus made representations in high places for a far more com-passionate attitude to Netherlands issues. As his own writings show, he became gradually informed by that irenicism already noted as characteristic of all who had connections with the Family.

He became a very good friend of Ortelius. In February 1576 he wrote to him from Rome (i.e. after his work in Antwerp was over) lines which say much about the sympathy between them:

> Though your letter arrived rather late, it was very agreeable to me as written by the man whom, among my Belgian friends, I hold dearest, and whose name I hear always among the learned. No one would believe with what close ties of affection I feel bound to you and those like you, ties which become the looser the further I am away from you. Although I am here among friends, men learned and devoted to me, yet by my absence from you I seem deprived of all the pleasure of life, to such a degree that if the hope of rejoining you some day or the greater wish of ending my days among you, did not sustain me, I should nearly have been overcome by grief.

The presence of this most distinguished man, near the powerful, but ambiguous and full of human sympathy, learned but mindful of ordinary people, divided in his relationship to the claims of tradition and new knowledge, pervades the *Theatrum* itself.

PART THREE
THE *THEATRUM*
AS A REALITY

Previous page:
New World/America *from the 1570* Theatrum. *The principal source for this was Mercator's world map of 1569. Ortelius comments in his text on the singularity of the continents being withheld from 'ourWorld' before Columbus. His admiration for the ancients made him anxious to believe that they had at least thought a western land mass might exist.*

CHAPTER ELEVEN

Ortelius was now in touch with many scholars in many countries – as a result of his own maps so well-received, and through his search for ones suitable for the atlas now underway. None of these learned men did he hold in greater esteem than the Welsh Humphrey Lhuyd (1527–1568), to whom he sent a copy of *Asia* while soliciting him for contributions. Humphrey Lhuyd's reply of 3 August 1568 ranks among the most moving letters ever written to Ortelius:

I received your description of Asia the day I had to leave London; and before I had returned home I caught a most dangerous fever, which has made me doubt of my recovery. But neither fever nor the prospect of death, nor an uninterrupted head-ache, were able to efface the remembrance of my Ortelius from my troubled brain. I therefore send you my map of Wales, not completed in all its details, but faithfully drawn, provided certain safeguards are observed, which I wrote down dying. You will also receive a map of England with its ancient and modern names, and another map of England tolerably accurate. Also some fragments of a description of Great Britain written by myself rather roughly, and imperfect, but based on the computations and authorities of the ancients, and which would have been completed if God had granted me life. Accept therefore the last remembrance of your Humphrey.

From Denbigh in Gwynedd or north Wales *Tuus et Vivens et Moriens* [Yours ever both living and dying].

A true scholar's disinterested passion for his subject frequently stays with him right up to the very portal of death. (Robert Louis Stevenson describes how in their last days both his father and grandfather went back and back to their great lighthouse engineering triumphs; Ortelius, too, was in due course to persist with his cartographic and bibliophile interests during his last infirmity.) Ortelius recorded that the writer of the above letter died on 31 August; in fact he was mistaken, 'his Humphrey' died on 21 August, seventeen days after writing him sentences at once those of a dedicated fellow professional and of a warmly disposed friend unafraid to face the truth of things.

Humphrey Lhuyd (his own chosen spelling for what's now usually written Lloyd) was a Welsh humanist whose part in the *Theatrum* is a particularly important one. Paradoxically he was in the cultural vanguard on account of his attitude to the past, especially the remote and primitive past. His antiquarianism, which was akin to Ortelius' own from his boyhood onwards, insisted on the preservation and scrutiny of past artefacts in order to arrive at the desired understanding of a land and its inhabitants. His native Wales, its history and language fascinated him in their own right. But they could also be used as a paradigm for other places and cultures, and no one appreciated this aspect of Lhuyd's work better than Ortelius.

Not much is known about Lhuyd's probably fairly eventless life. He was born in Denbigh and graduated from Oxford 1547/48, entering the service of the Earl of Arundel in 1553. He was responsible for the first proper map of Wales and for a seminal work of Welsh history, the *Cronica Walliae*, taking his native country up to the year AD680 and including in it the legend of the ancient Welshman, Madoc, who sailed the Atlantic, to discover a continent on its far side. (Not to Columbus nor to the Norse, then but to a Briton must go the honour of 'finding' the New World.) Lhuyd went on a tour of Italy with the Arundels, and passed on the way through Antwerp where he met Ortelius; the two of them, who had correspondence and friendship with Daniel Rogers in common, got on as though intimates for years (hence the tenderness of the above letter). After Lhuyd's death Ortelius contacted his heirs, and received maps for use in the *Theatrum*, but judged that, as far as publication in it was concerned,

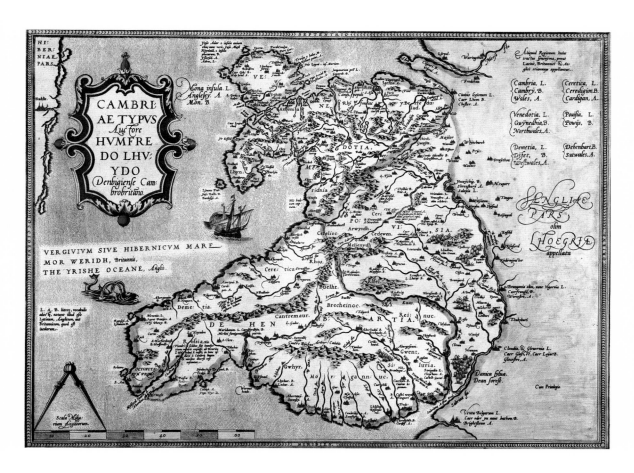

Map of Wales by Humphrey Lhuyd. It was with great pride that Ortelius included this beautiful and scholarly map by his admiring and distinguished friend in the 1573 edition of the Theatrum. *The learned commentary that accompanies it derives from information supplied by Lhuyd as well as from other and older sources, and though it goes in for generalisations by no means consistent with later thinking, it is admirable in its emphasis on the antiquity and independence of the Welsh language, that of 'Britain's most ancient inhabitants'.*

they needed further editing – which he proceeded to give them. An essay by Lhuyd on Anglesey (*Mon*) and its druidical inheritance he did include, however, in the book's first edition.

Lhuyd's maps were models of their kind, and they manifest the high value that not just he but Ortelius also gave to toponymy (the science of place-names); they understood that what a place is called is a valuable palimpsest of its history, aiding our knowledge of its foundation, its evolution, and often, through linguistic blendings, the ethnic or cultural tensions inherent in its make-up. The map of Wales bears names in three languages – Welsh (British), Latin (the language of the country's first conquerors) and English (that of its second). Certain names appear on it – Gwynedd, Dyfed – that would not be current again until the county- and placename reforms of the 1970s. And Lhuyd's essay – though it may at first appear a little extraneous to the contents of the rest of the *Theatrum*, and, for that reason, was never followed up by anything else of the same sort – provides an excellent illustration of what Ortelius made into a motto for his work, and the presiding one of the *Parergon* or historical supplement: 'Geography is the eye of History'. Read Lhuyd's essay, and the island of Anglesey on the map will acquire a new interest; here was a place once culturally significant. Look at the map in the light of the essay, and this culture becomes more intelligible because of its geographical circumstances.

That the work which brought Lhuyd and Ortelius together cemented a friendship alive with affection is evident from correspondence. But in truth one gets the decided impression, as one reads through the *Collected Letters* or the *Album amicorum*, that establishing contacts with the *Theatrum* in mind was at once intellectually stimulating and personally pleasurable – even fun. Another letter from London, dated Monday 21 June 1568, can be adduced here, its author a rather more practical character than Lhuyd, one Joannes Venduillius Douai, who includes Plantin in his expressions of goodwill, showing the solidarity among these humanist 'sets':

I desired to converse with you and Plantin and to form friendship with you, when I was at Antwerp at Eastertime. The Laurini are our common friends, and I take great pleasure in the study of history and geography. If your affairs should lead you to visit this or any place in the neighbourhood, pray come and be my guest. Count de Lalaing, who has returned from Spain, wishes me to procure some maps and books for him from Antwerp; send me therefore all that you have on sale of the things that he wishes for, with their prices, and buy that, which you have not yourself, through Speelman. You will receive the amount from my cousin Nicolas de Vendville, a merchant at Lille. Enclosed is a list of what the Count wishes to have; send also a copy of your universal map and its price. Send me anything written on the Southern region beyond the Straits of Magellan. Is it true that they are printing in Italy a very full description of Africa? Has our king founded any universities in America or the neighbouring isles? You will consider it rather uncivil in me to trouble you with all these requests, but you may feel sure that I will do even more for you, if it be in my power.

This letter provides good insight into the kind of person – well-educated, prosperous, with international connections – who went to form the *Theatrum*'s readership; this would prove to be sizeable, responsive, anxious to proselytise its values and interests, and widely distributed. We can note in this writer's lines many attractive qualities: a lively informality, an undisguised and galvanising curiosity, a willingness to turn acquaintance into something warmer and more generous-spirited – alongside an unflagging awareness of transactions, prices, rightful money value, all the ins and outs of commerce. This almost instinctual hard-headedness did not stifle the heart or the intellect of these men. But it imposed its own parameters of vision and lifestyle – as in due course we shall be forced to confront.

Through his persistent endeavours the maps continued to come in to Ortelius' Antwerp home, and built up and built up, until by 1568 the bulk of them were with him (though some, like Lhuyd's, he would hold over till later editions). Of the maps to be published in the 1570 *Theatrum* only eight have dates, these being all dates of their composition. Significantly none is later than 1568. We can look at them, then, as forming a kind of bedrock of the whole assemblage.

The maps are: *Bavaria*, from 1533, by Joannes Aventinus at Landshut; *Calais-Boulonnais*, from 1558, by Nicolaus Nicolaius Delphinas; *Wirtenberg* (Würtemberg), dated 1558, but in fact redrawn by Frans Hogenberg from an earlier model, perhaps dating from as far back as 1540; *Portugal*, from 1560, by Fernandus Alvares Zeccus; *Silesia*, from 1561, by Martinus Helwig Neissensis; *Russia, Muscovy and Tartary* (see page 173), from 1562, by Anthony Jenkinson (Antonius Ienkinsonus); *Transylvania* (see page 40), from 1566, by Johannes Sambucus Pannonius (the Hungarian); *Friesland* (northern Netherlands), from 1568, by Jacob van Deventer.

The authors of these maps were men distinguished in all senses of the word. Sambucus, for instance, the first person to hail Ortelius 'cosmographer', was a fellow numismatist, a physician of great standing, and humanist historian to the Holy Roman Emperors, first Maximilian II, to whom he was successfully to commend the *Theatrum*, then that great collector of intellectuals, often of an alchemical and metaphysical disposition, Rudolph II of Prague. In purely cartographic terms there were few more eminent than Zeccus or Deventer. The Zeccus map had actually been put out by Michael Tramezzini, from whose Rome publishing house Ortelius had obtained the majority of the maps which made up his compilation for Gillis Hooftman. The sources then are various, but they have one thing in common: they were unmatched for accuracy, conscientious detail – and manner of presentation.

There is not complete consistency of cartographic language or style among them, though there is far more than we could find within any previous or contemporary bound-together group of maps. The lettering is overwhelmingly italic, but the map of Bavaria, for example, retains Gothic for the names of provinces. Almost all maps to be used in the *Theatrum* are north-oriented, in this following Ortelius' ultimate mentor, Ptolemy, but that of Portugal has west orientation. This can be justified since, in fact, it serves brilliantly to emphasise the west-stretching Atlantic Ocean as the key to that country's character and destiny. All *Theatrum* readers, and particularly Netherlander ones, who'd benefited amply first from Portugal's successes and then from her failures, would have appreciated that without her earlier mastery of the sea-ways the Age of Discovery – and of subsequent exploration and colonisation – would be unimaginable. Jenkinson's map of the Russias is made vivid by many illustrations, whereas the others rely for their visual impact on the aesthetically satisfying disposition of carefully done symbols – the Alps of *Bavaria*, the downland and dunes of *Calais*; the magnificent German rivers of the *Wirtenberg* map (Rhine, Neckar and Danube) are especially commendable.

Indeed beauty is the outstanding attribute of all these eight maps, the beauty that proceeds from meticulous attention to detail and from scrupulous inner consistency maintained out of an unswerving belief in

Russia, Muscovy and Tartary. *One of the masterpieces of the* Theatrum, *1570, this is the work of the English diplomat–explorer, Anthony Jenkinson, first published in England in 1562. Of its many vivid and amazing pictorial features, justified by travellers' tales, none rivets the attention more than that on the extreme right, explained as follows: 'The Kirghiz live in troupes and hordes. They have the following custom. When a priest performs a religious ceremony, he obtains blood, milk and dung of a beast of burden and mixes it with earth. He pours this in a specific vessel and climbs a tree with it, and when there is a gathering he sprinkles it over the people, and this sprinkling is considered to be divine and is worshipped. When some one of them dies, that person is hung up in a tree by way of burial.'*

the importance of the completed work. Map-makers surely resemble practitioners of the art of fugue. They have to follow given rules which themselves serve given realities. They are therefore not at liberty, during the course of their work, to change either the rules or the assumptions on which they rest. The obligatory devotion, however, is rewarded in the formal perfection of what is produced, and its complete realisation of every single detail.

So conspicuous is the beauty of these productions that perhaps it doesn't need the stress I have laid upon it. I have done so because in watching Ortelius get together the maps for his atlas, canvassing, eliciting, choosing, rejecting, editing, we realise that over and above Ortelius the 'cosmographer', as Sambucus was pleased to hail him, is Ortelius the collector. We've seen that the collecting passion was his from an early age, inherited from his father, and he pursued it all his life – his coins, prints, pictures, *objets d'art* (not to mention books or maps) became famous. The collections were made not just with himself in mind, but with the delight and instruction of others; people would speak of a *Museum Ortelianus*.

It was Ortelius the great collector, the recognised connoisseur of first-class work, the arranger of interesting pieces so they were set off to individual advantage and yet shed light on their fellows, who came into his own in the mid-1560s as he prepared for the work that would give him – and his chosen form – a place in posterity.

In his close friend Frans Hogenberg he had found the perfect engraver for the maps in his books, a man of harmonising yet complementary gifts, patience and artistic judgement. Ortelius gave him those maps which he himself – initially with Radermacher's enthusiastic aid – had, with intense application, redrawn to meet the specifications required for the book as he planned it. The preparation of these on to copper-plate was itself a highly skilled and delicate art, but there was no greater exponent of this art in all Europe than Hogenberg.

But for all the help he received from such gifted and conscientious colleagues, most of the decisions necessary for a work so organic and so ambitious in scope only Ortelius could be responsible for. And he didn't spare himself. The scale of reduction, the kind of commentary to appear on a map's verso, its length, its bibliography, the order in which the maps should be placed – he wrestled with them all.

It's therefore hardly surprising that, though only in his early forties, Ortelius suffered from palpitations of the heart, invariably an indication of stress. We can read about his problem in a letter of 12 July 1568. His London physician friend Thorius offered him a medical explanation of this disturbing and often frightening phenomenon: 'This arises,' he told him, 'from tightness of the heart caused by the surrounding veins and arteries being obstructed. A cure can only be effected by aperients,' and he wrote down a 'mixture' for him. 'Have the vein of your left hand opened which is above the ring-finger,' he advised. (We don't know whether Ortelius followed Thorius' instructions.)

And, of course, on top of the strain of so much hard work was the strain of living through such painful times in the Low Countries, suffering to a real degree because of their virtues, because of their having built up so sophisticated, strong and enterprising a society: 'the present most deplorable times'. They had brought illness also to Christophe Plantin, and – when we consider what he had to go through – small wonder.

Ortelius must have been working almost as hard on the maps that would make up the atlas as Arias Montanus and his helpers on the *Biblia*. Radermacher, though now in enforced absence from Antwerp, has left us vivid testimony to the intensity of the years of patient work on his older friend's part to get the atlas ready. To this we ourselves may add the varieties of the areas of judgement necessary. But by 1568/1569 – as distressed by public events as Plantin, though not as personally threatened by them, and probably even more personally pained by the diaspora they'd produced – he had ready all the maps he wanted to use for the book he felt society needed.

CHAPTER
TWELVE

The solution to the question of their sequence Ortelius found in his primary and most admired source, Ptolemy's *Geographia*, as he himself declares in the Introduction to the *Theatrum* which he wrote in early 1570. He was, he says, 'following Ptolemy the prince of geographers'. It is impossible to understand the significance of the *Theatrum* without knowing something of the extraordinary story of the *Geographia* and the Alexandria in which it was conceived and produced.

It is a double paradox, an irony of intellectual history, that the *Theatrum*, a true watershed original, is at once unimaginable without the earlier work, and yet through both its resemblances to it and its departures from it, was the publication that ended its hegemony, indeed its currency, for ever. Ortelius' admiration for Ptolemy (c.90–168) was second to nobody's, except possibly Mercator's with his devout reverence. All during Ortelius' work, Ptolemy had enjoyed an unassailable-seeming eminence. But after the *Theatrum*, thanks to its merits, Ptolemy would become the concern of geographical historians only.

For this is the strange truth: that Ptolemy, important in his own times and place, the second century AD in Alexandria, then became – after an enormous lacuna – important again, over 1,200 years later, to a culture he could never have anticipated, and which had, in fact, developed for over a millennium without any benefit of the knowledge he himself had accumulated and presented. No parallel for this fascinating pendulum swing suggests itself. But as Ortelius and his co-workers in his field applied themselves to examination of him, many similarities with Ptolemy's situation, and with that of Hellenic Alexandria itself, must have occurred to them. Today they appear even more conspicuous, impressive, and curiously poignant.

Alexandria was founded, as its name commemorates, by Alexander the Great, in 331BC, beside an excellent harbour and on a promontory where for over a millennium a modest Egyptian town had existed. When he died, Alexander's body was brought back to Alexandria to be buried at the crossroads at the centre. In the consequent break-up of his empire, one of his generals came to rule Egypt: Ptolemy, a Greek-speaking Macedonian later known as Ptolemy Soter (Saviour), who inaugurated a long line of kings ending, anti-climactically, with Ptolemy XVI or Caesarion, the bastard son of Julius Caesar and Cleopatra.

The geographer Ptolemy's surname suggests some connection to the former Egyptian royal family, but by the time of his birth Alexandria had, in fact, been a provincial capital within the Roman Empire for more than a century. It hadn't lost its importance as a disseminating centre of civilisation, however; it was the richest, busiest and biggest city of the Eastern Mediterranean; in other words, it occupied much the same position as Antwerp inside the Hapsburg Empire. Like Antwerp, Alexandria was a cosmopolitan entrepôt whose citizens spoke a different language from their real rulers. Prosperity, internationalism and a strong sense of cultural identity united in both cities to stimulate the acquisition and systemisation of objective knowledge. Both were great book citadels; the reputation of Alexandria's Library kept traditions of scholarship and learning strong, and in both places the production of geographical works was well to the fore.

Ptolemy wrote with authority on many subjects – music, optics, ethnography, astrology, placenames (he would have felt at home with Mercator, Radermacher or Ortelius himself) – but his two greatest works, whose influence on posterity is incalculable, are his treatise on astronomy, the *Syntaxis Mathematike* (known subsequently as the *Almagest* after its Arabic title of *Al Madjisti*), and our own concern, the *Hyphegesis Geographike* or *Guide to Geography*, in its later lease of life successively

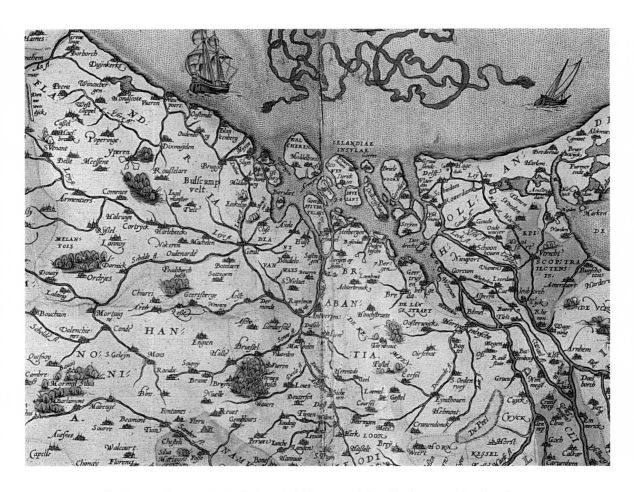

Brabant/'Germania Inferiore'. *This map of Ortelius' own region for the 1570 Theatrum derives principally from that of 1536 (1558 Antwerp reprint) by his compatriot, the great geographer Jacob van Deventer (1500–1575). Antwerp is honoured in the text. 'Antwerp, situated on the Scheldt, [is] the most famous market not only of Germany, but of all Europe and one of the strongest cities in the world, much beautified by the steeple of St Mary's, built to an incredible height with marble.'*

entitled the *Cosmographia* and the *Geographia*. In both works Ptolemy quite consciously saw himself (much as Ortelius – rather than Mercator – did) as one sifting through and evaluating a huge mass of accumulated information, thought, intellectual exchanges, experiments and calculation; the greater part of all this was of eastern Mediterranean (including Alexandrian) provenance, just as work on the *Theatrum* focused on the findings of Ortelius' fellow Netherlanders such as Jacob van Deventer. He stands therefore as a synthesiser of preceding and contemporaneous endeavours in his fields, as a crucible through which a long, multi-stranded and magnificent tradition has been passed. This is one reason why well over a millennium after his death he came to have such near-mystical authority, reminiscent of that exercised somewhat earlier by Alexander the Great's tutor, Aristotle, and by the last royal Ptolemy's great contemporary, Virgil. Not that Ptolemy himself isn't very much there in his productions, working things out, passing judgement on others' computations and theories, assessing the relationship between *idée reçue* and fact. It is from the calendars he used for his own calculations that we know what his main period of activity was – AD125–151 – while as for the passing of judgement, it's no exaggeration to say that the history of discovery itself, of our contemporary world's evolution, would be wholly different had he not made certain key decisions about the material he was examining.

The intellectual territory he surveyed included work accomplished at that institution for which – its lighthouse, the fabled Pharos, apart – Alexandria has enjoyed such legendary prestige: the *Mouseion* (Museum), started by Ptolemy Soter and controlled, largely to its benefit, from the palace itself, its central feature being an immense library. The whole can be likened to a great university college, and indeed teaching was carried out there, though not as an essential occupation for employees. It isn't hard to imagine Ortelius and Plantin's response to the intimate connection between a mighty library and course-setting cartography; it was a relationship they represented themselves. And Ortelius' Museum was actually compared by friends to the *Mouseion*.

The very catalogue of the library's books (probably over half a million) took up 120 volumes, and was largely the work of one remarkable man, Callimachus (Kallimachos – c.300–240BC), scholar, critic, controversialist and celebrated poet, who, in this curious time-spanning story, touches geographical history again later.

As far as posterity is concerned Callimachus was primarily a poet, and one with enormous impact on the evolution of Hellenic literature. He eschewed such grander older forms as the epic ('big book, big bore' he said) in favour of epigrams and other, rather more lyrical 'shorts', most frequently on the allure and pursuit of boys. He was verbally dextrous, with a range of emotions and intellectual perceptions at his command. A bitter-sweet tribute of his to a dead friend became popular in late Victorian England in the song-like version of William (Johnson) Cory:

They told me, Heraclitus, they told me you were dead,
They brought me bitter news to hear and bitter tears to shed.
I wept as I remember'd how often you and I
Had tired the sun with talking and sent him down the sky ...

Callimachus greatly disliked an epic written by a slightly younger man, a probable pupil of his, Apollonius, the *Argonautica* (*Voyage of* Argo) – he thought it too long and too portentous. So great was the derision of it that he orchestrated that the author went off in dudgeon to Rhodes (hence his usual name of Apollonius of Rhodes) where he taught rhetoric and reworked his long poem, with such success that not only did Rhodians greet it with enthusiasm but his own Alexandrians also. Apollonius had been director of the great library, a position superior to Callimachus' there, a situation which fuelled their literary disagreements.

Apollonius' epic once enjoyed a reputation second only to Homer's; he influenced Virgil's *Aeneid*. Its narrative of the one-sandalled hero, Jason, fighter and healer, aboard the *Argo*, voyaging in search of the Golden Fleece and succumbing to the bewitching charm of Medea, takes us over a goodly section of the world as contemporary geographers, and for that matter Ptolemy himself, were to see and delineate it. In it we traverse the Mediterranean eastwards from Tunisia on the North African coast and Liguria on the Italian, voyage round Crete and past the Aegean islands, pass through the Dardanelles and the Bosphorus (the 'Clashing Rocks') to enter the Black Sea. Colchis, home of the Fleece and Medea, lies on the Black Sea's further, eastern shore, part of today's Georgia. Jason is compelled to voyage inland too, on European rivers: the Danube, the Sava, the Po, the Rhine, the Rhône. Though there are geographical errors, improbabilities and trips away from reality – these all accentuated by the stylistic elaborations that persisted even into Apollonius' second version – the *Argonautica* is incomparably more tied to a measured and mapped world than the far earlier Homer. And the ship herself is paid handsome tribute, as is only right from a man who grew up in a great port. The epic begins with the start of a voyage and ends with return to home base (Pagasae in northern Greece). The world is shown as full of curiosities and dangers but it can (says the poem) be encompassed in a single story, a single vision. Besides, as its blind seer Phineus says, 'Zeus himself intends a prophet's revelations to be incomplete, so that humanity may miss some part of Heaven's design.' Beyond the interest of the (just about) known there is always the fascination of the unknown, the uncharted. It is hardly surprising that the work later interested Antwerpers used to travellers' tales and is referred to by Ortelius in his *Parergon*.

While Apollonius was achieving epic, Callimachus, not content with book-cataloguing and prolific poetry composition, was compiling lists of, and collating facts about, living creatures, natural phenomena such as rivers and winds, and also sports, an excellent example of the Alexandrian passion for informative classification, which Ptolemy abundantly inherited, and which can be found again, long afterwards, in the Antwerp of Plantin, Mercator and Ortelius. A theory was circulated by Callimachus' twentieth-century editor, Rudolph Pfeiffer, that scholarship – which Mercator, Plantin and Ortelius so dedicatedly served – actually originated in Alexandria, with the desire of the city's numerous poets for a thorough understanding of the laws and history of their own art.

Callimachus, to his disappointment, never became head librarian at the *Mouseion*. After his death the directorship went to Eratosthenes (c.275–194BC), no more important figure than whom exists in geographical history. Eratosthenes had been tutor to the son of the reigning king (Ptolemy III Euergetes) and he, too, was a poet (among many other accomplishments, it should be said). His favoured form was the *epyllion* or pocket epic but he also wrote epigrams, including one on how to double the cube. However, it isn't his literary productions that have given him his long-lasting significance, but his dazzlingly ambitious work in astronomy and geography. He was the author of many books that have survived through the discussion of them (often entailing strong disagreement) by others, notably by another eminent Greek geographer working (if only briefly) in Alexandria, Strabo.

Eratosthenes knew the world to be a sphere, a conviction that not only was the later Ptolemy's own, but which he shared with many influential thinkers considerably predating him – among them Pythagoras (born 570BC and significantly active in the southern Italian city of Crotone); his followers, the Pythagoreans, whom Plato visited; and Aristotle (384–382BC), who found proof in the circular shadow always cast by the Earth on the surface of the moon during an eclipse. (Aristotle also noted that travellers see different stars as they travel northwards from those visible on a southbound journey.) Eratosthenes believed we could measure the circumference of our round Earth. The experiment he carried out has become one of the treasured icons of the history of science.

It had been observed that at midday on the summer solstice a well in the town of Syene (Aswan) received the rays of the sun at this moment exactly overhead. No shadow proceeded from the upright pointer placed nearby. Alexandria was, according to Eratosthenes' reckoning, due north of Syene (in fact it is some 2 degrees north) by some 5,000 stades (a stade equals 200 ancient feet). He, therefore, on that day, at that hour, measured in his own city the shadow cast by another upright pointer. It turned out to be 1/50 of a circle, and therefore the whole circle's circumference could be put at 50 × 5,000 stades (250,000). There are differences of opinion about the length of a classical stade, but it's usually agreed that Eratosthenes' total is somewhere between 29,000 and 27,000 miles – in distinction to the real one of 24,902. However, there's a school of calculation according to which the director of the Alexandrian library in fact got even closer still, to within a few hundred miles of the true figure. Whatever the small difference between Eratosthenes' estimation and the finding of our times, his is an astonishing achievement. It was one, however, that Ptolemy chose to reject, with the most serious consequences.

He also rejected another conviction of Eratosthenes: that more of the surface of the Earth is occupied by sea than by land, that the central mass of the three continents, Europe, Asia and Africa, was therefore encircled by ocean. Paradoxically, Ptolemy's erroneous disagreements with his great predecessor derive from the increased sophistication of his age, from living within the Empire of the practically minded Romans who, far less interested in mathematics and theory than the Greeks, had established in relation to the vast sweep of territory under their jurisdiction an efficient system of communications and of the measuring of distances between places. Knowledge of the lie of land inside the *Pax Romana* both supplemented and supplanted the information the Greeks had acquired through their preferred means of sea travel. Psychologically and culturally, as well as literally, Ptolemy was an inhabitant of a larger world than Eratosthenes (who hadn't been a Roman citizen), and it was a world to an unparalleled degree cohesive: organised, controlled and even discovered, by land.

This was surely the factor that made him, as mapper of the known world, give superiority to landmass over sea, that made him landlock the Indian Ocean by stretching southern Africa eastwards to meet up with south-east Asia. And this regard for the land – connecting to a natural pride in what the civilisation and political set-up to which he belonged had achieved – was partly responsible, too, for the other great mistake already recorded. His estimation of the world's circumference is about thirty per cent less than the real figure. It was clearly difficult for him to envisage so much lying beyond the ken of the great Empire into which he'd been born and reared.

Yet for all the magnitude of these errors, a society which knew them for what they were – and knew too the bitter costs they had incurred – positively venerated Ptolemy. And it seems only just that they should, for he had a stature and a breadth that made him not only surpass his own predecessors but theirs also. Ptolemy's *Geographia* offered his rediscoverers of the fifteenth century a fuller, clearer window on to our world than any other available work, and so impressed the next century that it became an indispensable, galvanising (and for a considerable time a permanent-seeming) point of reference. Its author, for all his remoteness in date and place, was outstanding for purity of intention: all he wanted to establish, to show forth, was the objective truth. He didn't bow to mere supposition, let alone to superstition, nor did he give in to fanciful conjecture or cherished myths. And appreciation of this obviously puts a very different complexion on where he *did* go wrong, indeed virtually exculpates him.

As important as matter was Ptolemy's manner – his advice to the geographically curious. Ptolemy offered systematic methodology; he was a unique guide as to how best to present the world to readers. And that didn't exclude the question that preoccupied all map-makers of the sixteenth century: how to present a spherical body on a flat surface.

Ptolemy agreed with Eratosthenes that the inhabited world – the *oikoumene* – lay for the greater part 'in one of the two northern quarters' of a sphere that could be divided into four by an equator and a line of longitude (meridian). The *oikoumene*, as he perceived it, was far longer east–west than

The oikoumene, *or known inhabited world according to Ptolemy (c.AD150), in the famous Ulm reprinting of the* Geographia, *c.1486.*

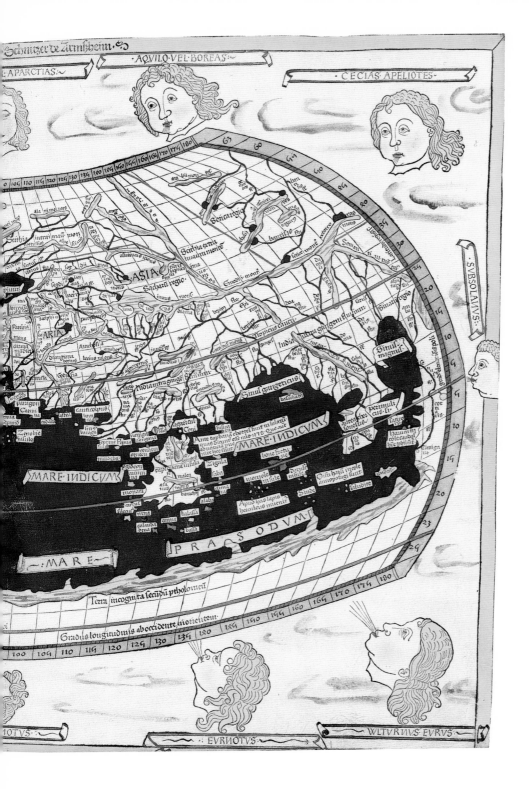

it was broad north–south, and therefore could be best envisioned as rectangular or trapezoid. Its clear correspondence with the known world of Ptolemy's rediscoverers must have seemed extraordinary to them.

We have, unfortunately, no maps of Ptolemy's from his own times, let alone his own hand. The *Geographia* is a treatise in eight books. The first of these gives the famous distinction between 'geography' and 'chorography', and lays down the desiderata for good map-making: the most accurate possible measuring instruments, access to the latest information, acute personal powers of observation. He presents his own ideas on the dimensions of the Earth and two methods of projection, both of them essentially conical, not the cylindrical favoured earlier and to be later used again, of course, by Mercator. In the second to seventh books he lists places – first general areas with their various divisions, then towns in the order of those on the coast, those on big rivers, and those far inland, all with co-ordinates. Only in Book VIII – amid astronomical matters and generally accepted theories about climate zones and habitability – does he tackle the question of how to make a map of our world.

Many have thought the original *Geographia* didn't contain maps, merely extremely detailed instructions for the making of them. This is very possible. Myself, I think otherwise, finding convincing the arguments of the scholar of classical mapping, O. A. W. Dilke. Examining the text, he notes that in the first and second books the author uses the first person plural, future tense, suggesting an intention that he and his readers will see realised. While in the eighth book Ptolemy announces that *the maps have actually been made* (though not necessarily, it must be added, by himself). From this it would seem more than probable that the original offered a world map followed by twenty-six others, ten showing the component parts of Europe, four those of Africa and twelve of Asia.

His mistakes acknowledged then, the recognisability, the truth of the *oikoumene* Ptolemy gives is indeed remarkable – and if we view it, recreated with fifteenth-century eyes, accustomed to the deliberate distortions, the subjection of geographical realities to religious hopes and beliefs that characterise the medieval *mappa mundi*, it becomes the more so.

His opening world map is north-oriented, reflecting the relationship of Alexandria to Rome and, for that matter, to the major part of the entire

Empire. Reading it as we do text, from left to right, that is from west to east, we begin with the *oikoumene*'s westernmost end, the coast of Portugal, and move eastwards all the way to Indochina ('the Golden Chersonesus') and a coast-less China. To the north, beyond an inaccurately drawn but nonetheless identifiable British Isles, we find Thule – probably Shetland, as established by that Greek explorer from Marseilles, Pytheas, who landed there, commenting on its Midnight Sun, on one of his two extensive northern Atlantic voyages (c.330BC). (He circumnavigated the British Isles on the first of these.) Thule is placed absolutely at the top of the map; latitudinally the island is level with the wastes of northern Scythia (Russia). Ptolemy (and his sources) are ignorant of Scandinavia, apart from a misunderstood Jutland, here resembling the head of a heron whose body is the Low Countries. Pytheas on his second voyage almost certainly explored the Baltic, but Ptolemaic representation of even the southern and eastern shores of this sea hasn't learned much from his experiences.

The most casual inspection of the opening world map shows the *oikoumene*'s most vital areas as the surrounds of the (far too elongated) Mediterranean, with extensions to Asia Minor, Mesopotamia, Arabia Felix, and the Persian lands of the Medes, Hircanians and Parthians. The impression is confirmed when we turn to the individual twenty-six maps themselves.

True, Italy is tilted at too marked a west–east angle, and the 'boot' of the country is wrong, with the Gulf of Taranto a lesser affair than in reality; true, the relative sizes of the Black Sea and the Sea of Azov are way out (though not their shapes nor their interconnection). But an almost joyous satisfaction, a palpable sense of long-standing human relationship with a given terrain, can be apprehended in the maps of Iberia, Italy, Greece (a splendidly full one, this), from those four dealing with North Africa from the Pillars of Hercules and Mauretania to the Nile delta just to the east of Ptolemy's native city. As a Hellenic Roman citizen, Ptolemy would, in presenting the most civilised areas of the *oikoumene*, have been honouring the Empire of which he was legally a part. If we put ourselves in the place of later pioneering enthusiasts for Ptolemy's work, we see that their view of the 'civilised' and 'non-civilised' areas of the world were all but coincident. One emotion the rediscovered *Geographia* promoted must have been something not unlike blessed relief. So many centuries of confusion, destruction, of enemies without, within, and without again, so many cruel power-struggles, and at the end of them, a view across a 1,200-year gulf of a society, cultured and intellectually agile, and a world with which they could identify.

Such feelings would have undergone a change – even more so for later readers of the *Geographia* – when the eye travelled over the southern and eastern sections of Ptolemy's world-map and surveyed maps devoted to their components. From Ptolemy you can't learn either the real shape or comparative size of India, and China lacks a sea. Taprobana (Ceylon, later Sri Lanka), whose famous pear- or teardrop-like form the *Geographia* honours, is huge in proportions, almost the same length from north to south as Arabia Felix, and the Equator runs through its southern regions.

The rediscoverers of Ptolemy would probably have shared his disregard for Africa south of the Nile, and for the west of that continent (though Portuguese ventures were to begin in earnest in the not too distant future). About that southern *Terra incognita*, the long indented coastline of which stretches between southern Africa and south-east Asia, there would have been division of opinion.

In truth, Ptolemy, who made careful use of many travellers' accounts of Saharan Africa, was perfectly well-positioned in time and place to have known about early circumnavigations of Africa. These had been made, sailing clockwise, by Phoeniceans over half a millennium before (between 609 and 594BC). Perhaps the omission of any material based on data from such voyages is less a question of knowledge (or lack of it) than of priorities, of what was deemed important enough to be followed up and followed through. Those who pored over the printed editions of Ptolemy in the later fifteenth century and after – more particularly, Ortelius and his fellows in Antwerp – would have regarded the Ptolemaic failures here from a vantage point of information far closer to our own than to that of second-century Alexandria. A closed-in Indian Ocean, no hint of land on the far side of the Atlantic – these would have been as alien to them as to us. Alien but not alienating – their moral and mental attitude to the maps of the *Geographia* would have been quite different from ours.

Confronting Ptolemy's *oikoumene*, readers of the mid-sixteenth century would have seen a resemblance between the vast sway of the Hapsburg Empire and the Roman Catholic Church – a sway now established far beyond the Mediterranean heartland – and the great Roman Empire of the first and second centuries AD. Even the sundering struggle between the

Catholic Church and Protestants could, on one line of vision, be regarded as an event within a single culture, whose differing groups acknowledged the same founder, the same traditions. Greece and Rome, too, had been unlike each other, yet the unparalleled extent of the known – and administered – world in the *Geographia*, and of disseminated information about its many parts and practices, sprang from precisely that inspirited fusion of these two often acutely contrasting *Weltanschauungen*: the Greeks contributing a disposition to theory, a genius for mathematics and philosophy and a long-standing vigorous maritime tradition; the Romans a strong empirical practical approach to life, unsurpassed military expertise and legal organisation, and an interest in exploration of land interiors from Britain to Dacia (if for primarily functional purposes).

Contemporary Europe could come up with a comparable synthesis of mores and talents – indeed wasn't it already doing so? And wasn't Antwerp, where Portuguese, Spanish, French, Italians, Dutch, Germans and even English met up so regularly and profitably, a supreme instance of this? Ptolemy's atlas could therefore be seen as an icon of the human ability to know and have mastery over the globe. It was a wonderful, admirable souvenir of the world's greatest civilisation to which they were – no question of it – heirs in the fullest sense. And on top of that, where was more akin to Alexandria in geographical investigations than Antwerp itself? Ptolemy's map, of course, was not perfect, and, psychologically, it was better for everybody that it wasn't. The *Geographia* was a spur as well as an icon, a brilliant encouragement to continue the exploration and the representation of the world, which their own abilities and determination had so dramatically increased and improved.

The range of the *Geographia* is best seen from its contents:

1. World Map
2. British Isles
3. Spain
4. Gaul and Belgica Galliae
5. Great Germany
6. From the Danube Lands to Macedonia
7. Italy
8. Sardinia and Sicily
9. Sarmatia (from the Vistula to the Don)

10. Dacia, Thracia and the Black Sea
11. Greece
12. Mauritania
13. Carthage to Libya
14. North Africa to Egypt
15. Libya and Ethiopia (North and Central Africa)
16. Asia Minor
17. Sarmatia Asiatica (Southern Russia)
18. Armenia Major
19. Cyprus, Phoenicia, Holy Land
20. Medea and Persia
21. Arabia
22. Scythia
23. Farther Scythia (Central Asia)
24. Arachosia (present-day Pakistan)
25. India
26. Ganges and China
27. Taprobana (present-day Sri Lanka)

If, standing on the bisection of the Equator by a meridian running through the Fortunate Isles (Canaries), you deemed the inhabited world as essentially within the north-east quarter of the globe, what about the rest – the remaining three-quarters? Ptolemy didn't dismiss any possibilities about its constituents; another great continent was certainly a possibility, though, accepting prevalent thinking about climate as the key to human life, he tended to doubt many people could exist outside the *oikoumene*.

Sphericity as the truth about the world never died. Rather, it went underground. Therefore for the fifteenth-century educated – and their sixteenth-century successors – Ptolemy's adherence to it was one of his most admirable qualities. Medieval cartographers simply did not see the Earth's roundness as a key feature; their religious interpretation of existence and their aesthetic ideals and notions of pictorial convenience led naturally enough to their maps showing disc-like earths (often in the pattern known as TO – the O being the round disc, the T the convergence of the three continents, with Jerusalem at the very centre as Scripture stated; the *mappa mundi* in Hereford Cathedral is of the TO type).

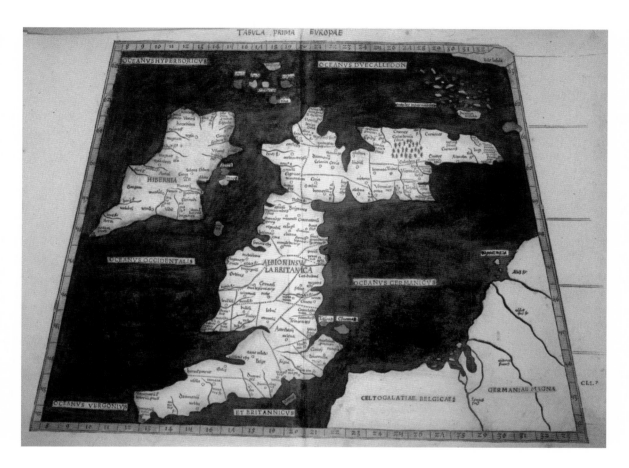

The Ptolemaic view of the British Isles in printed fifteenth-century form (Ulm, 1486).

Alexandria itself went under; its once dazzling and numerous lights were dimmed, and centuries passed when they could be only very faintly perceived, even by scholars. A great modernist poet, Alexandrian Greek like Ptolemy himself, tried to place the death of his city's former great civilisation into some kind of context:

When at the hour of midnight
an invisible choir is suddenly heard passing
with an exquisite music, with voices –
Do not lament your fortune that at last subsides,
your life's work that has failed, your schemes
  that have proved illusions.
But like a man prepared, like a brave man,
bid farewell to her, to Alexandria who is departing.
Above all, do not delude yourself, do not say that it
  is a dream,
that your ear was mistaken.
Do not condescend to such empty hopes.
Like a man for long prepared, like a brave man,
like to the man who was worthy of such a city,
go to the window firmly,
and listen with emotion,
but not with the prayers and complaints of the coward
(Ah! supreme rapture!)
listen to the notes, to the exquisite instruments of
  the mystic choir,
and bid farewell to her, to Alexandria whom you are
  losing.

Cavafy (Constantine Peter Kavafis, 1863–1933;
translated by George Valassopoulo)

In the West, Ptolemy enjoyed a limited underground reputation before his centuries-long submergence. At the court of Theodoric the Goth in Rome both Cassiodorus and Boethius (c.480–524) were admirers of the *Geographia*, and Boethius for his part made translations of Ptolemy from Greek into Latin. But effectively, he was forgotten about. In the East, though, it was quite otherwise.

The Arab world appreciated Ptolemy's works as storehouses of learning and theory, and the Abbassid cultures, centred on the cities of Baghdad and Samarra, took up his ideas on map-making as well as on the relationships of heavenly bodies. Both the great mathematician al-Khwarismi's maps, with their placenames and co-ordinates, and the achievements of the man known indeed as the 'Arab Ptolemy', Ishaq ibn Hunayn, testify to this. The earliest known copy of the *Geographia*, from the twelfth century, is in Arabic. But it was Byzantine interest in Ptolemy that had the more direct effect on the West. A monk, Maximus Planudes (c.1260–1310), dedicated student of Greek geographers, indeed of Hellenic culture generally, hunted for manuscripts of the *Geographia* but was unable to find any which had maps attached. This remarkable man we have to thank too for his rescue of the Greek poems in that treasure-trove known as the *Greek Anthology* – and thus through him the lyrical poems of Callimachus and of Eratosthenes came back, for humanity's enrichment. To the monk Planudes must go credit also for serious interest in the fables of Aesop.

Rather than despair at finding no extant maps of the *Geographia*, Planudes remedied the lack by drawing them himself, interesting the Byzantine Emperor in his work. So Ptolemaic cartography passed from the private enthusiast to the imperial court, and examples from the latter survive to this day.

In 1395 Constantinople needed help against the Turks. It sent an eminent scholar, Manuel Chrysoloras (1350–1415), to Venice to plead its cause. Here he got to know two young men from Florence, both passionately ambitious to study Greek. One of them, Jacopo d'Angelo da Scarperia, became Chrysoloras' personal student and went back with him to Constantinople to immerse himself in his chosen subject. In February 1397 scholar and disciple returned to Italy, for through Jacopo's persuasions Chrysoloras had received an invitation from the University of Florence to teach Greek there. They brought from Constantinople a number of manuscripts, among them Ptolemy's *Geographia* which had already aroused Jacopo's interest.

Chrysoloras began translating this himself, but in the end handed the work over to Jacopo, now working as a copyist in the Roman Curia. It took him a good long while to finish, but he did so in 1406, a key year therefore in the history of the atlas, for without Ptolemy, without Jacopo and his successors, it's impossible to envisage a *Theatrum*. Jacopo did not render the title of *Hyphegesis Geographike* as *Geographia*, but as *Cosmographia* by which the work was known for decades to come. This is a pity, for it suggests

Ptolemy's other interest, that culminating in his *Almagest*. But from the late fifteenth century onwards the more obvious name was reinstated.

Many manuscript copies of the work were made; Chrysoloras and Jacopo's belief in its importance was abundantly vindicated. Ptolemy, it was said – the rhapsodic tone is that which later greeted Ortelius and his *Theatrum* – had drunk of the ambrosia of Jupiter himself. But the real success of the *Geographia* came with the printed editions. The first of these appeared, without maps, in Vicenza in 1475; two years later, Bologna printers, hearing that a house in Rome was to put out a fully pictorial version, published the first Ptolemy with maps. It was a rushed job; fame has preferred its successor, the Roman edition of 1478 with its handsome copper-plate engravings. (This is undoubtedly the one to look at.) Other printings followed, in Germany (Ulm), in the Low Countries. Ptolemy became an indispensable part of an educated person's inheritance, and geographers felt it virtually incumbent on them to conduct a dialogue with him (sometimes as scholarly editors of his work).

Outstanding among those who thus conversed with Ptolemy were: Martin Behaim (maker of the first extant globe, of 1492, showing the world, so to speak, that Columbus left), Martin Waldseemüller (whose globe and world map, as we've seen, honoured and indeed named America), Gemma Frisius, Sebastian Münster, Giacomo Gastaldi and Gerard Mercator – as well as Ortelius himself. So much did they admire his methodology – for he and he alone had advocated and used co-ordinates, the meridian, north orientation and related scales – that they felt almost religiously obliged to re-present and respectfully supplement him wherever possible. Whatever may have been the true reason for Mercator's delay in preparing his own atlas – affection for Ortelius and a concomitant desire to let him have a good run, or simply (surely the greater factor) knowledge of the immensity of the task in front of him – Mercator produced in 1578 an edition of the *Geographia* edited by himself. Already his friend's *Theatrum* – because of what it drew on from the accumulated knowledge of a century of discovery, because of the particular attitudes to the history and nature of humanity informing it – was reducing appetite for the great second-century work. Mercator's was a task of sheerest scholarly love and scrupulous attention, the maps as faithful to Ptolemy's as possible, and beautifully engraved, too. With that done, Mercator felt freed to pursue his goal: his own great *Atlas sive Cosmographicae Meditationes* got underway.

CHAPTER THIRTEEN

Pieter Bruegel 'has been taken away from us in the full flower of his age', bemoaned Ortelius of his friend who died in 1569 from an unspecified illness, 'should we attribute this to death, who because of his mastery of his art, judged him sufficiently aged? Or to nature who was fearing that one would mistake her because of the perfect and ingenious imitation he had carried out? It's difficult for me to decide.'

On his deathbed Bruegel was anxious, his biographer Karel van Mander tells us, to have destroyed any paintings with too overt a political content lest his family suffer. Whatever perished as a result of this considerate order of his, what has been left for us of his intense, original and bold work of his last years provides the bitterest, most haunting commentary on the time he was living, and dying, in.

In the early part of the decade Bruegel had painted a view of Antwerp, *The City of Antwerp with Two Monkeys* of 1562 (see page 198). It is the classic vista as discussed earlier, though the waterfront, the 'roadstead', runs south-east/north-west here, to disappear before the distant bend that will swing the Scheldt round still more fully north-west, bringing it to the estuary and the North Sea.

The foreground of the painting shows us, sitting in an arched niche in a wall (which provides the necessary elevation), two charming but chained guenon monkeys, such as you could buy, together with other exotica, in

Antwerp markets. (Bruegel's patron, the very powerful Cardinal Granvella, owned some in his personal zoo.) No painting does greater justice to the mighty width of the river and the maritime nature of Antwerp. The monkeys, so realistically rendered in posture and expression, could stand for any beings absorbed in their own predicament (children, visitors, immigrants), but dependent on Antwerpers' wealth. Yet they have a meaning beyond this. The monkeys are tethered, a wretched plight for them. Essentially they are prisoners mourning their loss of freedom (and they've finished their meal of nuts). Bruegel was deeply concerned about the deteriorating political and religious situation of Antwerp and the southern Netherlands. He saw the possibilities of economic depression, of the 'chaining' of people preventing them from expressing their true feelings and beliefs. All this the guenon monkeys are warning us of; they're telling us a troubling fact about the great city beyond the niche in which they're captives: that what has actually happened to them is hanging over it just as the sky does. In the distance, river, buildings, land, meeting up, recede in that sky's milkiness, the imminent future ...

Bruegel was to feel his pessimism justified. His great later works are ample testimony to this. *The Massacre of the Innocents* has often been seen as a representation of the Spanish *tercios* forcing their way into the wintry southern Netherlands countryside of Flanders and Brabant. The leader of the vicious battalion at the picture's very centre, killing children by Herod's order, has been identified with the hated Duke of Alva himself. But in fact the *Massacre* may have been executed before the Iconoclasm and its punitive aftermath, in which case it is a work of prescience rather than artistic protest. Certainly we can find in all those winter scenes of the mid-1560s, from the treacherous ice of the frozen rivers and ponds in *The Numbering at Bethlehem* (1566) to the driving snow of *The Adoration of the Magi* (1567), a land in the grip of fierce life-denying forces it cannot withstand.

But the mysterious symbolic paintings from the end of Bruegel's life, their subject matter often derived from Flemish proverbry – executed in a more lapidary, Mannerist-influenced style than earlier works, without sacrificing any of the humanity or emotional energy of these – testify to the artist's despair at the prevalent situation, which is at the same time curiously spiritually exhilarating. *The Parable of the Blind* (c.1568) was inspired by the adapted biblical saying, terrifyingly apt in the historical circumstances, that 'If the blind lead the blind, they all fall in the ditch.'

And this is what is happening in the picture: five unseeing vacuous-faced figures cannot synchronise their movements – some push forward, some stumble, and the last is tumbling over the unfortunate sixth who has already fallen, helpless, his head below the rest of his body. The church stands in the background, aloof from the sorry scene. The monk in the same year's *Misanthropist* walks in grim isolation along a country way while a plump crouching young man hooped in a circle surmounted by a Christian cross tries to steal his wallet. But who is the true hater of humanity? The sly thief robbing an innocent religious man, or the latter so inattentive to human beings that he doesn't see them? Meanwhile, as remote from the episode as the church in the other picture, a shepherd tends his flock (the Church again?).

The young men of *The Land of Cockaigne* (c.1567) lie foolishly like spokes of a wheel round a laid but all messed-up picnic table, in a drunken stupor, exposed to any number of dangers great and small, yet can we blame them for having wanted pleasure? They are at once, like so many people in Bruegel, badly behaved yet pitiable, gross yet likeable because so like ourselves and our associates. The eponymous *Cripples* (1568) – products of the violence of a time of conflict and cruelty – have no limbs with which to dance, or even with which to move properly on the ground, yet they form a strange choric group, a touching yet horrifying parody of the peasant-dance, the *kermess* that Bruegel had during his working life so loved. The cripples are also the *mutilés de la guerre*, a horrid reminder of what violence begets, what soldiers and civilians can expect from its ravages.

Oddest of all perhaps is *The Birdnester* (c.1568) where a somewhat complacent-faced young peasant points knowingly, almost gleefully to a birdnester up in a tree on his right (to get him into trouble?) while himself being on the point of tripping over and falling into the stream in the extreme foreground. In the southern Netherlands of virtuous law-breakers and unvirtuous law-makers where does innocence begin and end, who are those deserving of punishment?

These are all paintings of a fallen humanity that contemporary history is causing to fall still further, still lower. Dignity and honour are daily being robbed from all alike, young and old, men and women, with usually the most lusty and physically vigorous – young working men – as the most signal victims. Yet who could be so cruel as to deny them caring thought, let alone eventual redemption. (It's hard not to believe, as supposition has

Pieter Bruegel: The City of Antwerp with Two Monkeys. *The guenon monkeys tethered in the foreground belonged to Bruegel's powerful patron, Cardinal Granvella (Granvelle), who kept them in his menagerie in Mechelen. They are represented with a naturalist's fidelity, but they surely mirror the freedom-loving but captive people of Antwerp, the City-on-the-Scheldt, whose geographical setting provides the vivid background.*

it, that Bruegel did not have affinities with the Family of Love.) These paintings are great arguments, some of the most powerful ever made, for the ultimate but difficult acceptability of the human race, even when as wretched or contemptible as so often shown in these strange, inexhaustible canvases. They are pleas for that inherent and God-given ability in the most obscene or deformed of our fellow beings to appreciate and enjoy the diversities of the physical world – for the two have been made for each other. The year after Bruegel's death, his friend Ortelius was to present his world also as a splendid and various theatre.

The year of Bruegel's death, 1569, was also the year in which Mercator published a world map (of which only four impressions are extant) using a new projection. This had been developed by himself after exhaustive study of all other available methods of projection, but its principal source was Mercator's own globe of 1541, which had been constructed with navigation significantly in mind. History has made 'his' projection inseparable from Mercator's very name – even above the great atlas that began to come out in 1585. So it comes as a surprise to realise that this map of 1569 was the only one he issued to employ what's come to be seen as the single most far-reaching achievement of sixteenth-century cartography.

Mercator, of course, solved no problem, he only, very substantially, relieved it. We use the term 'lines of latitude' but these parallels to the equator are in truth circles; we use the term 'lines of longitude' but these meridians are arcs which meet up at the poles of our spherical world. Whatever system is employed for representation of the globe on a flat sheet of paper, some distortion must inevitably arise.

Mercator's is a cylindrical projection, like that of Marinus of Tyre against whom Ptolemy argued in the first book of his *Geographia*. That is to say, the globe has been wrapped round by a sheet of paper in the form of a cylinder, and its circles and arcs projected on to this as straight lines intersecting at right angles. In Mercator's projection, not only are the meridians stretched east–west (straight verticals unable to meet) but every parallel (line of latitude) is made equal in length to the Equator itself. This necessitates the progressive stretching north–south between them in order to balance the east–west stretching of the lines of longitude. This means, therefore, that the further from the equator, and the nearer the poles, the greater the distance between the parallels. There's an ineradicable distortion in area (but not shape) of the more northern or the more southern regions of the world. Greenland, only one-ninth the size of the continent of South America, actually appears on a map using the projection to be the larger of the two, and has become perhaps the most famous instance of the exaggeration it imposes. On the other hand, Mercator's methods enabled the maintenance on the surface of the map of the straight line of compass bearing (a carry-over from work on the 1541 globe).

The southern hemisphere being so much emptier than the northern – and even more so in Mercator's day, before the discovery of Australia and New Zealand – the distortion favoured those very parts of the world which were, during the years following the belated adoption of the projection, engaged in expansion of themselves: Holland, Britain, Sweden, Russia. Since the later twentieth century, this has been held against the projection, with some justice, and even against Mercator himself, with, it seems to me, no justice at all.

The world map itself, like the globe, was made with seafarers principally in mind – and their part in the colonisation of the world by the West is, of course, beyond estimation. Empires arose from their endeavours. The new projection aided the charting of ships' routes, it made for far greater safety (the stubbornness of sailors in taking it up seems from our perspective positively perverse). Seamen planning a voyage could now hold a ruler on the map between their point of departure and their point of arrival and with the aid of a magnetic compass proceed straight ahead. Mercator himself admitted to his pleasure in this, in his own comments on the 1569 map, though in his honesty he also warned that the length of the line would require recalculation.

The sphericity of the Earth had not been overcome, and there were limitations even in this new and long-lived way of coping with it. But it had been, for map-makers and map-users, tamed, incorporated into our furniture of the mind (along with, one has to say, a false image of its proportions). Europeans, especially given the prominence to the eye of their own homelands, acquired through the projection a sense of mastery of that sphericity, which they proceeded to turn into literal, acquisitive fact, a sense that was to result in great misery and injustice for millions, as well as benefits from a more 'advanced' society.

Arno Peters' projection, which superseded Mercator's in the second half of the twentieth century, is judged today not only more satisfactory from the standpoint of accuracy, but for ideological irenicist reasons (that would probably have pleased the generous-minded Mercator). But Mercator significantly expanded our sense of possibility in relation to the world, as surely as did those thousands upon thousands of seamen, Dutch, French, British, Scandinavian, who were to succeed the Portuguese and Spanish as the explorers, openers-up and colonisers of the world. Ortelius did not, in fact, use Mercator's projection in his *Theatrum*, but an oval form (which does better justice to the poles as facts of the Earth's physical identity). And as we have established, the atlas was nearing completion, as far as the editing of its contents was concerned, by the time Mercator's historic world map came out. Nevertheless there seems a rightness that the first atlas did not appear until this biggest step in dealing with the roundness of the world had been achieved.

On 23 October 1569 Ortelius received his first 'privilege' (licence) for the *Theatrum* – guaranteed for ten years from the Secret Council of the Spanish Netherlands. On 21 February 1570 he received a second 'privilege' from the Council of Brabant. Both these are printed at the end of the atlas. In order to satisfy the authorities Ortelius would probably have had to show them a plan of the whole and perhaps one or two maps, though it's unlikely that any text – which Ortelius wrote himself – would have been ready by either of these dates. Paper for the book was ordered from Christophe Plantin in September 1569 and between then and January Plantin's records show that Ortelius received 47 reams.

By May 1570 the book had been printed, at Ortelius' own expense, in the workshop of Gillis (Egedius) Coppens van Dienst, a master-printer with over thirty years' experience of cosmographical works, maps and atlases behind him. Coppens van Dienst it is who recorded the publication date as 20 May. Christophe Plantin sold his first copy on 13 June. As his ledgers show, this was to be the first of many, very many.

As has already been observed, the book would have been more often than not sold unbound, as a collection of collated sheets, and offered to the client 'plain' or 'coloured'. Despite his own and his sisters' excellence at colouring, in later years Ortelius was to tell Ortelianus that in truth he preferred 'plain'.

So now the theatre is ready, the play of the whole known world can be staged. But first things first – there's the title to consider. Why had Ortelius fixed on *Theatrum* as the name of his great enterprise?

CHAPTER FOURTEEN

The Latin word *theatrum*, from Greek *theatron*, means 'a place to see shows' (the Greek noun deriving from the verb 'to see'); these shows, in distinction to those at the more popular amphitheatre, being either serious drama or religious rites. If we want any endorsement of the primacy of the visual in the atlas, it is here in the very title Ortelius decided on for his book. It will, he's announcing, put on a show for us of all the countries of the world (*orbis terrarum*), and it will be a serious affair, as much so as the solemn plays of the ancients which took human destiny as their subject or as those rites which connected us to our sense of place. The idea of the show is not, of course, unrelated to the more modern one of armchair travel, as a poem written by Christophe Plantin in French for the 1581 edition makes clear. Addressed to the '*débonnaire spectateur et lecteur du Théâtre*' ('the kindly spectator [member of the audience] and reader of the Theatre'), it apostrophises the atlas' editor in rhyming couplets:

> *Combien doit-on chérir nostre ABRAHAM ORTEL*
> *Pour nous avoir dressé ce grand oeuvre spectacle*
> *Nommé DE L'UNIVERS LE THEATRE; où les Cartes*
> *De tout le Monde sont? Auquel; sans que tu partes*
> *Du sueil de ta maison, quiconques sois; tu peux*
> *Apprendre le chemin pour aller où tu veux.*

Et si, sans te bouger, tu aimes mieux apprendre,
Où le Marchand s'en court chasque denrée prendre,
Icy tu verras sans courir le danger
Des chemins périlleux, ni de la haute mer
Les flots impétueux.

('How much ought we to cherish our ABRAHAM ORTEL[IUS] for having made this great show called THE THEATRE OF THE UNIVERSE where are maps of all the world? In which without leaving the threshold of your house, whoever you may be, you can learn the way to go where you want and if, without moving, you prefer to learn where the merchant ventures to get hold of each commodity, here you will see [it all] without running the danger from perilous roads or the raging waves of the high sea.')

But these delights mustn't obscure the high seriousness of the artefact, just as enjoyment of an entertainment mustn't obscure the theatre's solemn origins.

As an intellectual of his time, as a committed humanist, Ortelius, his life through, took the widest, deepest interest in multiple aspects of the classical world; its architecture was as important to sixteenth-century humanism as its geography. Vitruvius – he who'd advised the Emperor Augustus on the grand rebuilding of Rome – was as revered a figure as Ptolemy, and his *De Architectura* (c.27BC) as raptly pored over as the other's *Geographia* (with influential new translations into Italian, Dutch and French); Book V, chapters iii–ix of this work, deals with the building of theatres. The earlier humanism saw classical drama – like so much else from Greece and Rome – in terms of a new and secular freedom to express ideas and emotions which contrasted welcomely with older forms – with the church settings of medieval religious plays or with the waggons in streets and squares for their more popular equivalents, the Town Guild Mysteries. It was like comparing the trapezoid Ptolemaic world map, which could be adapted to accommodate modern knowledge, with the theologically imposed distortions of the old *mappa mundi* which defied it. In Italy, in particular, in the 1550s and 60s, the time of Ortelius' visits, interest in the ancient theatre and its restitution was strong – for obvious reasons. The architect Andrea Palladio (1508–80), who'd made drawings for a new edition of Vitruvius, devoted himself in his last decade of life – the first decade of the *Theatrum*'s – to a fine recreation of the classical model, the Teatro Olimpico in his home town of Vicenza.

But in fact, the theatre as it developed moved away from the strictly followed ideal of Palladio. The *skena*, the elevated portion of that round O which the Greeks had called the 'orchestra', became emphasised and marked off by an archway, the proscenium arch. Behind this took place the real drama, the rite proper. Appropriately enough then, the frontispiece to the printed *Theatrum* has a design recalling a proscenium arch; from behind it will emerge the show of the world's countries.

Inspired doubtless by the round shape of the classical theatre, the shape of our globe itself, the sixteenth-century mind was much taken up with the idea of the world as a species of theatre, and they found precedents for it in the writers of Greece and Rome, especially among the Stoics (Athens, third century BC, Rome, first century BC to second century AD, with Seneca, c.4BC–AD65, presidential over Renaissance intellectual activity, a major exponent). Of this conceit a theatre which represents the world – like Ortelius' book – constitutes a wholly logical (and often complementary) inversion. The events of a stage play occur as a result of decisions made by the dramatist; we the audience observe how its characters cope with them (and how the actors discharge their roles). So in 'real' life: 'Those decisions are fixed and permanent,' insists Seneca in number LXXXVII of his *Letters from a Stoic*, 'part of the mighty and eternal train of destiny. You will go the way that all things go. What is strange about that?' He is speaking of the culmination of all lives, all events: death. 'This is the law to which you were born; it was the lot of your father, your mother, your ancestors and of all who came before you as it will be of all who come after you. There is no means of altering the irresistible succession of events which carries all things along in its binding grip.'

No medium can bring home to us more directly or hauntingly than the theatre the stark truths governing our existence. Says Seneca in Letter XCI, after speaking of the unexpectedness, the terrifying suddenness of so many catastrophes in life: 'All the terms of our human lot should be before our eyes; we should be anticipating not merely all that commonly happens but all that is conceivably capable of happening, if we do not want to be overwhelmed and struck numb by rare events as if they were unprecedented ones; fortune needs envisaging in a thoroughly comprehensive way.'

A world obeying laws of time as well as of space is, then, the *Theatrum*'s object of study.

The age was inclined to attribute the notion of world-as-theatre ultimately to Pythagoras (sixth century BC) in his sojourn in southern Italy. In an English play of 1564 by the Oxford academic Richard Edwards, *Damon and Pithias*, we come across the following lines: 'Pythagoras said, that this world was like a stage,/ Whereon many play their parts.' As Pythagoras is the first man we know about to have held that the world is round, it is nice to think of him as the originator of this powerful and durable image. Edwards' lines suggest, of course, one of the most famous speeches in all Shakespeare, Jaques' in *As You Like It* (1599/1600) (first played most probably, appropriately enough, at the Globe Theatre):

All the world's a stage,
And all the men and women merely players;
They have their exits and their entrances,
And one man in his time plays many parts ...

On to the spherical world, just like *dramatis personae* appearing before the spherically seated audience in Greek theatre, human beings are sent out, each allocated a part – a unique identity, a unique body – but each, in common with all others, put through a preordained sequence of experiences broken only by some calamitous happening: birth, infancy, childhood, puberty, maturity, child-begetting and -rearing, ageing, dying, death. In the Christianised version of this, the merits of your performance in these successive situations determine your eternal fate, your redemption. The round Earth, governed by its immutable physical laws, was designed for these human performances just as a round theatre for actors and the dramas devised for them.

Ortelius would have thought thus, since the image was integral to the view of life of the Family of Love. In fact the phrase 'world-as-theatre' was to members of the organisation rather what 'architect of the universe' has been for Freemasons, a means of self-annunciation and of recognition of fellow members. Those in the know about the Family – a category which extended well beyond the members themselves, to people like Guillaume Postel – would recognise the title *Theatrum* as a term of the profoundest significance to men and women of deep spiritual commitment, and so perhaps be moved to cosmological thoughts in accordance with theirs.

For the first buyers and readers of the *Theatrum* there's further significance still in the first and all-important word of its title – it was a bang up-to-date term for all those interested in the phenomena of memory and cognition. 'Theatre' was a contemporary metaphor for the brain, for that storehouse of information and recollections we all carry about but which needs cues for its goods to be released. In the real theatre actors recite lines and perform actions which emanate from, and add up to, a completed whole – i.e. the play itself, an analogue for amassed knowledge.

It's not at all hard to endow the atlas with the qualities of 'the theatre-as-brain'. We turn over its pages, and country after country, city after city reveal themselves – to call forth a host of associations, facts, desires, questions. And just as the already written play precedes its performance, so the already measured world (the subject of the very first 'spread' of the *Theatrum*) precedes the various different maps of its component parts. Furthermore, the atlas consists of visual matter, of images which impress themselves on the mind, become part of its natural (and permanent) gallery. Ortelius himself realised this when he wrote of his maps as *imagines agentes* (image-agents), a point underlined by the leading contemporary expert on the arcana of the *Theatrum*, Giorgio Mangani of the University of Ancona.

But one can't leave the topic of the aptness of the term 'theatre' without saying something else. Through the art of catharsis, a play (as Seneca by inference observed) does us good. It arouses our powers of sympathy, its situations address our moral sensibility. Likewise the atlas. It stimulates our fellow feeling for all those who share the world with us. It should increase our appetite for peace, our will for harmonious living. In this respect the *Theatrum* does indeed approach the original religious nature of the drama; it is an act of virtue, made by a man who believed in the obligation to be virtuous.

The other two words of the title – '*orbis terrarum*' – seem to me to need less comment, though R. A. Skelton pointed out that all three words occur in a different order in Cicero's *In Verrem* (*Against Verres*, a corrupt Sicilian functionary whom Cicero prosecuted – Book V, XXXV): '*Ut me quaestoramque meam in aliquo terrarum orbis theatro versari existimarem.*' ('So that I thought that I and my quaestorship [an official position] were being exhibited on some theatre of the whole world [the lands of the world].') Ortelius would undoubtedly have known this passage; the words, consonant with what has been outlined above, may well have reverberated in his mind. But in fact, the Romans and their succeeding Latinophones employed the phrases *orbis terrae, orbis terrarum* often with the habitable area of the world (*oikoumene*) in mind. In 1570, however, the word *orbis* would contain not just the world's sphericity but the task of dealing with this.

With its title absorbed in all its many and deliberate implications, we can now examine the 'prelims' of the *Theatrum*. In all editions they were to have the same order – though there were to be additions and (for the English edition of 1606) subtractions. Their sequence is as follows:

1. Frontispiece (title page). This, after the fashion of the day, is an allegorical engraving, which encases the book's title and forms an annunciation of its subject.
2. Dedication – to His Majesty Philip II of Spain.
3. Poem by Adolphus Mekerchus Brugensis (Adolf van Meetkerke of Bruges). This both summarises Ortelius' achievement and explicates the frontispiece, so revealing the close attention to visual material expected of readers (who would have also been keen purchasers of the popular illustrated *Emblem* books such as Plantin himself liked to publish). We, heirs to that starvation of the optic sense which followed the Industrial Revolution, have perhaps more need of this – admittedly rather curious and unsatisfying – verse commentary than the original perusers of the book.
4. In editions after 1579 only, a portrait of Ortelius, engraved by Filips [Philippe] Galle.
5. Introduction, in which Ortelius explains his concept of geography/ cartography and the intellectual importance of these disciplines, and outlines his intentions for the whole work.
6. After 1573 only, the letter from Gerard Mercator recommending Ortelius' work and speaking of its likely longevity.
7. The *Catalogus Auctorum* (List of Contributors), acknowledging the sources for the various maps in exemplary fashion.
8. *Index tabularum*. A list of the places covered by the *Theatrum*.

Then come the maps, all with text on their versos. The volume ends with a list of the names of places as they were in classical antiquity, and that essay already mentioned by Humphrey Lhuyd, *De Mona Druidem*, and, finally, the patent of the author and his colophon.

Pietatis vis,

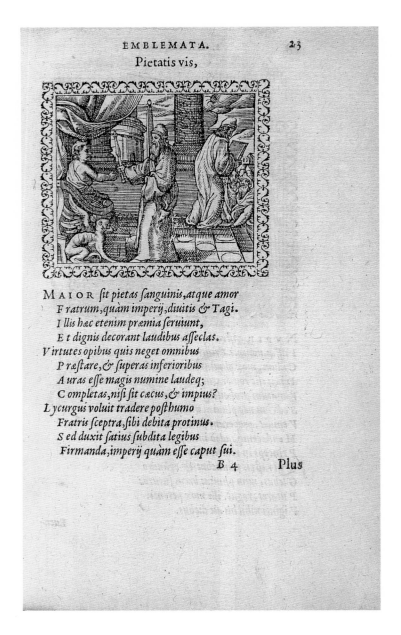

MAIOR *sit pietas sanguinis,atque amor*
    Fratrum,quàm imperij,diuitis & Tagi.
Illis hæc etenim præmia seruiunt,
    Et dignis decorant laudibus asseclas.
Virtutes opibus quis neget omnibus
    Præstare,& superas inferioribus
    Auras esse magis numine laudeq;
    Completas,nisi sit cæcus,& impius?
Lycurgus voluit tradere posthumo
    Fratris sceptra,sibi debita protinus.
    Sed duxit satius subdita legibus
    Firmanda,imperij quàm esse caput sui.
                  B 4   Plus

Emblem books were very popular in the mid-sixteenth century, and Plantin was an eminent and very successful publisher of them. An emblem has been described as a 'speaking picture', usually with a moral purpose. Collected in a book, emblems were usually accompanied by mottoes or verses pointing up the visual lessons.

The frontispiece was almost certainly by Frans Hogenberg, the obvious candidate since it was he, a well-known graphics artist, who was responsible, as Ortelius' preface makes clear, for the engravings throughout the book. But it has also been attributed to Filips Galle and to Joris Hoefnagel. Because Mekerchus' poem provides such a detailed commentary on it, and in so doing supplies a mind-set for the whole volume ahead, it will be taken in conjunction with the artwork. The Bruges-born Mekerchus (1528–1591) was an alderman of his native city, a jurist, a diplomat, a truly learned hellenist, with particular expertise on how the Greek language was pronounced, a Familist – and, of great consequence in his life, a Calvinist. He'd written many poems and witty epigrams for Ortelius' close numismatist friend and neighbour, Hubertus Goltzius, and for Ortelius himself; hence the choice of him for the *Theatrum*. For the *Album amicorum* his verse, headed *adelphos* (brother), has a certain high-minded charm, superior to anything of his in the *Theatrum*:

What a thing a brother is!
Oh, it's sweet three or four times over
To see under the same roof
Brothers living together,
And bound by a bond
Of love and peace.

Suitable words indeed for the enterprise to which he contributed, though his own lines for it don't particularly advance the cause.

I've already compared the design of the frontispiece to a proscenium arch. But it's equally like a funerary monument with the title boxed in the centre where the name of the deceased and the epitaph should be. The theme of the allegory is the four continents. Mekerchus, in his accompanying poem, proudly observes that the Ancients had thought there were only three of these. But within the lifetimes of people still alive, a fourth continent had been 'uncovered, a New World' (the two Americas being considered as one).

Each continent is represented by a female figure, with Europe at the top of the arch/monument, Asia and Africa as the plinth-supported columns on either side of the title-tablet, on our left and on our right respectively, and – at the foot of the whole construct, supine on the ground – America.

The title page, engraved by Frans Hogenberg, of Ortelius'
Theatrum orbis terrarum *of 1570.*

No spectator of the *Theatrum* could so much as glance at this tableau and fail to find Europe the most commanding, the most august member of the quartet. So elevated is she that she scarcely belongs to the same order of being as the others – and perhaps in truth does not.

She is sitting as one enthroned underneath a U-shaped arbour, under a trellised arch all entwined with vine leaves and bunches of grapes – symbols of plenty, of Nature husbanded, in both Classical and Christian traditions. Hellenist Mekerchus sees this Europe as a worshipper and beneficiary of Bacchus, but surely at least implicit in all the fruit so abundantly depicted around her are the many images from grapes and wine informing both Christ's sayings ('I am the true vine') and His acts ('This is my blood...'). The picture of Europe also embodies an idea still current today that European civilisation is intimately bound up with viticulture.

Flanking Europe on her marmoreal elevation are two globes. In her right hand we see a sceptre, in her left what Mekerchus calls a 'rudder' (but its shape is the Christian cross). With this rudder she can steer a third (and larger) model of the globe, itself patterned with the Holy Cross (even if its proportions are somewhat unorthodox). Poet Mekerchus sees this as showing her ability to extend her boundaries 'up to the lands of the Britons who are separated from the Continent'. Thus, on the very first pages of the first-ever world atlas, the question still emotionally debated today as to whether Britain is or is not an inextricable part of Europe is raised (and as Mekerchus fled to Britain for safety, we must conjecture that at the time he was glad of a negative answer to the question). Mekerchus, having raised the subject of European expansion, feels obliged to expatiate on the achievement in this respect of Spain (about which his feelings must have been equivocal to say the least, considering the tie-up between Calvinism and separatism). 'Spain,' he says, 'has dared to extend Europe's empire across the unknown sea and to discover new kingdoms and new nations, now called the New World.'

Europe is the only figure to be seated, (though America isn't standing, she is recumbent); she is the only one, too, who looks across at us – the other three have downcast eyes. She is crowned, sharp-breasted, imperial and proud in attitude, surrounded by the blessings of a long-practised, civilised agriculture, and patently in charge of the Christianisation of the entire world. If we needed just one figure to embody sixteenth-century Europeans' belief that they had been not just permitted but divinely appointed to discover and develop the whole globe, because they alone could bring the one true religion to it, then we can do no better than turn to Europe on the *Theatrum* frontispiece – and read the lines on her.

And such a view of her will be vindicated when we pay attention to her sisters. Hogenberg's Europe – it will be obvious from the most casual inspection – bears no detectable resemblance to the Europa of Greek mythology and Ovid, who was seduced – or raped, according to which version you prefer – by Zeus in the form of a bull. This story in all its brute sexuality came to alarm the lofty-minded of the sixteenth century, who considered it an affront to their spreading and proselytising civilisation to persist with a name commemorating a vile act of bestiality. Ortelius would seem to have been of their number. See his dismissal of the classical origins of Europe in his commentary to the map of the continent. His friend Guillaume Postel proposed that the name be changed, his choice being Japétie, after that son of Noah, Japheth, responsible after the Flood for the Europeans. But Postel's proposal never caught on.

Asia is amply dressed as Africa is not, in a charming flowing ankle-covering garment, recalling to the commenting Bruges poet Assyrian robes, and therefore painted Tyrian purple by the colourists. In 'plain' copies of the book it would seem that her midriff is bare, in 'coloured' copies this deficiency is remedied and a brooch-fastened covering is allocated her, giving her therefore a rather more conventionally civilised appearance. On her gracefully coiffured head she wears a coronet. Both body- and head-wear should be taken as manifestations of her comparative cultural (and even economic) closeness to Europe, and the state of the midriff can be seen as indicating the varying degrees to which she was, or could be, thought this. But it'd be fair, surely, to describe her as courtier to Europe's monarch.

Africa, by contrast, is scantily clad, with just enough to cover her loins, though the garment worn for this purpose clearly extends over her back and backside (we can see a fold of the drape on her left shoulder and her left upper arm). Round her head the rays of the sun form a kind of natural casque, a spiky halo. This refers, as the poet reminds us, to the dominance of the sun over Africa, thanks to the misadventures of the sun-god, Phoebus Apollo's son, Phaeton. Phaeton took over the chariot of the sun, was overturned, fire spilled out, the fertile land of Libya was turned into barren desert, and the inhabitants of the continent harmed, burnt black by the heat. The figure we see here is negroid in features, rendered black by the colourists.

Both Asia and Africa are holding up one object in one hand; theirs are attitudes (for all Asia's civilised apparel) of supplication – or is it homage? – to the Europe raised so high and unassailable above them. Poet Mekerchus sees Asia in terms of Arabia: what she is holding is a thurible full of incense (you can see the smoke rising up from it); she smells sweetly, he says, of 'Arabic spices'. Her graceful figure thus suggests the lively and demanding European–Eastern spice trade, evidence of which was daily available in Antwerp and swelling its coffers.

Africa carries in her hand a large spray of balsam, that resinous plant with medicinal properties still in use today for colds and respiratory problems, and then believed to grow only in Egypt. It'd surely be impossible not to find in both these 'lower' continents a distinctly feminine charm denied the haughty Europe, who, for all her prominent but rather hard-seeming breasts, has a chaste, not to say sexless, quality. Asia and Africa are more full-bellied (suggesting fecundity) and freer limbed.

How limiting these representative figures are! For all her charms, the female allegory of Asia scarcely suggests the sophistications of achievement to be witnessed on the vast continent. For example the extraordinary – and contemporary – empire of India's Akbar (1524–1605) who, only the year before the atlas' publication, 1569, had established his capital at Agra from where he proceeded to make sweeping, enlightened reforms the aim of which were wider tolerance and the creative pooling of different religions and philosophies. It was an experiment in syncretism from which the western Europe of the time, so riven by bloody and chronic religious conflict, could well have learned, conflict against which the nervous, limited ecumenicism within the Family of Love couldn't, unfortunately, prevail. Still less does Hogenberg's Asia bring to mind China, even then the most populous nation-state in the world, and that with the longest cultural pedigree. Yet navigators from Ming China had, over a century before, made at least seven voyages to East Africa, the distance of each of which was somewhat longer than that of Columbus' crossing of the Atlantic (and, Gavin Menzies has uncovered, reached Australia and America, achievements which were discounted at home). And in 1541 (printed in 1555, with seven later editions) there appeared China's first major book of maps – the *Guangyu Tu* or *Ming Atlas*.

Likewise the frontispiece's Africa has nothing to do with such Malian centres of trade and learning as Timbuctu or Gao (Mali's ostentatious gold-based wealth had dazed earlier Catalan map-makers who'd paid it decorative homage, while Gao employed Andalusian marble-carvers and poets). Or with Benin, familiar to Europeans from the late fifteenth century onwards, with its highly developed sculpture in cast bronze, brass and ivory, its lively visual presentation of its own history (reliefs on plaques in important buildings) and its grouping of the population of its chief city according to the crafts they pursued. Looking at Africa's downcast expression we should remember that in the earlier 1570s the Portuguese, after the sack of East African ports, tried to take the upper Zambesi valley state of Mwene Mutapa, so rich in gold and in disciplined soldiers, and failed – and then failed again.

But, however reductive their delineation, both Asia and Africa make a most favourable contrast with their American sister, whom we find at the base of the monument, a slumped figure with her back and right arm touching the plinth that supports Asia, and her bottom and legs on the marble floor. (Perhaps a reference to America's conjectured geographical and racial connection to the largest of the continents.) She is entirely naked, unless you count a curious bracelet worn round her left leg – perhaps a shackle of some kind. Her hair reaches down her back, flowing into, as well as considerably below, her groin. One of her legs (her left) is arched over two crossed arrows; a bow lies close by; her right hand holds a long club-ended rod, but it's what is being held up in her left hand that's so significant and eye-catching. It is a severed head, and the head of a bearded and wise-faced European at that. Nearby there is a bust of another young woman – clearly of the same racial type as America herself – mounted on a small pedestal over the top of which hang her prominent breasts, and below which a little burst of fire is mysteriously rendered.

Mekerchus' lines on this section of the tableau make fascinating – and very disturbing – reading. America the continent was, he says, a 'nymph' whom Amerigo Vespucci, after whom she was named, 'captured by force and then embraced ... with tender love'. His description of her (prose rendering here) has a most curious gloating quality:

> In her right hand she carries a club with which to kill fattened prisoners of war. She roasts their bodies, torn to quivering pieces, in smouldering flames, or she boils them in a hot copper kettle. Or, should the frenzy of hunger overcome her, she might devour their limbs, still raw and

freshly slain dripping with black-red blood. Their limbs, still warm, are crunched under her teeth. She feeds on the flesh and on the blood of the wretches: a crime horrible to see and horrible to relate. What barbarous impiety does this evince! What contempt of supreme power! In her left hand you see a severed head, evidence of a recent killing. There you can also see her bow and the swift arrows which on being launched inflict mortal wounds and certain death to men. When tired of hunting men, she wishes to sleep, she mounts a bed woven with wide meshes like a net which has been fixed at both ends to a stake. She climbs into it, and within its ease she lays her head and body to rest.

Note the fervid eroticism which has entered the Bruges poet's style. The young woman's cannibalism has as much dark, covert appeal as the charms of her body as detailedly imagined in naked repose. The ultimate source for this young woman is almost certainly the reports Vespucci brought back from his expeditions of 1499 and 1501, which made a great impression on Europeans with their pictures of the eating of human flesh (a man was met who had eaten over 300 of his fellow beings) and of female promiscuity and cunning sexual know-how. One is tempted to say, judging by its wide and long reception – exemplified here by Mekerchus – that the first had an even more compulsive hold on the western imagination than the second, as if cannibalistic desire was somehow a buried component of the European psyche.

Mekerchus now turns his attention to the female bust nearby:

Her looks are like a virgin's, and she has well-formed breasts. Her hands and feet are truncated because she is scarcely known. The Iberian Magellan is said to have fallen in love with her when sailing under the Austral wind through the Straits, and to have called her MAGELLANICA after his own name. He happened to see this incautious virgin once, in the glitter of flames when she was preparing some solemn festivities. Thereupon the deeply blushing virgin immediately hid her face and concealed herself in dark smoke and in the shadows of a dull mist. And, in order not to be detected unawares again, she lit this flame as a memory under her breast.

Here again the expatiation is superfluously detailed, though it can't be said to lack interest – and the inclusion of Magellanica may well have been

GRONL — Baier flu — ANDIAE PARS — Monasteriu. S. Thom. — MARE SE

OCEANVS HYPERBOREVS

ISLANDIA TVLE

DEVCALIDO NIVS OCEANVS

SCRICFIN NIA

FINMAR

LAPPIA

BODICVS SINVS

SVECIA

GOTIA

SVEVI CVM MARE

FARRE insulæ

SCETLANT insulæ

ORCADES Insulæ

HEBRIDES insulæ

SCOTIA

OCEANVS GERMANICVS

DNE MARCA

HOLSI

IRLANDIA

Man

Anglesey

ANGLIA

FRISIA WES GERMANIA

POL

BOHEMIA

AVSTRIA

EVROPAE

Brasil.

Demar

OCEANVS BRITANNICVS

NORMANDIE

BRETAIG

BELGIC

FRANCE

BOVRGO

SVISVA VARIA

OCCIDENTALIS OCEANVS

CANTABRICVS OCEANVS

AQVITANICVS OCEANVS

POICTOV

GALLIA

LIA

VOIE

DAVPHINE

PROVENCE

ISTRIA

MARE ADRIATI

GALICIA

CASTRA

ARRAGON

HISPANIA

PORTVGALIA

GRANADA

ITALIA

CORSICA

SARDINIA

SICILIA

MARE

BARBARIA

Africa

MEDI

TRIONALE.

OCEANVS
SCHYTICVS

Nouo Zemla

Colgoieue

Vagatz

Ob fiu

SINVS
GRAN
VICVS

BIARM
IA.

CORE
LIA.

CONDORA

Pechora

Pusterora

Cingolo

Lampas
Sloboda

Zena mundi montes

Sybir

I A

Crustuma

KITA
IA LA
CVS.

Kowloi

S. Micha

Micola

PERMIA

Permeuelick

Teron

Kondori

Temis
Chira

S. Nicolas

Shenkoria

Vsting

Vstiug

IVGA.

Voichoda fiu

TARTAR

VOLOGDA

Chogbloma

Nisnouo
gorod

Vasbugorod

Cazane
gorode

ASI

TVMEN

MOS KO

Cassin gorode

Terboue

Shabogs
har

Cham

Camai fiu

NOVOGA
RDIA

VIA

Donke

Blagar

Lechi

Samar fiu

LITVA
NIA.

ZEVERA

Tanais nunc Don fiu

Vich

TVRCHE STAN

Volgha Rha. vel Edel fiu

Bessima

PODOLIA

CUMANI.

CABAR
DI
Palestra

La Tana

Achas

Nabarz

Baxcuchi

Cahar

CATTA
CHI.

AE

Mechet

MARE
DELLE
ZA
BACHE

Locopa

Astracan

Sara

S. Maria

Salacinit

Risan

MOLDAVIA

GAZ
ARIA

Zechia

Anagoffa

Coro

Zauatopoli

GEOR
GIANI.

Derbent

Bachu

MARE DE
BACHV olim
CASPI
VM.

WALAC
HIA

BVLGARIA

MARE MAGIORE

Faffo

Lonati

Gonea

Quica

Santina

Manuidaua

Araf

ME
DIA.

Machmu
abat

Seruani

ROMA
NIA

BOLLI.

Sinol

Carossa

Chij
sonda

Trebisonda

TVRCO
MANI

Igril olim Tigris fiu.

AMASIA

NATOLIA.

AIDINELLI.

CARMANIA

PARS.

MESOPO
TAMIA.

PER
SI
A.

Aleppo

Soldino

Laiazo
Alexan
dretta

Tripoli
SOR
Damasco
IA.
Baruti

Frat. olim Epphrates fiu.

Bagdet

CANDIA.

NEVM

Zaffa

Irrusalem

intended as a bow in the direction of the fifth continent, the Great Southern one that Mercator himself believed in, and of which the island of Tierra del Fuego (just south of the Strait mentioned) was believed to be a part.

If one turns from America and Magellanica and the verse commentary on them back to the illustration as a whole, one finds that the proportions, the emphases of the whole composition have undergone a decided and troubling change. *Now* it seems that the whole construction rests on the relationship between that figure atop the arch or monument and that at its base – with her living bust companion. They are the deliberately counterpointed opposites and between them is the lettered plaque announcing the imminent 'theatre' of all the countries of the world. That, the picture suggests, is the true story of the show – Europe's superiority to, and dominion over, America. The other two continents are, quite literally, side-shows to that.

The top and bottom figures of the frontispiece illustrated a split in humanity – in the inhabitants of this world of ours – so great as to be beyond dialogue, beyond reparative communication altogether. For what can be said to someone who enjoys crunching human limbs under her teeth? It's hard for us inheritors of twentieth-century psychology not to find enthroned Europe the super-ego, cannibalistic America the id – and the world between the two the ego awaiting the resolution of their struggle. Or in Jungian terms, the more valid as these personifications are feminine, Europe as that half of the anima that is pure, virginal and brooks no moral failings, no male coarseness or laxity (the Catholic Church of the Counter Reformation) and America as its other half of rapacious sensuality, of sexuality as it flourishes in non-Christian societies, the polar antithesis of the rational and the law-abiding.

This imagery and its stated significance will prove impossible to forget altogether – for all the many excellences and delights ahead. After all, isn't the very point of an engraved frontispiece (and of an introductory gloss on it in verse) the provision of *imagines agentes* for use when reading the work proper? The distortions these representatives of America constitute

Previous page:
Europe. *This could be seen as the emotional iconographical centrepiece of the 1570 Theatrum and of subsequent editions too, with its many carefully collated sources: Olaus Magnus' map of Scandia of 1539, Mercator's Europe of 1554, Anthony Jenkinson's Russia of 1562 and various productions of Gastaldi's. The text is erudite and fulsome in its praises of Europe's favoured situation in God's world.*

will remain with us – and it should be added that there will be no single map of any part of America in any edition of the *Theatrum* before 1579, a distortion in itself considering how much the fortunes of Antwerp were dependent on money made there (though the absence can, and perhaps should, be attributed to Ortelius' extreme punctiliousness where geographical reliability was concerned).

To Amerigo Vespucci (1451–1512), friend of Columbus and part-responsible for the financial backing for his second and third voyages, must go the credit for realising during the course of a nine-month-long voyage, 1501–02, that the continent down whose coast he was sailing – and on which he 'discovered' and named Rio de Janeiro and Rio de la Plata – was not the Asia of those earlier suppositions of his he'd shared with Columbus, but another continent altogether, a New World – as he proclaimed in his *Mundus Novus* of 1505. The great cartographer Martin Waldseemüller honoured Vespucci as this 'world's' true discoverer by naming the continent after him in his ground-breaking world map, globe and accompanying text of 1507.

And to Magellan – also paid tribute to in the frontispiece and poem – goes the credit of having rounded the continent for the first time, of having passed in 1520 from Atlantic to Pacific Oceans and so understanding its extremities – after a terrible Patagonian winter and a fearsome navigation of the twisting straits now named after him.

But a great deal had happened in and to the New World since Vespucci and Magellan, and the interesting thing is that there is no recognition of this in the engraving at all. Nothing of the great civilisations that the Spanish had brought down, the Maya, Aztec and Inca, nothing of the many other indigenous peoples, less sophisticated than those great nations but with cultures of their own – though their sufferings would have been familiar enough, if only in very general terms, to the first readers of the *Theatrum*, thanks not least to certain conscience-troubled men among the Spaniards themselves. No mention, let alone iconography, from North America.

But we have only to turn to the first document ever of the West's confrontation with the Americas to realise how wilfully partial the frontispiece is in respect to them. Columbus, under the impression that he'd arrived at Zipangu (Japan) or Cathay, or, at any rate, at their outposts – wrote a letter to his commissioners, their Spanish majesties, during his homeward voyage (when off the Azores) in February 1493; it was published, and in no fewer than nine editions, that same year. It gives us a decidedly appealing picture of the peoples of 'Cuba' and 'Hispaniola', who (like Hogenberg's America here) 'go naked, as their mothers bore them, men and women alike'. They were peaceful, unmaterialistic, shared property and possessions, were constant to their partners, shy but strong, and proved friendly once they'd overcome their fear of men they believed had arrived from the sky. 'They were,' said Columbus, 'of great intelligence, for they navigate all those seas, and give a marvellously good account of everything.' Vespucci, some eight years later, spoke in similar terms about a similar people, singling out for praise their ability equally to share property.

However, Columbus, so he says in that first letter, had heard of people in a neighbouring island (probably Dominica) very unlike those he'd actually encountered, who were 'regarded in these islands as extremely fierce and who eat human flesh'. These men, long haired and savage, took women from what we now call Martinique. 'These women do not follow feminine occupations but use cane bow and arrows like those of men ...' Very like, in fact, the figure in our engraving. It is as if the Western mind had to extrapolate from any descriptions of the New World only what marked it out as barbaric and backward, what made it resemble the frightful habits of folk in pre-literate lore and classical legend, and – most important of all – showed them as so far steeped in savagery that the only way open for the Christian powers would be their subjugation or suppression.

Mekerchus rounds off his introductory Latin poem with a recapitulation of the atlas' appeal akin to the quality praised later by Plantin in his French verses already given. So now the reader was returned to his European safety and comfort (ironic or self-deceived lines, considering contemporary history and Mekerchus' own sufferings within it).

The dedication won't require translation or explication:

D. PHILIPPO/ AUSTRIACO/ CAROLI V AUG/ ROM. IMP F/ INDIARUM HISPA-/ NIARUMQ. ETC RE-/ GI, OMNIUM AETA-/ TUM ET TOTIUS/ ORBIS AMPLISSI-/ MI IMPERII MO-/ NARCHAE,/ ABRAHAMUS/ ORTELIUS/ ANTVERPIANUS/ EIUS MAIESTATIS/ GEOGRAPHUS, DED./ CONSECRATQ

Not for nothing have we seen the *Theatrum* in the same company as the great *Biblia*. Both required and benefited from Philip's blessing.

Yet, of course, there were strings attached. At this very time, reluctantly (he was percipient enough to realise that the situation in the Netherlands had by no means come to a final decisive stop), Plantin was in the process of agreeing to accept, in the wake of the great Bible, the proffered post of *Prototypographus*, king's printer. This meant that he had to watch over the activities of other Antwerp printers, a difficult task in such tense times, and print at the royal command such pro-Spanish, pro-Roman Church matter as successive Indices of prohibited books – an ironic fate, indeed, for a pluralist humanist. However as time went on the position tended more and more towards being a sinecure. And Ortelius was rewarded for his contributions to mapping by being made Royal Geographer, a title, judging by others' references to it in the *Album amicorum*, of which he was rather proud.

How could this book – in nine years' time to be printed/published by the *Prototypographus* himself – avoid having the dedication it bears? It couldn't, obviously. No argument about it. And yet we have only to bear in mind how inimical Philip's regime, indeed his very position, was to many of the finest minds to contribute to the *Theatrum* – from Mekerchus, who had to flee to England, to Mercator in his self-banishment in Duisberg, or Radermacher in permanent exile – and the grandiloquent Latin dedication rings very hollowly indeed. To say nothing of the fact that by the time Plantin's edition came out, Philip's soldiers had brought suffering to Antwerp on a scale that seems terribly and near literally to fulfil the ghastly visual prophecies of Bruegel's *Dulle Griet*.

After the dedication we find Mekerchus' poem. In later editions of the *Theatrum* the next prelim featured a portrait of Ortelius himself. The first edition to do so was that of 1579, published by Plantin. The engraver was Ortelius' old friend Filips Galle (another to whom the dedication could not have been wholly pleasing) and his portrait depicts the architect of a great humanist work: the high intellectual forehead, the facial lines suggesting hours of long, arduous work, the eyes contemplative, looking away from us into the near distance – or possibly into some invisible but nameable abstraction. It is a kindly face, and an admirably grave one.

Is there anything in his expression, though, to tell us that Abram Ortel was a shrewd, not to say canny, businessman? Could we know from it the ruthlessness with which he would see to it that a rival atlas, assembled soon after the *Theatrum*, had its publishing 'privilege' delayed? Or that he would pursue his influence further and all but ensure that the rival atlas' sales were poor – from Plantin, for example, who admittedly doesn't appear himself to have thought much of the book. Or to indicate the periods of fence-sitting that the times, his family and his own nature imposed on him, requiring constant careful assessment of situations and, to quote that Skelton poem again, 'the lizard [lying] lurking in the grass'?

If we turn to the portrait Rubens painted of him thirty-two years after his death, we can fancy certain shades of these qualities in the visage. But these must be offset by the dignity of his posture, with the strong fingers of his left hand grasping the globe.

Ortelius' own words follow on from Ortelius' picture – and indispensable they are to any understanding of the *Theatrum*, expressing as they do most of the thought processes we have been tracing as we have followed Ortelius to the bringing-out of the atlas. Too long to be quoted in full, the Introduction can be indicated in select quotations, in the seventeenth-century English of his translator and editor, 'WB'.

Seeing, that as I think, there is no man, gentle Reader, but knoweth what, and how great profit the knowledge of histories, doth bring to those which are serious students therein, I do verily believe and persuade myself, that there is almost no man, be it that he have made never so little an entrance into the same, and touched them never so lightly, that is ignorant how necessary, for the understanding of them aright, the knowledge of Geography is, which in that respect therefore which is of some, and not without just cause, called the eye of history.

This so necessary a knowledge of geography, as many worthy and learned men have testified, may very easily be learned out of geographical charts or maps. And when we have acquainted ourselves with the use of tables or maps, or have attained thereby to some reasonable knowledge of Geography, whatsoever we shall read, the charts being placed, as it were certain glasses before our eyes, will the longer be kept in memory, and make the deeper impression in us; by which means it cometh to pass that now we do seem to perceive some fruit of that which we have read.

We were not moved to undertake this labour by any covetous desire of getting much of by it, but even of a willing and forward mind that we had to help and further those that have a love for these studies, not any whit respecting the gainsaying of any vainglory and commendation by other men's labours. For what need we to make new maps, when as the old maps of other men, now extant, would serve our turn? Some there are peradventure, which will look to find in this our *Theatre* more descriptions of particular countries (for every man naturally for the love that he beareth to his native soil, would, I doubt not, wish that it were here generally described among the rest) but let them know, that those which are here missing, are not left out and omitted, either by our negligence, or for that we were loath to be at that cost and charges; but because that we never saw any such, or at leastways for that there never came any such to our hands. If there be any man, which either hath any such, or knoweth where they may be had, him we would earnestly entreat, that he would be the means to help us unto them, assuredly promising him, that we will, at our own cost and charges, not without great thanks to him, and a most honourable mention of his name, cause them to be cut and imprinted apart and by themselves, that hereafter they may be inserted into this our book, either in their own place, elsewhere, as any man shall like best.

... Thus far of the maps themselves: now let us speak a word or two of the backside of the same. Because we thought it would be a thing nothing pleasing to the reader or beholder, to see the backsides of the leaves altogether bare and empty, we determined there to make a certain brief and short declaration and historical discourse of every map, in the same manner and order as we said we observed in the maps themselves; [not] omitting nor concealing any man's name, that we had occasion to use. Moreover to these also, we have added a table of the names of all the authors, that ever we knew or had; out of which, those that are so disposed, may fetch a more ample and larger discourse and description of the several countries handled by them. Wherefore the students of geography shall have here, in the authors thus named in order, and in the catalogue of the authors of the geographical tables or maps, which we have set before this our work, and lastly in these tables themselves, a certain shop, as it were furnished with all kinds of instruments necessarily required in suchlike business; out of which, if peradventure there may seem anything wanting, in his judgement, either to the finishing of any book of that argument, or more fuller descriptions of any countries whatsoever, very easily, or indeed without any labour at all he may see, from whence it may, by and by, be fetched.

We all live, says Ortelius, contexted by history. But in order to understand that history – i.e. to understand ourselves – we should have knowledge of the places in which events occurred or lives unfolded, for they were determinants. Besides, envisaging the places that other people knew is imaginatively enlarging.

If the above applies to ordinary human history, it is equally valid for the divine intervention into history, the happenings recorded in Holy Scripture. Again, our understanding is expanded. Now the events of the Bible could be seen in topographical and cultural terms, not just as sequences of the miraculous. This emphasis was part of a whole new approach to religion, both to its considerable enrichment and of course to its demythicising and its secularisation.

'The maps of the atlas are like mirrors, and play the part of images,' Ortelius writes. When you look at a map, it's as though you're confronting a mirror, a reflection of the part of the world in question, which then affixes itself to the mind. So that within us (within, if you like, that interior theatre that is memory) there's a pertinent and constant image which we can take out for use when we desire (this is the idea of the *imagines agentes* mentioned earlier). If we are thinking, let us say, of Spain, then – according to Ortelius – we apply to our memory to receive the image of the appropriate map in the *Theatrum*; it stands before our mind's eye as we consider whatever aspect of Spain it is that is exercising us. It was this usage of 'image' that was in John Donne's mind when he wrote, splendidly relating humanity in its present geographical condition to humanity in its spiritual destiny:

> At the round earth's imagined corners, blow
> Your trumpets, Angels ...

Ortelius' deep love of travel books led him to summarise in their vocabulary the journey he would take his readers on around the world. He adopts a travelogue manner, an accent of active movement. This is certainly a book intended to have a creative constructive effect on readers. So his invitation to readers to make good his omissions by submitting maps of their own is of particular importance. Ortelius says that he will fully accredit any he publishes, just as he has those he has already taken into the book. He is thus appealing to the readership to become a fellowship of like-minded and mutually helpful minds.

In editions of 1573 onwards Ortelius' introduction is followed by a letter by Gerard Mercator commending the atlas.

> I have examined your *Theatrum* and compliment you on the care and elegance with which you have embellished the labours of the authors, and the faithfulness with which you have preserved the production of each individual, which is essential in order to bring out the geographical truth, which is so corrupted by map-makers. The maps published in Italy are especially bad. Hence you deserve great praise for having selected the best descriptions of each region and collected them into one manual, which can be bought at small cost, kept in a small space and even carried about wherever we please.

The original, 22 November 1570, charmingly continues:

> For your work will (I believe) always remain saleable whatever maps may be reprinted by others. That you prefer me to other recent authors, I regard as due to your partiality for me, as there are many who have made more learned maps though perhaps fewer in number than I.

Next comes the *Catalogus auctorum*, the list of contributors to the book, to become a model for editorial punctiliousness. Ortelius always wanted to acknowledge those responsible for the maps he offered – to give credit where credit was due – but obviously the roll-call of names did much to boost the reputation of both the *Theatrum* and himself, for the names cited are illustrious, men widely known for their intellectual probity. One example can suffice here. The one map specially done for the volume – of Southern France (*Gallia Narbonensis*) (see page 257) – was, like that already executed of Spain, the work of Charles de l'Escluse or Clusius (1526–1609), who, later a professor at the new Dutch university of Leiden, became perhaps the foremost botanist of his time. Eighty-six such cartographers/geographers are honoured on Ortelius' list for the first, 1570, edition.

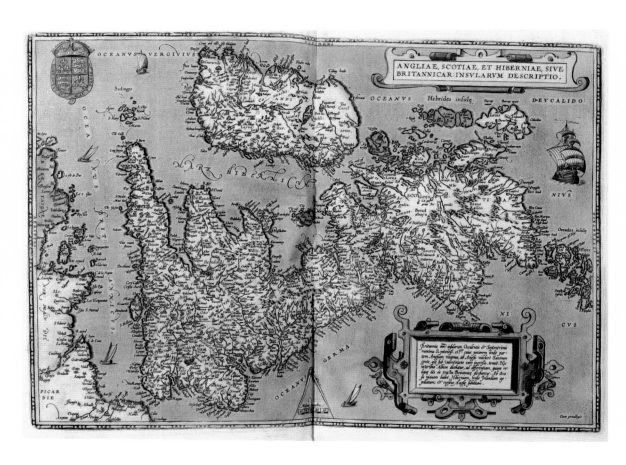

British Isles. *Mercator (in his 1564 map of the British Isles), Humphrey Lhuyd and Christopher Saxton are cited as sources for this map in the 1570* Theatrum. *Of Britain 'the most powerful part …we call Anglia'. In the west – the map is west-oriented – 'it has Hibernia as its neighbour which is nowadays called Ireland, and which is subject to the Rulers of Anglia'.*

Following the list of contributors is a table of contents, *Index tabularum*, giving the different countries and regions covered (the figures refer to sheets not maps):

1. Typus Orbis Terrarum [World Map]
2. Americae sive novi orbis, nova descriptio [America, the New World]
3. Asia nova descriptio [Asia]
4. Africam Graeci Libyam app. Africe tabula nova [Africa]
5. Europae [Europe]
6. Angliae, Scotiae, et Hiberniae, sive Britannicarum Insularum descriptio [England, Scotland, and Ireland, or the British Isles]
7. Regni Hispaniae post omnium editones locupletissima descriptio [Spain]
8. Portugalliae que olim Lusitania, novissima et exactissima descriptio [Portugal]
9. Galliae regni potentissimi nova descriptio [France]
10. Regionis, Biturigum exatissima descriptio; Limaniae topographia [the region of Bourges; the Limagne]
11. Caletensium et Bononiensium ditionis accurata delineatio; Veromanduorum eorum quer confinium exactissima descriptio [Calais and Boulogne; Vermandois]
12. Galliae Narbonensis ora marittima Recenter descripta; Sabaudiae; et Burgundiae Comitatus descriptio [Narbonne and the southern French coast; Savoy; Burgundy]
13. Germania [Germany]
14. Descriptio Germaniae Inferioris [the Low Countries]
15. Gelriae, Cliviae, finitimorumque locorum verissima descriptio [Geldern, Cleves]
16. Brabantiae, Germaniae Inferioris nobilissimae provinciae descriptio [Brabant]
17. Flandria [Flanders]
18. Zelandicarum insularum exactissima et nova descriptio [Zeeland]
19. Hollandiae antiquorum Catthorum sedis nova descriptio [Holland]
20. Oost ende West Vrieslandts beschijvinghe. Utriusque Frisiorum regionis novissima descriptio [East and West Friesland]
21. Daniae regni typus [Denmark]

22. Thietmarsiae, Holsaticae regionis partis typus; Prussiae descriptio ante aliquot annos [Schleswig-Holstein; Prussia]
23. Saxoniae, Misniae, Thuringiae, nova exactissimaque descriptio [Saxony, Meissen, Thuringia]
24. Franciae Orientalis (Vulgo Franckenland) descriptio; Monasteriensis et Osnaburgensis episcopatus descriptio [Franconia; Münster and Osnabruck]
25. Regni Bohemiae descriptio [Bohemia]
26. Silesiae typus [Silesia]
27. Austriae Ducatus chorographiae [Austria]
28. Salisburgensis jurisdictionis, locorumque vicinorum vera descriptio; Urbis Salisburgensis genuina descriptio [Salzburg; city of Salzburg]
29. Tipus (sic) Vindeliciae sive utriusque, Bavariae, secundum antiquum et recentiorem situm [Augsburg; Bavaria]
30. Palatinatus Bavariae descriptio; Wirtenbergensis ducatus vera descriptio [the Palatinate; Wittenburg]
31. Helvetiae descriptio [Switzerland]
32. Italiae novissimia descriptio [Italy]
33. Ducatus Mediolanensis, finitimarumque regionum descriptio [Duchy of Milan]
34. Pedemontanae vicinorumque regionum [Piedmont]
35. Larii Lacus vulgo Comensis descriptio; Territorii Romani descriptio; Fort Iulii, vulgo Friuli typus [Lake Como; Rome and Lazio; Friulan]
36. Thusciae descriptio [Tuscany]
37. Regni Neapolitani verissima secundum antiquorum et recentiorum traditionem descriptio [kingdom of Naples]
38. Insularum aliquot Maris Mediterranei descriptio [Islands of the Mediterranean Sea]
39. Cyprus Insula; Candia olim Creta [Cyprus; Crete]
40. Graeciae universae secundum hodiernum situm neoterica descriptio [Greece]
41. Schlavoniae, Croatiae, Carniae, Istriae, Bosniae, finitimarumque regionum nova descriptio [Sclavonia (Slovenia), Croatia, Carinthia, Istria, Bosnia]
42. Hungariae descriptio [Hungary]
43. Transilvania [Transylvania]

44. Poloniae finitimarumque locorum descriptio [Poland]
45. Septentrionalium regionum descriptio [the Northern Regions]
46. Russiae, Moscoviae et Tartariae descriptio [Russia, Muscovy and Tartary]
47. Tartariae sive Magni Chami regni typus [Tartary and the kingdom of the Grand Cham]
48. Indiae Orientalis, insularumque adiacientum typus [India and adjacent islands]
49. Persici sive Sophorum regni typus [Persia]
50. Turcici imperii descriptio [the Turkish Empire]
51. Palestinae sive totius terrae promissionis nova descriptio [Palestine]
52. Natoliae, quae olim Asia Minor, nova descriptio; Aegypti recnetior descriptio; Carthaginis Celeberrimi sinus typus [Anatolia; Egypt; Carthage]
53. Barbariae et Biledulgerid nova descriptio [Barbary – North Africa]

Then begin the maps, with text on the verso, and the *Theatrum* proper opens. The play is now in progress.

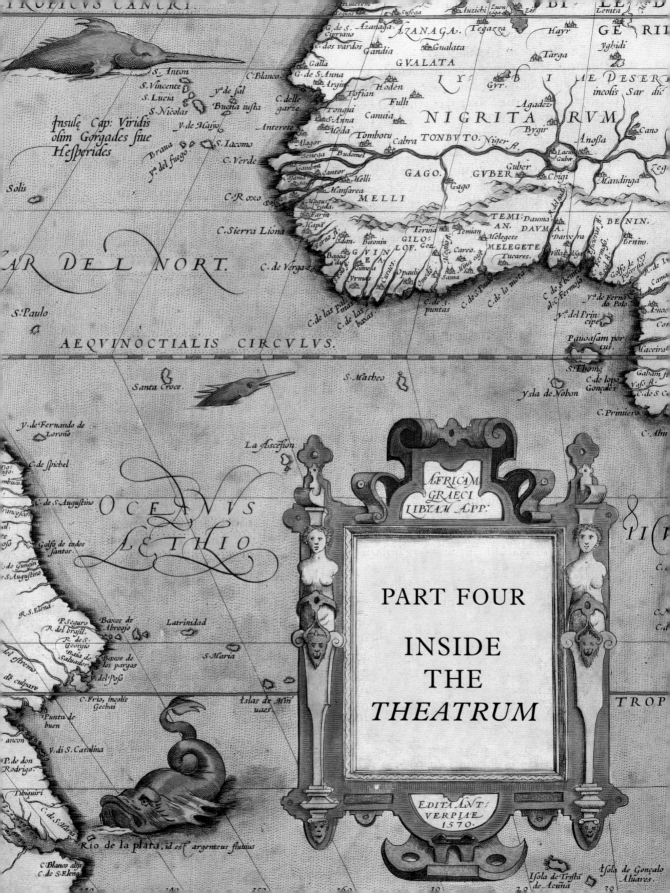

PART FOUR

INSIDE
THE
THEATRUM

AYMAN olim
Arabia felix.

MAR ROSSO, ol Sinus Arabicus.

NVBIA
Regnum olim Chri
stiana religione im
butum; hac tem
pestate vix
ullam reli
gione
agnos
cunt.

DAFILA

BARNA
GASSO

AMAZEN

Hic longe lateq, imperitat
magnus princeps Presbiter
Iöes totius Africæ
potentiß.
Rex

BELLE GVAN

ZE

FATIGAR

MAGADAZO

FVNGI

MELINDE

SINVS BARBA-
RICVS, quä et Asse-
rum mare Ptol:

MARE

RVBRVM

Mecha, hic
Mahometis sepulchrum
visitur

Babelmandel fre
tum et insula

Zacototera insf. ol:
Dioscuriada

de Guardafu olim
Aromata Prom

Isolas que hallo Vasco
de Acuña

S. Francesco

Hæc insula ab incolis Madagasc
ab Hispanis. S. Laurentij, olim
nuthias Ptol. Cerne forte Plin.
dicitur

MADAGASCAR

DAGAS

CAPRICORNI

MOZAM
BIQVE

CEFALA

ZANZI
BAR hæc pars
friæ meridionalis
nē veteribus in
cognita fuit, a Persis
rabibusq, scrip-
ribus vocatur.

Deserta

C. de Buona
speransa.

Ja de Iuan
de Lisboa

Los Romeros
insule

CHAPTER FIFTEEN

Ortelius opens his atlas with a world map, just as Ptolemy's *Geographia* advises. Drawn by Frans Hogenberg, this *Typus Orbis Terrarum* is largely based on the world maps of Mercator and Diego Guttierez, but Ortelius uses the oval projection of Gastaldi's world map. In no way does this deny us the desired awareness of Earth's sphericity – quite the contrary, it beautifully brings it home. The *Typus* gives us an equator twice as long as the pole-to-pole meridian that bisects it. To the right and to the left of this central longitude line there extends a sequence of eighteen arcs, each of them running pole-to-pole and placed equidistantly from one another. Arresting and clear (though Ortelius was personally to redraw it for his edition of 1587), it seems to us now a fitting annunciation for the theatre's drama.

Contemporary readers felt a distinct sense of pride as they surveyed the *Typus*. So much here that had not been known before their own century, so much indicated that could be fuller still if accorded further exploration in the spirit of the age. Christopher Marlowe famously described his play *Tamburlaine* as a great game of chess with kings and conquerors for the pieces and the *Theatrum orbis terrarum* for the board. An odd compliment perhaps to pay the irenicist Ortelius, but not an inapt one. For, undeterred by distance or remoteness, determined to have every possible part of the world scrutinised and rendered (a determination that persisted till his death), concerned with particulars whether placenames – for which, assisted by his Cologne bookseller friend, Arnold Mylius, he scrupulously compared current usage with the older forms – or the real shape and quantity of the islands that make up Japan, Ortelius showed an amplitude of vision and a patience quite worthy of Marlowe's triumphant protagonist, even though his were so entirely constructive in intent.

It's hard, in fact impossible, to survey the *Typus* today without acute, and sometimes obstructive, awareness of what it does *not* show, of what it actually gets wrong. Our concern here very interestingly mirrors that of Ortelius as expressed in his text when he reflects on the large-scale ignorance of the world that had prevailed for so long and in the most distinguished company before his own century.

We should confine ourselves to the most spectacular instances of what troubles us in the *Theatrum*'s world map. The lower portion of the world's oval is taken up by a vast southern continent such as Mercator and colleagues believed must counterbalance those great tracts of land to be found at the top of the world. (These last are by no means accurate either, with a Greenland smaller than reality and a huge Nova Zemblya, focus of much misplaced speculation.) Ortelius' *Terra Australis Nondum Cognita* ('southern land not yet known') has the shape of a great bowl with a jaggedly broken rim. At its extreme left it reaches out to New Guinea; later it takes in Tierra del Fuego (already referred to in Mekerchus' introductory poem), includes one enormous bay longitudinally to the south of the Indian subcontinent, and many times bigger than Hudson Bay in the north as adumbrated here, while in the east, at its extreme right, it rises into a peninsular country mysteriously designated *Beach* and situated about as near to Java as the Egyptian coast is to Greece. ('Beach', together with 'Lucach' and 'Maletur' are mentioned by Marco Polo, though – obviously – he never went there, and for this reason they featured on Mercator's world map the previous year. Marco Polo had an undeserved reputation as a sort of permanent authority on the part of the world he purported to have visited.) True, the extremities of this *Terra Australis* as shown here could be thought to suggest some (very limited) experience of the real Australia by Portuguese sailors (and by those they encountered in the East Indies), but for the greater part, with all its numerous curiously named indentations, the continent partakes, one cannot but feel, more of fantasy (if not Ortelius' own) than of serious conversation or reasoned conjecture.

Erroneous inclusions are always more bemusing to later generations than erroneous exclusions – which can simply be attributed to the fact that western adventurers had not yet reached the places in question. We feel no surprise at finding an absence of a recognisable Alaska; European sailors hadn't ventured as far as that yet – which makes the *Typus'* sharp separation of Russia and America the more admirable. But how to account for the obstinate presence of Friesland? – by which the northern Dutch province, with its offshore shoal of moving islands, is not meant – but somewhere altogether more detached, more independent.

Friesland here is an island-country, a little larger than Ireland but situated, below Iceland, to the south-west of the Faeroes. It was even provided with cities by those certain of its existence; there they are, lettered for any peruser of the *Theatrum* to plan a journey to and alluring in their names: Ocibar, Sorand, Godmec, Ran. 'Altogether unknown to ancient writers,' as Ortelius admits, it was documented, pretty thoroughly, by a Venetian, Nicolao Zeno, who in 1380, after being 'tossed around by bitter storms, arrived on this island'. Subject to Norway, its inhabitants living principally by fishing, it abounded in orchards and gardens and springs with water that turned into sweet bitumen. In its hold over a map-minded public, Friesland resembles the southern continent's kingdom of *Beach*. In fact *Beach* went on being shown on some maps even after Australia had become an established geographical fact.

There's a lesson for us, surely, in both the charted non-existent and in the omissions. Before the twentieth century and the ability to see land from above, now endorsed by satellite image-transmitters, so much about the lie of land and sea was taken on trust, indeed had to be taken on trust, by even the most sceptical readers of books that purported to be learned or even authoritative. And if we try to stand back from our perceptions now, soberingly we are forced to realise just how much geographical or historical information we hold that we never have questioned – because we have never had cause to. When crises occur in places far from the nerve-centres of the west, in the Falklands, in Rwanda-Burundi, even, for all its European situation, in Kosovo, it's always revealed that a majority of people don't know where these trouble spots are actually situated – sometimes it's a case of imprecision about specifics, in other cases their lack of knowledge is more total. But even without explosions from the news, an hour with an atlas invariably highlights misconceptions of the relationship between places,

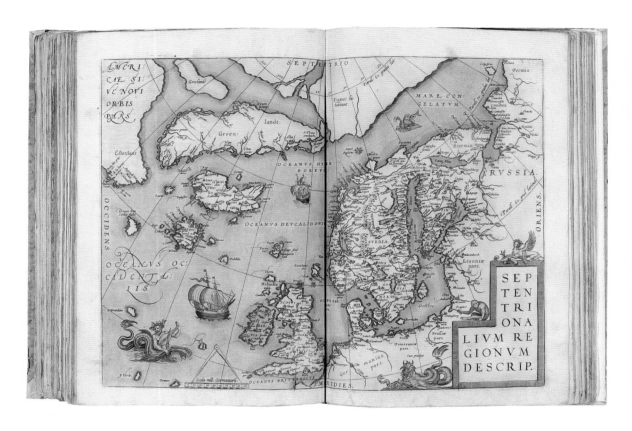

*The Northern Regions (*Septentrionalium Regionum*) from the 1570 Theatrum.
This fine map had many sources including maps by Englishman Anthony Jenkinson
of 1562 and by Mercator of 1562 and 1569. The non-existent island of Friesland is
included in the northern ocean by the authority (among others) of one Nicolao Zeno,
a Venetian wrecked here (so he said) in 1380. The inhabitants live by fishing, and the
volcanic nature of their land clearly resembles that of Iceland, but 'the orchards and
gardens… are always green and flourish almost all year long, with all manner of
flowers, kinds of corn and fruit'.*

usually deriving from some error or misleading circumstances of earlier years – and we have correspondingly to readjust, often a difficult, and, in my experience, not always a durable process. And yet ... While we believed, say, that Cork was further south than Bristol (instead of being slightly further north) was the validity of our recognition of both these cities seriously in question? Would it have affected our dialogue with inhabitants or our reaction to some incident in either place? Almost certainly not, and yet there are matters in which the gentle difference in latitude between them could be of determining importance. To ponder such questions is, I believe, to shed light on our whole relation to the world in which we live and the way it conditions our sense of identity. In order to feel truly a part of it we need to carry about with us a stock of information about it. But if that information is wrong ...

Ortelius was troubled by a related difficulty articulated throughout the *Theatrum*. Soaked in the great classical writers, in Plato, Aristotle, Pliny, Strabo, and himself a devout Christian, well-versed not only in Scripture but in the Church Fathers, Ortelius was obliged to come to terms with a painful fact. These foundation layers of his own humanist culture had known nothing, absolutely nothing, about important realities of the world on which they had so inspiringly and confidently pronounced – and on which he was himself now conferring so much intellectual energy. Whole peoples had been found to exist in countries unknown to and unsuspected by these ancients; civilisations had arisen making no use whatever of tenets that they, and generations of their disciples, had considered indispensable truths.

The Spaniards, looking for the first time at the Aztec capital city of Tenochtitlán, had been overcome by awe at the sophisticated order, beauty and splendour that lay before them, of this lake-city approached by great causeways and set in a fertile and well-tended countryside. Nothing in their education had prepared them for the fact that a culture outside any they knew about (and itself wholly ignorant of these) could achieve anything of such a spectacular nature. In their brutal actions against it, can one not read an emotional resentment born of so radical a challenge to their identity?

The question the 'Great Discoveries' and their later consolidations posed was a twofold one: why had revealed truth not concerned itself with so considerable a portion of the world God had made? And how could any culture, worthy of the God who was the source of that truth, flourish without knowledge of Him?

Attempted answers to these led either into sophistry (principally in dealing with the first question), never good for intellectual health, or (principally applicable to the second) into something far murkier and more dangerous. Sophistry lay in making oneself believe, as wise Mercator did, that biblical writers knew all about the Americas (obviously the chief stumbling-block in all these troubling debates). Ingenuity has to be expended on readings from Plato or Pliny that back up such a view, for there's no hard data, no access to banks of contemporary knowledge these great men could have drawn on. The honourable fruit of genuine moral perplexity in the cases of Mercator and Ortelius, it fathered whole schools of twisted, specious and downright fallacious arguments, not wholly dead to this day, serving to give traditional religion a bad name on the one hand and a totally unwarranted authority on the other.

But in the case of the second question the answer arrived at was only too often far more gravely undermining of an appreciation of humanity's varieties. It was asked how a non-classically-rooted, non-Christian culture could be accorded respect, how it could have flourished? And the response came that it should, on account of its deficiencies, *not* be accorded respect, *not* be permitted to flourish. The astonishing Maya achievements in mathematics and astronomy, the Aztec genius for urban planning and engineering (including exemplary sanitation systems far superior to anything in the conquistadors' Spain), the fascinatingly complex sound-world of Indonesian *gamelan* music for shadow theatre (Sir Francis Drake attended a concert during the course of his circumnavigatory voyage) – did these enter the European educational systems as examples of human culture at its most inventive? They did not. Instead the reverential glance was encouraged to go backwards – backwards above all to the Mediterranean of antiquity – rather than westwards or eastwards. Alexandria but not the Yucatán, Athens but not Hangchow, Rome but not Tenochtitlán.

That Ortelius was greatly exercised by these matters is evident from the verso of the *Typus* itself. He writes that the first map of the volume:

containeth and representeth the portraiture of the whole earth, and of the main ocean that environs and compasseth the same: all which earthly globe the ancients (who were not as then acquainted with the New World, not long since descried) divided into three parts; namely *Africa*, *Europe* and *Asia*. But since that discovery of America, the learned of our age have made that a fourth part, and the huge continent under the South Pole a fifth. Gerard Mercator, the Prince of modern geographers in his never-sufficiently-commended universal table or map of the whole world, divides this circumference of the earth into three continents: the first he calls that which the ancients divided into three parts [Africa, Europe, Asia], and from whence the holy writ bears record that mankind had their first original, and first was seated: the second, is that which at this present is named America or the West Indies: for the third he appoints the south main which some call *Magellanica,* as yet on very few coasts thoroughly discovered.

Ortelius then reminds us that the ancients got the measurement of the world more or less right ('in circuit where it is largest 5,400 German or 21,600 Italian miles, antiquity hath taught, and late writers have subscribed to their opinion'), so virtually exculpating them from any pejorative charges of ignorance they might incur from their failure to write about the Americas as the sixteenth century knew them.

The second map of the *Theatrum* actually has America as its subject, following the Ptolemy–Lafreri principle of moving west-to-east, left-to-right. This is explicitly titled NOVUS ORBIS, the New World, nomenclature that imaginatively reverberates for its readers throughout the book. The word 'new' could be applied to the continent(s) only by Europeans, but how many of them appreciated this? For them the world was new by dint of their having 'discovered' it. And that had made the whole world new for them by reflecting back their increased wealth, extended power, enhanced self-esteem and expanded living space. Their very picture of it had altered, along with their own different roles on it. Looking at the atlas in the light of this change, with America as the focus, every reader could see himself a kind of *Tamburlaine.*

This map of America seems to have derived from Mercator's lost one of the continent(s), and is impressive artistically, with the four winds at the four imaged ('imagined') corners. Friesland makes an appearance, just touching latitude 60; the coast of Brazil ends with the great Plate estuary. The Galapagos islands – almost three centuries later to overturn traditional ideas about life on Earth as radically as the discovery of America itself – are there. There is fine representation of shipping on the Pacific, prophetic of so many later world-changing enterprises – in 1600 the Dutch were to arrive in Japan from the east. In Mexico the capital city is given its rightful Aztec name, Tenochtitlán; we can find the Yucatán peninsula there, too. The accompanying text reads:

That this hemisphere or half-roundel (which is called America, and in regard of the large extension, the New World) should lie concealed from our ancestors till the year of Christ 1492, at what time Christopher Columbus, a Genovese, first discovered the same, is a matter surpassing the measure of human admiration. For considering both the diligence of ancient geographers in describing the world, and the commodious opportunity of most large empires for the searching out of new regions, then also the insatiable avarice of mankind, learning nothing unattempted for the attaining of gold and silver, wherewith these countries incredibly abound, I have often wondered, how it could so long have been hidden from our world. Some there are which suppose that this continent was described by Plato under the name of Atlantis: myself also am of opinion that Plutarch speaking of the face in the body of the moon [the Earth's shadow], makes mention thereof under the name of a main continent. Some think that Seneca, ravished with a poetical fury, presaged the discovery hereof in these prophetical verses [in the very end of the second act of *Medea*].

> *Long hence those years will come,*
> *When th'Ocean shall disclose*
> *Nature's fast bonds and bars.*
> *Then shall huge lands appear,*
> *Typhis shall then detect*
> *New worlds; nor Thule then*
> *Shall bound the paths of men.*

In later editions Ortelius will mention historians' views that North America was colonised by 'certain Indians, forced thither by tempestuous weather over the South Sea – the Pacific. But to me it seems more probable ... that this New World many ages past was entered upon by some islanders of Europe, as namely of Greenland, Iceland and Friesland; being much nearer thereunto than the Indians, now disjoined thence (as appears out of the map) by an ocean so huge, and to the Indians so unnavigable.'

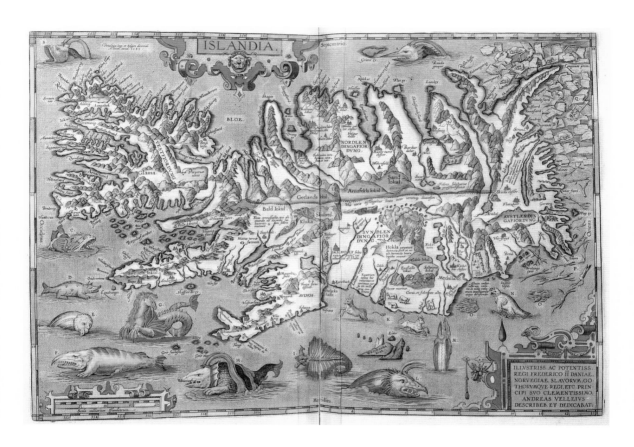

Iceland, *first shown in the* Theatrum *of 1585 and a map remarkable for its accuracy of detail and its many imaginative touches, especially the monsters of the seas. The volcano Hekla features. Ortelius received the map from Anders Sorensen Vodel (1542–1616). Heartily denying its correspondence to the Thule of the ancients, Ortelius shows himself well informed about Iceland's colonisation and history – even though he does include in this a rebuff of an attack by Zichni, king of Friesland.*

As we now know, there was migration into the 'New World' from Asia, if not from India, and Scandinavians did colonise along the continent's east coast – and some of these indubitably operated from Greenlandic or Icelandic bases. What is interesting for us here, in consideration of what kind of show is being staged in the 'Theatre of the countries of the world', is not so much whether Ortelius was right or wrong on this or that subject (or, for that matter, whether prevalent contemporary opinion was right or wrong), but the kind of emphases, the insistences being made for the readers. And, sadly, it would seem that for Ortelius it was more important to stress that presiding classical geniuses of his age, Plato and Seneca, had probably known about America than to consider any achievements of pre-Columbian America itself, whether Inca, Aztec or northern Native American, with so many elaborate cosmogonies (about all of which enough was known to have been set down).

Reflection on the mystery of the withholding – by God Himself? – of the Americas from Christian Europeans until the arrival of Columbus is to come near to the Genovese's own interpretation of the event (even though he believed himself to have encountered subjects of Cathay): that with him the hour had been judged right for the Christianisation of the world beyond that known by the ancients.

On one level, of course, there's no need for any speculations about divine purpose. The 'Great Discoveries' began as a consequence of certain mid-fifteenth century advances in ship-building, and of their adoption by the one kingdom which combined a major Atlantic coast with access to Africa, and, more particularly, the Africa south of Cape Bojador (famous for both storms and fog, and long thought of as the very extremity of the habitable world) – Portugal. The traditional Portuguese ship, the *falua*, had evolved into the *caravel* and then into the *carrack* with its several decks and square rigging. Vasco da Gama's historically determining voyage made use of *carracks*. But to the religiously inclined even such inventions required explaining. Why so long before oceanic crossings and circumnavigations of the world were possible? And why had the present been chosen for the problems, challenges and blessings in their wake?

Ortelius, however concerned with the intricacies of places and their representation, was always mindful of the need to see everything – the world and the human treatment of the world – *sub specie aeternitatis* (under the mirror of eternity). In the text for the *Typus* already quoted from he says:

And these so manifold portions of earth (saith Pliny in the eleventh book of his *Natural History*) yea rather, as some have termed them, the prick or centre of the world (for so small is the earth in comparison of the whole frame of the world) this is the matter, this is the seat of our glory. Here we enjoy honours, here we exercise authority, here we hunt after riches, here men turmoil and tire themselves, here we move and maintain civil dissensions, and by mutual slaughter make more room upon the earth. And to let pass the public tumults of the world, this in which we force the borderers to give place and remove farther off, and where we encroach by stealth upon our neighbours' lands: as he that extends his lands and lordships farthest, and cannot abide that any should seat themselves too near his nose, how great, or rather how small a portion of earth doth he enjoy? Or when he hath glutted his avarice to the full, how little shall his dead carcase possess? Thus far Pliny.

Ortelius has been vindicated by history in his choice of classical author here. In common with all thinking people in his expansionist age he was perfectly familiar with what drove and characterised colonisers and colonialists especially in the New World. He was after all a prominent and a sociable member of a European community second to none in its dealings with the Americas, and whose wealth and repute rested on them. He was a subject of Philip II, to be his Royal Geographer, and through his extensive Spanish contacts had access to numerous accounts of how the New World had been won for Spain, and how it had since been colonised, retained, and profitably – and extortingly – run. Bartolomé de Las Casas' *Short Account of the Destruction of the Indies* had come out, to phenomenal attention and sales as far back as 1542, and gone into many subsequent editions.

This conscience-provoking work was dedicated to Philip himself in the hope that, emulating his own father, Charles V, he would be moved by what it recounted, moved to attempt effective change. Las Casas' 'long' account of Spanish activities in the New World had to wait for posthumous publication; it was too shocking and too subversive; the 'short' one had proved quite strong enough meat. Las Casas (1484–1576) had gone to the Americas when only a boy; his presence at a massacre of Indians had led, via a sermon heard from a visiting Spanish cleric, to a religious conversion and to self-dedication to the cause of the wronged indigenous peoples. Even in its shorter form, and written without any particular verbal power or distinction, his history (from Cuba to Peru) appals, both in its general thrust and in the particulars chosen ('Wriggle, you little perisher!' Spaniards in Hispaniola amused themselves by exclaiming as they threw babies seized from their mothers into the nearest rivers).

In a later edition of the *Theatrum* Ortelius was to give readers a map of New Spain (Mexico) with a commentary on the verso beginning: 'This province was about the year 1518 forcibly subdued to the Spanish government, under the command and conduct of Fernando Cortez; who with the great slaughter of his own people, but far greater of the inhabitants fighting for their liberty, conquered the same ...' He goes on to speak of the greatness of its capital city 'taken by the Spaniards one hundred and forty years after the first foundation thereof; Montezuma at the same time being king, the ninth in number. A wonder how in so few years it should grow to such largeness and magnificence.'

One should compare this with the beginning of the first of the two chapters on New Spain in Las Casas' *Short Account*, to which book indeed it must owe its information:

New Spain was discovered in 1517 and, at the same time, great atrocities were committed against the indigenous people of the region and some were killed by members of the expedition. In 1518 the so-called Christians set about stealing from the people and murdering them on the pretence of settling the area. And from that year until this ... the great iniquities and injustices, the outrageous acts of violence and the bloody tyranny of these Christians have steadily escalated, the perpetrators having lost all fear of God, all love of their sovereign, and all sense of self-respect. The heinous outrages and acts of barbarity have been so vile, the violence so intense, the murders so frequent, other acts of despotism so extreme, and the havoc and devastation so widespread throughout the kingdoms of the Mainland that what we have so far set down in this account is as nothing compared with what went on in New Spain, and the scale and nature of the atrocities committed without a break from 1518 right up to this day beggars description.

There is evidence, I think, from that citation from Pliny alone that Ortelius realised to what cruelties and immoralities the greed for gold and property had driven, and was still driving, the more advanced nations in the territories that they had 'found' and 'claimed'. The *Theatrum* is by no means the only place in his work where the strangeness of the late arrival in European awareness of great tracts of the world is commented on. Perhaps by expressing his marvelment at this he was hoping to instil a gentler approach to colonies in the inhabitants of these among his readers, especially his Spanish or Spanish-dominated ones, a generally more developed conscience towards all fellow humans, even those seemingly so far down civilisation's ladder. That Ortelius was by inclination and principle a compassionate man there can be no doubting. But Philip II did not significantly share his own father's (or for that matter his grandparents') moral anxieties, and the prevalent mood in Spain itself – though there were plenty of men aware and troubled – was not conducive to radical moral reappraisals. (The crimes of Holland and England, generally performed where the older powers of Portugal and Spain were perceived to be weakening, were largely still to come.) Ortelius and his colleagues made a general dissociation of authority in the form of crown and church and the perpetrators of the atrocities (by which it benefited): common adventurers, the riffraff who made up so big a proportion of all ships' crews and invading armies. (Columbus' later voyages had taken on men with criminal records; they, more than most others, were willing to put up with hardships and to brave dangers in exchange for freedom and opportunity.) It was a convenient dissociation.

Exploration, in the most literal sense, gave the world-show of the *Theatrum* its special imaginative edge. The book was up-to-date with contemporary venturesomeness. And its maps, its images, were enticements to its continuation. On the verso of the New World map Ortelius was able to boast: 'All this part of the world (except the north tract thereof, whose coasts are not yet discovered) hath in these last times been sailed round about.'

Wouldn't the effect of such a sentence be to make the reader vow to complete that sailing round about? And indeed in 1576 and 1577 the Englishman Martin Frobisher (1535–1594) did make an attempt at completion of it, in his quest for a north-west passage leading to the great lands of the East.

As for the other continents, Asia is seen in terms of the 'great empires by which it is governed'. This is at healthy variance with the imagery of Hogenberg's frontispiece. There's no sweet demure compliance about the five empires listed: the Muscovite, 'bounded by the frozen sea, the river

Ob, the lake Kitaia, and a line drawn from thence to the Caspian sea, and by the isthmus or neck-land [Georgia, Azerbaijan, Armenia] between the Caspian and Euxine [Black] Seas'; the Tartar empire of the Great Cham; the 'progeny of the Ottomans or Turkish Empire', the 'kingdom of Persia', the 'Indies' [India].

The Far East empires of China and Japan are done considerably less than justice, though Ortelius sought to remedy this later. The exploratory voyages of the Chinese to East Africa, remarkable in distance and endeavour, and germane to the *Theatrum*'s general theme, did not impress as yet, any more than did China's stupendous cartographic tradition – even if confined mostly to representation of territory inside its own frontiers. In fact Chinese nautical charts would have been available (a copy is preserved to this day, of those for the Cheng Ho voyages of 1405–1435, the reached destinations of which ranged from Vietnam to well south of the Horn of Africa). Of China, however, Ortelius observes that it is 'in a manner possessed, or made tribute to the Portugals' – a great exaggeration, despite Macao.

Of those Asian empires named it was the first which, even though it could (geographically, and perhaps from the point of religion) be considered European, was the least-known to atlas-readers. 'Russia, Muscovy and Tartary' is accorded one of the most visually fascinating – and long-lived – of all the maps of the *Theatrum* (its illustrations haunt the mind and became icons associated with the country for at least a century after publication). It's the work of a man who played a key active part in the investigation of this Empire. In 1557 the Englishman Anthony Jenkinson journeyed on behalf of the Muscovy Company to the Russia of Ivan the Terrible, and the following year was granted permission to make a great journey down the Volga. He was horrified by what he saw, the poverty, the slavery – and his general view of the barbarity of the Empire wasn't much ameliorated by his second visit of 1561 to the Caspian regions. There is little on the map to indicate (the sheer size of the regions apart) the great potentiality of Russia, and much to encourage a horror of life beyond inner Muscovy: the Kirghiz scene, exquisitely done, shows men hanging from trees in a grove, a depiction of a traditional way of disposing of the dead. Here is a society not just beyond all civilised order but innocent of it. (There is, however, a sort of untutored charm in the neighbouring glimpse of an encampment of yurts and horses.)

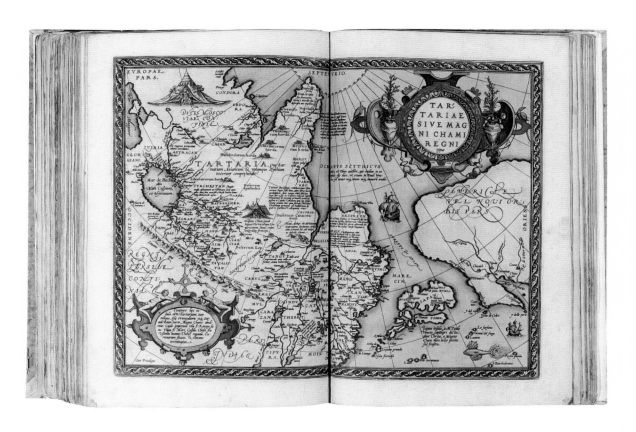

Ortelius based his map for the 1570 Theatrum *on his own 1567 wall-map of Asia, itself in part derived from Gastaldi. Ortelius' text is full but was expanded for the editions of the following year. He pays tribute to the strength of the five empires into which he sees Asia essentially divided, to the potential and actual wealth of Asia's islands, especially the 'East Indies', and to the fact that the 'Human Race was first created [in Asia], betrayed by the Devil and fallen, and resurrected by Jesus Christ'.*

He was also aware of the inaccuracies in the presentation of Japan. These he considerably remedied in the 1595 edition, with a new map by the Portuguese Jesuit priest, Father Luis Texeira, an improvement on all previous maps of the country.

The map of Africa was almost certainly the last to be ready for publication in the *Theatrum*. Readers return to Africa for maps only on the last two sheets: and these will show them Egypt and the hinterland of Carthage, on sheet 52, and Barbary and Biledulgerid (what would be later called the Maghreb) on sheet 53. Setting aside Ptolemy's mistaken reading of a southern Africa sealing off the Indian Ocean, we find Ortelius' Africa, in its emphases, not so greatly different from the *Geographia*'s, or from that of those Arab cosmographers who treasured that work early. 'The land of *Numidia*,' Ortelius tells us, 'is so full of dates the Arabs just call it the "Date-bearing region".' But there were other Africas than the Saharan, and they had been known for some time, and yet were not singled out here for special attention.

One fact that comes to mind is that as much as one hundred and twenty years before this atlas (between 1444 and 1448) over forty Portuguese ships had sailed along the west African coast to bring back about a thousand Africans then sold as slaves. 'Portolan' sea-maps from this time must have been available; a map of West Africa, full of conjectures though sections of its interior would have been, couldn't have been too difficult to produce and include. Yet one was not sought. Whereas Egypt and Numidia were presented, they having the oldest and closest European links.

The map of Europe (the last continent in the *Theatrum*'s opening section) was again based on one by Mercator, used in conjunction with Olaus Magnus' ground-breaking 'Scandinavia'. It heralds the major part of the atlas. Of its 53 sheets 42 deal with European countries (counting Russia among these) – an emphasis that speaks for itself. Even so, Europe's superior merit *is* spoken of, Pliny proving once more a valuable mouthpiece. The readers' own continent is 'nurse of the victorious and conquering peoples of all other nations of the world, most beautiful and far surpassing the rest'.

This would seem (and indeed is) entirely consonant with Hogenberg's image of Europe as we encountered her on the title page: dominant, mighty, virtuous and martial. But in fact, when we turn to the maps and commentaries, it is not *Europa victrix* that strikes us, but Europe the industrious, the productive, the blessed by Nature with a fertility that its fortunate and long-civilised inhabitants have gone on diligently and commendably to husband.

In France the province of Anjou, we are told, 'is everywhere beautified with rivers, mountains, woods and meadows. It aboundeth with cattle and

Barbary and Biledulgerid *from the 1570* Theatrum. *This is principally based on an unattributed Venetian map derived from Gastaldi. The text accompanying it paints a vivid picture of the harshness of Arab life as lived in desert country.*

fish.' The people of Touraine 'are held to be one of the richest people in all France, both for the fruitfulness of their fields (which they deservedly call the king's garden) and also for their excellent manner of government, and the industry of their citizens who are especially addicted to traffic, for which purpose their navigable river [the Loire] stands them in great stead.' (Plantin himself gave Ortelius assistance on the maps of France, so St-Avertin near Tours, his birthplace, may be concealed in this charming, laudatory description.) Picardy 'yieldeth such plenty of wheat as it is called by an usual proverb, the Barn or Granary of Paris', and as for Lorraine (through which Ortelius personally journeyed, writing a travel book as a result) 'for tall men and beautiful women, and all things necessary for man's life, it is inferior to no other country'.

The standards for appreciation of the urban were virtually those applied to the rural. What is important are the gifts that fortune bestowed and the use made of them by responsible inhabitants. Seville, richest of Spain's cities, and that most closely connected with commerce with the Americas, brought forth an awed jubilant response in the writer, who sees the place as a kind of tie-pin jewel fastening the two hemispheres of our world together:

> Now Seville both for churches and houses is the gallantest city in all Spain, and for the neat attire of citizens and a kind of seemliness to them only peculiar is inferior to no city in all the world. Here religion, the study of liberal arts and the practice of gentleman-like exercises are in their prime. And so infinite are the riches and treasures included within the walls of this city, as never the like in old time could be found in any kingdom or Empire, how great soever, the Roman only excepted … largely distributes over all Christendom that unspeakable wealth, and before these last times never dreamed of, which it fetcheth as it were from another world, that from hence was first discovered. Wherewith also it abundantly furnisheth the very barbarous and savage nations, inhabiting the inmost part of Africa and Asia … the neat houses of citizens with their crystal fountains, green arbours and odiferous gardens; with silence I omit the ancient water-streams diffused by arches through all parts of the city, and those later ones, which by the infinite cost and industry of the senators and citizens of Seville have for public delight been conveyed to the place commonly called

Hercules' Pillars; where by planting of trees they have converted a large fenny quagmire into a most beautiful grove, leaving fair and broad spaces for men to walk, run and disport themselves in. Now the gardens without the city, fraught with all variety of pleasures, and those stately houses in the fields, bordering upon Baetis [Guadalquivir], who can sufficiently commend? Out of which they may daily behold ships coming in from both the old and new world.

France (particularly the south of the country), Spain and Italy all had, for Ortelius and for a majority of his readers, the inestimable advantage of having been previously extolled by classical writers. It was different when you turned your attentions northwards (though there were always, of course, the far austerer Caesar and Tacitus to read as sources). Yet surveying Germany as a whole gave Ortelius no cause for dissatisfaction:

This country of Germany which for the present is adorned with the title of the Roman Empire, is so replenished with beautiful and strong cities, castles, village and inhabitants, as it is no whit inferior to Italy, France or Spain: for corn, wine and rivers abounding with fish, it may compare with the most fruitful regions ... no country shall ever go beyond it. Moreover you shall nowhere find more courteous and civil behaviour, more honest and comely attire, more skill and furniture for the wars, nor greater store of nobility. This is the place that whilom (as Tacitus affirmeth) was either darkened by woods or drowned with lakes. *Such changes can succeeding time afford*, saith the poet ...

Ortelius' priorities with respect to landscape are clear enough here, indeed the passage could stand representative for his general pervasive attitude. It's a case of Alexander Pope's 'Nature, yes, but nature methodised'. With application of the virtue of patience, not just the dangers but the infertilities, the uselessness of the wild can, and will, be overcome, the rightful desideratum. Regarding its people (and, like Mercator, Ortelius himself had roots in Germany) he shows himself very percipient: 'The nation is very popular and mighty, ruleth far and wide the world over and in greatness is second to the Scythians or Tartars. Wherefore if they were at concord and under one Prince, then might they well be deemed invincible and want nothing.'

With Germany his own southern Netherlands homeland of Brabant has become imminent. Of Liège (which then included Maastricht) we are told, 'It is a region exceedingly pleasant and fertile of all things, especially in the north part where it joineth to Brabant.' At this point 'it becomes overspread with woods. This is the natural hue of the country, but in the entrails and bowels thereof it is enriched with metals and sundry kinds of marbles – as also with sea-coals, which they burn instead of fuel.' (This is a pointer to the heavy industry in which Belgium excelled early.)

But Brabant, with Antwerp its capital, was an even more rewarding region to contemplate. Not just the land, though that indeed was 'goodly and pleasant, and exceedingly fertile', but the people of the land who had worked it so well and, even better, had the capacity to enjoy it:

> The people are so jocund, as they seem scarce to feel the inconvenience of old age; which frolic disposition of theirs hath given occasion to their neighbours round about to use this jest: the longer the Brabant lives, the more fool he. The air is exceeding wholesome; for when the plague hath been most vehement in all the regions adjacently, Brabant hath often most wonderfully remained free. Antwerp is situated upon the Scheldt, the most famous mart not only of 'Germanie' [the north of the continent's mainland] but of all Europe: and one of the strongest cities in the world, being much beautified with the steeple of St Mary's [*Onze Lieve Vrouwekathedraal*] built an incredible height of white marble. The palace [town hall] is scarcely to be matched in all Europe.

We can legitimately see this sheet as the centrepiece of the *Theatrum*. The map is one of the most appealing of them all. In a fertile country, graced by a mighty navigable river, a people – one of the most enterprising and prosperous in the world, and in the *Theatrum*'s specific fields of geography, chorography and ethnology unsurpassed – are even able to defy premature death through disease and to cock a snook at old age. An underlying assumption in this piece is that a folk is fortunate because God has willed it so. But side by side with this is another belief, that of the favoured much is expected. And haven't the Brabanters paid back divine providence with all that they have done, even to the gracing of their chief city with spectacular and innovative buildings? And isn't there, too, a plea here that so civilised a part of the world should be spared further suffering?

The tone of the verso commentaries matches the aesthetic harmony of the maps themselves. One couldn't deduce from either text or visual material the appalling tensions known by so many regions of this most favoured of continents. Nor the frequency with which these tensions turned into downright conflict and misery. How right Pietro Bizzari was when he said the maps of the *Theatrum* constituted a new kind of world-machine for the promotion of peaceful co-existence. Seeing these long-cultured regions – and the ancient lineage of their towns and monuments is often stressed – how could anyone fail to cherish them, fail to allow them the freedom of religion, thought and mores that would ensure them their natural pleasantness of life and its creative continuation?

But how wrong Bizzari also was, and in the short term how dramatically so. Just short of two years after it had produced the first theatre of the countries of the world, the Netherlands became a theatre of the bitterest war.

CHAPTER
SIXTEEN

During those two years the *Theatrum* had done spectacularly well, as the exemplary researches of M. P. R. Van den Broecke (1996) have enabled us to appreciate.

Three hundred and twenty-five copies were printed of the first Latin edition of 1570, and of these Christophe Plantin sold 159 in his shop in six months, at an unusually high price, too. Forty of these, we know from records, were personally delivered to his bookshop by Ortelius himself (on 17 June, just under a month after publication day). Other Antwerp booksellers as well as Plantin stocked and sold the *Theatrum*. A second edition came out that very first year, with another, also in Latin, the next. The year 1571 also witnessed the publication of the first of the vernacular-language editions, this one appropriately enough in Ortelius' own Dutch: the *Theatre oft Toonneel des Aerdtbodems*. This had an initial print-run of 275 copies, the first of three. In the accounting period 1571–2 nearly a third of further Latin editions received by Plantin from Ortelius were transported by his orders to Paris, where his 'brother' Porret's bookshop played its part in their distribution. Thus the book's reputation quickly began to spread well beyond the City-on-the-Scheldt. A French-language version, *Théâtre de l'univers*, appeared as soon as 1572.

The enthusiasm the atlas aroused was unprecedented by any comparable publication. 'All extol your *Theatrum* to the skies and wish you well for it,' the effusive but sincere Pietro Bizzari informed Ortelius, adding that, for himself: 'I shall live a worshipper of your name.' Pietro Bizzari (1530–1590) was a complex individual, devious but strong-principled, and a man of influence not least where the *Theatrum* was concerned. A Protestant convert, this poet and historian left Italy for England, where, in addition to teaching at Cambridge, he worked as a government spy. He later stayed in Antwerp, and had learned books published by Plantin himself. In England he'd won the friendship of the powerful state secretary William Cecil (Lord Burghley) who became one of the *Theatrum*'s greatest admirers. Among these surely only Philip II himself, who always wanted to have a copy of the work to hand whenever he travelled, commanded more authority.

Five years after his first rapt confrontation with Ortelius' atlas, Bizzari's proselytising admiration for work and author was if anything more fervent still. Writing on 26 September 1575 he declared: 'One must then exalt you by very great praises, very wise Ortelius, you who, blessed with the greatest gifts of the soul, have wanted to give immortality to your name and to work excellently for humanity. It's why you are very worthy of a happy and long life on earth since you have put into the light a world which many are ignorant of, and which now is visible to everybody.'

Plantin too appreciated the quality of his old friend's achievement with which he was increasingly, and by his own choice, professionally and commercially bound up. He realised that it owed all its lauded merits to some strong and noteworthy quality in Ortelius' character. For his *Album amicorum*, to commemorate Christmas Day 1574, he penned an honorific sonnet, accompanied by his own 'mark', a delightful design made up, suitably enough for the two of them, of divers books. No matter the poetic diction of the verses' language, its opening quatrain says much:

De bien long temps je me sens obligé
A tes vertus et grâces désirables:
Pour ce mon cueur s'est a toy engagé
D'un gage libre, et liens aimables.

('For a long time I feel myself indebted/ to your virtues and desirable graces:/ so that this my heart may engage with yours/ in a free manner and with pleasing bonds.')

And the poem commends his friend and colleague's *sainct labeur constant*, a phrase in truth supremely applicable to them both. It's applicable to Mercator, too, supplier of maps and of bases for other maps for the *Theatrum*. Some years later, wanting to provide Ortelius' *Album* with some 'symbol of perpetual friendship', personal and intellectual, on 1 October 1575 the great geographer came up with the motto *Suprema mundi optima* ('The very best in the world').

The *Theatrum* was, of course, a useful work too, even though so expensive and of such large dimensions. It helped people to find their bearings in the ever-expanding world and so themselves grow in experience and practical wisdom. Moreover, the maps as printed in the atlas could be sold separately. Ortelius usually waited until he had got a sufficient number of new ones together before publishing them as an *Additamentum* to the book proper.

A dear travelling companion of his who reminds us of this usefulness is Hieronymus Scholiers (1553?–?), a young Antwerp humanist and archaeologist, who in the disaster year of 1576 went to Spain and Portugal with the prelate Joannes Moflin, then acting chaplain to Philip II. He wrote to Ortelius: 'Our voyage went off very well; only the sea seemed a little strange to us, which may be condoned in us, it being (with the exception of Moflin) the first time, hoping to be so much the better for the next voyage. Your maps have been everywhere of great service to us, so that from town to town, we paid great attention to them, and their defect signified very little otherwise we should have noticed it, but no correction is wanted.'

No editorial statement or decision of Ortelius' had more consequence than that made in his Introduction to the *Theatrum* to the effect that – only too aware of what countries on the *Typus* had not received their cartographic due later on in the volume – he would like his readers to make good his reluctant omissions by submitting maps of their own. This invitation, he insisted, was of an entirely serious professional nature. He would fully acknowledge any he published, the names of the maker would go into that scrupulous *Catalogus auctorum* which, from the very first, presented itself as a model for other compilers. Thus, interested readers could, if their works satisfied the editor, join the distinguished ranks of such contributors as Mercator (author of the Flanders map), Jacob van Deventer (of Netherlands Friesland) or Johannes Sambucus (of Hungary and Transylvania). His request set up a fruitful dialogue between editor/author/ publisher and the public.

Gallia Narbonensis *or Southern France. This map has a special interest since it was drawn for Ortelius, with the atlas (the 1570* Theatrum*) in mind, by his friend, the later pre-eminent botanist Carolus Clusius/Charles de l'Escluse (1526–1609), to be the founder of Leiden University's wonderful and trend-setting Botanical Garden. The text makes much of the continuous nature of civilisation in southern France, especially from Roman times onwards.*

The 1570 *Theatrum* contained only one map from a hitherto unpublished model – that of *Gallia Narbonensis*. Eighteen more maps were added to the edition of 1573. And so the process went on, until the final edition that Ortelius saw through the press in his own lifetime, that of 1595, had 151 maps, eighty-one more than the parent volume.

Each submission Ortelius himself had to check against what other sources he could find. Here we find Ortelius receiving a letter from an Italian scholar, Caesar Orlandi (Orlandius), dated 15 May 1572: 'In your *Theatrum* you ask all persons who possess descriptions of particular regions wanting in that work to let you have access to them. Induced by such a reasonable request, and in order that my native place [Siena] may acknowledge itself indebted to you, I send you a map of it and the neighbourhood, sketched, some time ago at Rome, though not entirely finished; also a summary of a little book of mine on the origin of the city to be added (abridged by you) to your own record of it already found in your *Theatrum*, when you reprint that work which, I believe, will soon be necessary.'

Ortelius took up Orlandius' offer and his Sienese map was duly published. Not all writers were as amiable as Orlandius, who, writing in Italian, made use of the ingratiating charm of that language. Hiobus Madeburgus writing in March 1574 was blunter and more abrasive: 'The map of Meissen by Bartholomeus Schultetus is not worthy of your work; there is no art in it, and the courses of rivers and the sites of places do not often agree with the country. Similar errors are found in Johannes Cruginger's map of Saxony, who has put many things into his map just as others told them to him.'

In his procedure of canvassing maps – which coexisted with his own continuing search for them, with a special priority on East Asia – Ortelius was not just addressing an international intellectual community, he was helping to shape or consolidate one, and even to expand its ranks. And this procedure was emulated – quite consciously and early. In 1572 came the *Civitates orbis terrarum* (*Cities of the World*) – the very title is an intentional echo of that of the *Theatrum* – by Georg Braun of Cologne (dean of its cathedral chapter) and the *Theatrum*'s own Frans Hogenberg, who had now moved to that city. This work did for the particular entity, the microcosm, what Ortelius had done for continents and countries, the macrocosm. In the *Civitates*, too, the editors asked their readers for informed contributions, to remedy absences, and they were gladly supplied. The *Civitates* and its five splendid succeeding volumes – with each engraved city standing up before us, like a map coming to life, like a *veduta* at the very moment of its revelation of all intimacies – were the *Theatrum*'s first progeny, and like their progenitor, were immensely successful both in critical esteem and sales, welcomed by a truly sizeable public. Hogenberg brought his own unrivalled artistry to the work, but the contributions of that mutual friend of his and Ortelius, Joris Hoefnagel, are also noteworthy. His rendering of Brunn (Brno) in Moravia, and of Buda in Hungary, both show the importance of landscape to the total effect of the cities, to their atmosphere for both visitor and resident. Indeed the work as we follow it through suggests a deepening sense of the need for a real relationship between architecture and the natural world, reflecting a greater emphasis in the age itself on the importance of this last for the human sensibility (the portraits of Stockholm, for instance, by Hieronymus Scholiers most memorably and accurately convey the lake and sea which the city spans, and the low rocky hills around it).

The European culture which thought the whole world its legitimate theatre of operations took the greatest pride in making each individual disseminating centre of that culture something self-evidently significant, something both beautiful and magnetic, a pride that by the mid-century was almost as much an aspect of the north as of the south of the continent. We have seen how Ortelius, who rejoiced in Rome and Florence and Seville, felt the intensest admiration for his own City-on-the-Scheldt. In the *Theatrum* entry on Brabant he'd been pleased to sing the praises of some of its most splendid features.

But the first decade of the *Theatrum*'s book-life brought disorder and suffering to its place of origin. The moral of the atlas' harmonious pages had not been heeded; the book's royal dedicatee, Philip of Spain, however attached he might be to it, certainly did not follow its irenicism. The 'incredible height of white marble' that was Antwerp's cathedral was soon to rear above shattered and viciously ransacked buildings, and Frans Floris' grandiloquent town hall, crowning glory of his career with its 'romanist' and oriental features, the public edifice which all Europe couldn't match, was to be set on fire. 1572 and 1576 were burdening years in the history of the southern Netherlands: the first saw an insurrection that was never, at least in Antwerp, the success it should have been; the later date witnessed the Spanish Fury.

CHAPTER SEVENTEEN

In a letter, already alluded to, which he wrote to his cousin Emmanuel van Meteren back in December 1567 (just over a year after the *Beeldenstorm* or Iconoclastic Fury) Ortelius showed himself once again prescient. He actually named the source from which emanated the greatest trouble to disrupt his own society in his lifetime. The tone of the letter may seem a long way away from the celebratory prose of the *Theatrum* versos he was so soon to compose about the Low Countries, but in those he was striving for some ideal present, whereas here, to Emmanuel, he was putting out antennae to discover what future the instabilities of the times contained.

It will be remembered that Ortelius compared the southern Netherlands to a person terminally ill. '[The] patient will soon be entirely prostrate, being threatened with so many and various illnesses, as the Catholic evil, the *Gueux* fever, and the Huguenot dysentery, mixed with other vexations of black horsemen and soldiers.' His particular designations of the three principal conflicting social elements amount, when taken together, and in context, to a disturbing diagnosis of the current situation. Brabantine society, as he sees it, hasn't made up its mind on the issues devouring it – that is the real trouble. To pursue Ortelius' own metaphor, it is capable of experiencing all three diseases at once, to its eventual complete debilitation. The burgher prosperity and solid culture of Antwerp, which had made it for so long such an attractive place to live and work in, were to a considerable measure responsible for this. Now the city inclines to the Protestant (Calvinist/'Huguenot') outlook; now it's sympathetic to the freedom-fighting *Gueux*, to an independent and pluralist Netherlands; now it wishes to remain inside the age-old fold of the Church and, by so doing, not incur any further wrath from Philip and his appointed representatives. Now it turns away from the astringencies of Calvinism and its rejections of what was rich in the societal aspects of spiritual life; now it shudders at the behaviour of the Beggars, the *Gueux*, particularly the newer Sea-Beggars (*Waterguezen*), a wild lot, heavy-drinking, with a constant retinue of whores; now it realises just how intolerable, harsh and unyielding Spanish domination has been – and will continue to be.

The average Antwerper could think all these things at different times, or even at once. Nor were Plantin and Ortelius themselves free from this weakness. We have already witnessed their equivocations and accommodations, and the Family of Love – now breaking up under all the external pressures – practised an ecumenicism that couldn't really travel beyond its own clandestine conventicles.

Ortelius, it seems, appreciated a good deal of all this (and he was, after all, writing to a strongly committed Calvinist who had made a decisive break with a society he couldn't support and that wouldn't support him). Sooner or later, after the explosions of violence and immorality that the political instabilities would unleash, Brabantine society would exhaustedly, one might almost say cynically, simply settle for peace on whatever terms, because it had no appetite left to stand up for itself any longer. 'I expect that everyone,' Ortelius continues, 'after having done what he can in the way of robbing and murdering, will be so tired as to wish for the peace which he had formerly but did not value. All this we have deserved through our sins; for we are up to our heads in pride and ambition; everyone wishes to be called, but not to be, good; everyone wishes to teach others, but not to humble himself; to know much and to do little; to dominate over others, but not to bow under God's hand. May He be merciful unto us, and grant us to see our faults ...'

Whatever our dissensions from the vocabulary used here, one cannot but applaud the writer's moral insight. Insight of a more directly verifiable kind, however, is shown in what Ortelius goes on to tell his cousin – and this, with hindsight, is the truly remarkable passage in the letter: 'Two thousand men are at work here at the Castle, and the old walls are diligently pulled down.

When the whole is ready we shall probably get rid of the *lansquenets*, as the service of these German soldiers comes to an end next January, and it appears they will leave here and that the Spaniards will occupy the Castle.'

They did indeed. Ortelius, almost exactly nine years before it happened, is describing the provenance of the most traumatic event in the history of the Low Countries before their separation.

The measures carried out throughout the Netherlands by the Duke of Alva were deliberately designed to terrify and humiliate. Philip II had convinced himself that only through such means could the region become a Catholic society again, though he was prepared to admit that for it to be seamlessly Catholic was impossible. The Duke, however, was more concerned with the cowing of the populace, of whatever ideological hue, his main aim being that from hence forward it would do as its government told it to. Naturally enough – and the ferocity of Alva's repressions was extreme – all this greatly increased the appeal of, and support for, William of Orange. The ruthlessly thorough imposition on Netherlanders of taxes that they were in any case bound to resent, and the appointment of town councils, placed in psycho-socially impossible positions with regard to townsfolk, to implement the payment of these, made matters considerably worse – especially as one purpose for the money raised was the mainten-ance of citadels of armed men to keep the country in check. As so often happens in such situations, one tax in particular galvanised subjects into physically articulated fury: the infamous Tenth Penny tax, a levy of ten per cent of the region's sales. It became a rallying point.

In July 1571 the decree was made that the 'Tenth Penny' was law. The revolt against this of 1572 affected the northern Netherlands far more widely and radically than the southern. Aided by the exodus in the later 1560s of believers from south of the Great Rivers, Calvinism had emerged there as a far more socially unifying force than was possible in Flanders or Brabant with their very different social consistencies and histories. It has already been said that Catholic resistance to the iconoclasts, to all the angry protests against the corruption of the Church had been curiously lukewarm in Antwerp, but the obverse is also true – that opposition to Catholicism never hardened into a threatening militant force. Geography played its part. As was to be shown only too often and too tragically later, 'Belgium' was far more vulnerable to invasion than north of the rivers with its marshy, water-crossed terrain. But perhaps also too much of the past culture of the Flemish and Brabantine cities, of the liveliness of the *rederijkers* and of the guilds with their *ommegangs*, was tied up with the established Church. In that sense the equivocations of Plantin and Ortelius, exceptional men though they were, were quite typical – as Ortelius was perhaps trying to tell himself and his correspondent in his letter of 1567.

The insurrections of 1572 didn't directly touch Antwerp but they greatly affected the environs of the city. Holland and Zeeland rose up against Spain, roused by the energies of the Sea-Beggars, who, expelled from the English ports where they'd harboured, came in to seize first Brill, and then Flushing, on the Scheldt estuary. Brill was only a small town, and its capture by the Beggars, which passed into punning Dutch folklore, was primarily of symbolic significance. But Flushing was a key marine base. The rebels had cut Antwerp off from the mouth of its life-blood river.

The city was therefore plunged into an economic depression. Christophe Plantin, its most enterprising and successful businessman, had virtually completed his ambitious and beautiful Polyglot Bible, his hoped means of securing permanent good graces with the Spanish authorities; just the resetting of the last volumes was still outstanding. Plantin's worries that year, which included personal ones about his daughters, were further compounded by news of the Bartholomew's Day (23 August) massacre of Protestants in Paris, an event which, of course, irrespective of his own personal and commercial predicaments, was to have repercussions on southern Netherlands life, undermining hopes of Calvinist assertion there. Indeed Plantin came near to considering whether he ought not to put his entire Antwerp concern into liquidation.

However, as so often in the story of this astonishing man, this genius of printing and commerce – and quite contradicting the many letters of complaint he was now regularly writing to Spain, protesting manifold financial difficulties, corrosive illnesses (he sought further medications at Mons and Valenciennes), workplace difficulties and imminent poverty – he soon proceeded to do better than ever before. The seventies was the greatest decade of his whole career. The turmoils of the northern Netherlands he could keep off-stage: the heroic stands, the fierce conflicts, the savage reprisals, the seesawing of fortunes so that now it was a Spanish garrison whose inmates starved, now a Dutch city (most dramatically of all Leiden which suffered appallingly for many months and eventually

Painting by François Dubois of the St Bartholomew's Day Massacre – 23/24 August 1572 – of French Calvinists in Paris on the occasion of Henri III's marriage to Margaret of Valois.

won through not only because of the tenacity of the citizens but because of the eventual rains that forced the Spaniards to abandon their siege). All this did not really affect his business too pejoratively – in addition to which things in Paris were, from his own point of view, not as bad he'd feared. Despite everything the 'Porret' bookshop there was still a going concern. No need for him then to contemplate liquidation any further.

Instead there would be greater expansion – of machine, men, books and print-runs (and he was still supplying paper for the *Theatrum*). Moaning letters to the Spanish court produced payments from his patrons that might well otherwise have conveniently been withheld. Plantin himself was to claim (after another reversal of fate) that at this period he had 150 employees. This figure has been disputed by experts since inspection of his ledgers doesn't bear it out (and Plantin was most certainly capable of both exaggeration and underestimation if he thought either would serve his present purpose). But Voet in *The Golden Compasses* has worked out that to the printers, compositors and proof-readers itemised on the account books, we should add all those who worked in the bookshop and printing office, all those who did more occasional or *ad hoc* work for him – binders, engravers and domestics. These can add up without difficulty to the number later given.

And in June 1576 he moved into that splendid house on the Vrijdagmarkt which for well over four hundred years has acted as a lodestar for those who care about books, indeed about culture altogether. Until 1579 Plantin rented it from the Spanish merchant Martin Lopez. It wasn't until that year that Plantin set about altering, enlarging and generally improving the place. But maybe even from the first – it was officially described on the deeds as a '*groote huysinghe*' (a large dwelling-house) – it began to impart something of that atmosphere so palpable in it today. Jeanne Plantin was an excellent and economic housekeeper. The staff was numerous, the Plantin family was large and lively, and so was their circle of friends – with many fondly received, and often distinguished, guests coming to stay there. In 1576 Plantin gave the management of his book shops to his two elder sons-in-law. His eldest daughter Margareta's husband, the Calvinist scholar and proof-reader Frans Raphelengius – later to move with his family to Leiden and run the University Press there – was set up in a shop near the cathedral. To his second daughter Martina's husband, the Catholic Jan Moretus – later to run the whole Antwerp business and to lend his name to the mighty dynasty of Antwerper printers and *Hochburghers* that followed – Plantin assigned the premises he had just vacated in the Kammenstraat. Even in the matter of his sons-in-law he was able to play brilliantly the waiting political/religious game at which he was already so practised and accomplished a hand. There was a strange and convenient symmetry in their talents and their religious inclinations which, in the long run, served the whole family and their offspring well.

A further event of the year – 1576 – that was to end so terribly was the final approval given by the Vatican – through Benito Arias Montano's offices – to the Polyglot Bible. Plantin had certainly not anticipated the five years of objections, wranglings and in-fighting (the Salamanca theologians having made the strongest complaints to the Inquisition about both contents and contributors) that had elapsed between completion of this stupendous project and the bestowal of the expected and necessary *Imprimatur*. The *Biblia* did not therefore make quite the money for the press that had been hoped for, and it had involved too many stressful altercations and changes of official position – ended only by the enthronement of a new Pope – for Plantin to feel that it had strengthened for ever, beyond the point of daily anxieties, his standing in the eyes of Catholic authority. On the other hand it did bring honour to his House, and can stand alongside the *Theatrum* as one of the Golden Compasses' supreme achievements. It was a most handsome one as well, though its union of differing languages and types as a visual bibliographic counterpart of the harmony possible among believing people on God's Earth must have stood out ironically at the conclusion of that ghastly year in which it began its 'approved' life.

And the ironies promoted by reflection on the 'world-machine' that was the *Theatrum* must have been no less bitter – but no less modifiable by justified satisfaction in both the work and its exalted aims.

As for the engineer of the world-machine, Ortelius, he too had availed himself of the comparative calm that prevailed in Brabant despite the seizure of the Scheldt estuary by the *Waterguezen*. He worked on the editing and amassing of further maps, including ones of the Baltic region, Scotland and Wales (Humphrey Lhuyd's lovely and still operable one, acquired and worked on with the permission of his heirs). His friendship with Sambucus, now living in Antwerp, grew; their numismatism drew them together. He made another trip to Italy to study coins and other antiquities such as inscriptions and ancient monuments. And doubtless

IMAGINES
ET FIGVRÆ
BIBLIORVM.

IMAGES
ET FIGVRES
DE LA BIBLE.

BEELDEN
ENDE FIGVREN
WT DEN BYBEL.

Habitantibus in vmbra mortis
lux orta est eis. *Isaia* ix. 2.

Exprimebat Iacobus Villanus, Anno Domini M. D. LXXXI.

Frontispiece of Hendrik Barrefelt's Imagines et Figurae Bibliorum
*published by Christophe Plantin in Antwerp. The heart on the right encloses
irenicist images of the New Testament.*

his most sustained tribute to classical and biblical wisdom, the maps of the *Parergon*, were already germinating in his mind.

The political situation in the wake of the Sea-Beggars' triumphs played a part in the important schism of 1573 in the Family of Love in Antwerp. Ortelius and Plantin's former spiritual mentor HN now lived in Cologne, too far away and too out of touch. Embittered himself by what he considered failures in loyalty by his supporters, men whom he had personally (as he thought) lifted up, aided and made sacrifices for, Niclaes had increasingly infuriated earlier Familists with his messianic posturings – and possibly delusions. Instead they gave allegiance to a protégé of his, Hendrik Jansen van Barrefelt, who preferred to be known as Hiel (the 'life of God'); Familism in Antwerp now became Hielism. Hiel's vision is in truth not so different from HN's (at any rate from HN's in its earlier stages): irenicist, emphasising the importance of the inner life, of personal reception of Christ above any dogmatic or liturgical allegiances. Ortelius and Plantin were to feel the same devotion for it as they had towards HN's. If anything Barrefelt was more Nicodemist even than HN; Alastair Hamilton sees his position as still nearer the Catholic than the Protestant, and like HN, Hiel firmly rejected the Lutheran doctrine of salvation by faith. But he also (points out Hamilton) made fewer attacks on Protestant ideas or intentions than his one-time mentor, and certainly an English reader of his pronouncements, with their almost lyrical insistence on inwardness, remembers not just earlier German and Dutch divines but England's quietists of the seventeenth century who culminated in the Quakers. Plantin later published in 1584 Barrefelt's *Imagines et Figurae Bibliorum* (*Images and Figures from the Bible*), the double cordiform title page most memorably picturing scenes of ineffable peace, HN's *Terra pacis* given visual expression ... Yet it is only honest and honourable, however irritated or repelled we may be by his megalomania, to give HN the credit for the pervasion by this ideal of Ortelius' *Theatrum*.

CHAPTER
EIGHTEEN

But this ideal was as far from realisation in November 1576 as could be imagined – or dreaded. The event known as the Spanish Fury surprised and stunned, but, of course, it had nameable causes.

The Spanish exchequer was severely strained through over-expenditure on war on more than one front. So now there were insufficient funds to meet the maintenance or equipping of all the soldiers in the many Alva-installed fortresses throughout the Netherlands. The men had nothing to spend and almost nothing to eat, and yet were expected to carry out tasks – quashing rebellious towns, confronting insurgents – that were both demanding and dangerous. So they mutinied, and the form their venting of grievances took was the unleashing of their fury (for which the whole outbreak has been aptly named) on whatever and whoever was to hand. The States of Brabant were given permission speedily to raise scratch armies to deal with the sudden dilemma, but this response was too hasty and not substantial enough. In Antwerp on Sunday, 4 November, Spanish soldiers left the citadel to which Ortelius had referred in his letter to his cousin, marched in an orderly enough fashion until they reached the barricades which the States army had established, and then broke through into the city. And let rip.

Ortelius himself had realised a crisis was imminent and had left for England where he spent time with his kinsman, Daniel Rogers, and with

Engraving (1576) by Frans Hogenberg of the cruelties visited on Antwerpers by the Spanish in the wake of the insurrections of 1576.

Rogers' friend the antiquarian William Camden (1551–1623), 'a great admirer of antiquity, of geography and a fervent one of the name of Ortelius'. He left his Antwerp business in the hands of his sister Anne. As vivid an account as we can hope for of the dreadful events that happened in his absence (particularly if supplemented with the detailed and horrifying etchings of Frans Hogenberg) can be found in a letter written to his brother-in-law Jacob Cool by an Antwerp businessman, Gerraert Janssen, shortly afterwards:

> The Lord be thanked and praised for his mercy, which he has shown me in the oppressive times which we had in Antwerp last week, and from which He has so miraculously saved me, as I have never been so near death as I was at that time near being murdered, shot or burned ...[The] soldiers of the States [of Brabant] arrived in Antwerp and admitted the Count of Oversteyn and Champagny, the governor of Antwerp on Saturday November 3, about 10 o'clock in the morning, and as soon as they entered through the Cipdorp gate, they marched through the town till they came in front of the castle. Thereupon they searched for all the wool- and hop-sacks, mead-casks and dry casks, and collected them in great hurry in front of the castle to construct bulwarks of them to protect the town; and every citizen had to send man, boy or young woman thither to dig at these bulwarks. It was dark at the time through a fog, so that people in the castle could not see what was done at the town, so that in a very short time they had made a trench along the whole way.
>
> During the night and the whole of the next day till the afternoon following (which was Sunday) the castle briskly fired towards the town, so that they shot through many houses situated near the castle, and also several people walking about in the streets. At the same time the Spaniards and Germans, who had pillaged Maastricht, and also the Spaniards who had been quartered in Aalst, entered the castle from behind, so that they came at once, with all their force, without resting, through the castle into the town and attacked the bulwarks, where they fought very courageously with the soldiers of the States and the Germans of Oversteyn, many being killed on both sides; but the Walloons and the Germans had to leave the bulwarks, so that the Spaniards entered the town in various places, over the bulwarks.

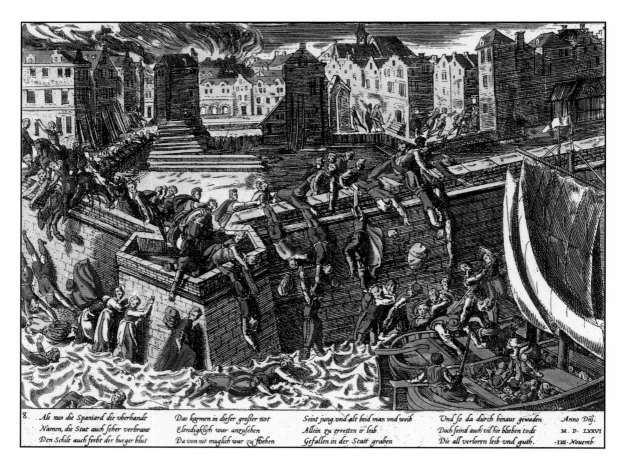

8. Als nun die Spaniard die vberhandt   Das karmen in dieser groſſer not   Seint jung vnd alt beid man vnd weib   Und ſo da dürch hinaus gewaden   Anno Dnj.
Namen, die Stat auch ſeher verbrant   Elendigklich war anzuſehen   Allein zu erretten ir leib   Doch ſeind auch vil hie blieben todt   M. D. LXXVI
Den Schilt auch ferbt der burger blut   Da von nit muglich war zu fliehen   Gefallen in der Statt graben   Die all verloren leib vnd guth.   ·IIII· Nouemb·

The Spanish Fury of 1576, as depicted by Frans Hogenberg.

The bell sounded an alarm so that also all the citizens put on their armour and armed themselves with guns; meanwhile the Spaniards with their Germans arrived, fighting, in the market-place, where they fought long with the German soldiers and the citizens who stood there, so that many were killed; the train-bands fired briskly from their rooms; but at last the Spaniards gained the market-place, and drove away the citizens and the Germans, almost throughout the whole town, so that most of the streets were filled with the dead; they drove away the Walloons, Germans and citizens, as far as the walls; so that many were forced, to save themselves, to jump down from the walls. Many were saved near the pesthouse in the New Town, who let themselves down into the water with cords and pikes, and got from there to land; many also were saved by boats from the New Town from out the canals, and many were drowned in the canals, who thought to save themselves in the boats. Some boats were so full of people that they sank with their weight, so that it is said that as many as five hundred men (mostly Germans and Walloons, but also many citizens, women and children) were drowned in a canal near the bridge. The Count of Oversteyn also was drowned in our Lady's Church. The governor Champagny and M. Havere saved themselves in boats, going to the ships of the *Gueux* which lay before the town; it is said that they have been in Zeeland with the Prince of Orange, and that they went thence to Ghent. The Count of Egmont is also imprisoned here in the castle.

When the Spaniards had gained the town and driven away and slain all their enemies, they attacked the houses of the citizens and the doors, which were not opened at once, were shot open or broken to pieces, and entering they rushed, with their naked rapiers and poniards, upon the inmates of the house, beating, stabbing, nay murdering many, as they wished to have all the money, and when they received all that there was, they demanded still more. When they had all the money, they pillaged the house unless a ransom was paid for as much as it was worth, so that they have impoverished and confounded and so spoiled the whole town that it will never be again as it was.

Nobody escaped except those of the Spanish nation; all other nations, English, Germans, Eastelings, Italians, Portuguese, have been pillaged.

The Spaniards caused also great damage by incendiarism, as they burned the new town-hall with all the houses around; the *pant* on the market-place is burned, also the *brayerystraet*, the *silverstraet*, the *keestraet*, the *suykeruye*, the beginning of the *hoochstraet*, also the houses where the old town-hall stood, the *vlasmert*, two or three houses on *St Peeter's* bridge, many houses near the castle, so that it is said that about four or five hundred houses have been burned down, which was sad to see and hear; no one can believe what an amount of property was burned, besides many persons, who are still found daily. The pillage lasted four or five days.

At our house we have lost all that we had; I saved nothing but what I had on, which were the worst clothes I possessed. I for my part have lost more than fifty pounds Flemish which suits me very little; I have indeed experienced misfortune enough this year; God grant that it may cease ...

There are many persons in Antwerp embarrassed, who were rich and mighty, but are now poor, and all things are so dear here, that I do not know what the poor people will do this winter; and as to moving to any other town, it is difficult to get away from here, as one must have a passport, and one does not know where to be well.

Plantin and his family, right there in central Antwerp, were witnesses of these atrocities and suffered from all the attendant mayhem. Soldiers and their horses were forced on them; the quartered men behaved badly and stole. Afterwards when Ortelius returned from the safety of abroad, he made an evaluation of what his friend had lost in the Fury – he estimated it at well over 10,000 florins.

The Spanish Fury is a dividing-line – one marked by fires and corpses and ruins – in the history of the southern Netherlands. At the time it was said that as many as 18,000 people had died during its three-day-long ravages – and Netherlands separatists were obviously keen to exploit such high figures – but later 8,000 would be the number more frequently adduced. It now seems probable that the deaths were most likely in the hundreds only. This hardly matters. As in the case of the attacks on New York's World Trade Center of 11 September 2001 the fact of fatalities when none have been expected is sufficient in itself to create a trauma in the collective psyche, and the quantifying of those killed or physically (or otherwise) deprived is a secondary, and possibly an irrelevant matter. Ever afterwards Antwerpers had to live with the knowledge that their great city –

as a pre-eminent financial capital and trade entrepôt by no means incomparable with twenty-first-century New York – was not invulnerable as generally supposed, but could go under in lethal explosions of human malevolence. This shattered confidence within and impaired for ever a shining reputation without.

Recovery did take place, of course, on public, commercial and private levels, but the city's life as a major centre of Europe, indeed of the world that Europe sought to control, was over. The Fury had done more than burn numerous fine buildings and kill numerous innocent citizens; it had destroyed a whole future. By the time the *Theatrum*'s life had run its course – 1612 – Antwerp was no longer even central to its own arts of cartography and book-production (for all the elegance and productivity of the continuing House of Plantin-Moretus and the involvement with it of Antwerp's great painter-son, Peter Paul Rubens). Too much that was forward-looking and energetic had gone north to Holland, to that new seat of money and trade, power and culture, Amsterdam. From there came achievements and discoveries to match those of Ortelius (a fitting forebear for them) – a tribute not only to new geographical excellences but to the solicited intake of eastern cultures, notably, at last, China and Japan.

Only a matter of days after the Fury, the Pacification of Ghent was agreed by the States General, the united councils of the Low Countries. There came together in common purpose the northern Netherlands provinces of Holland and Zeeland – Protestant, passionately separatist, with the Sea-Beggars' successes to stoke their sense of the righteousness of their cause – and the southern Netherlands provinces of Flanders and Brabant where Catholicism still prevailed despite all, where there was still a nobility nervous of antagonising Spain, and the experience of large-scale suffering was not even yet a memory. Religious freedom was obviously a prime desideratum, but how to arrive at it without incurring further Spanish repression? It was agreed that Protestantism should be permitted in private everywhere, and that all anti-heresy laws must be repealed; that said, Protestant worship in public was only permitted in Zeeland and Holland and thus the separation between the north and south Netherlands, which has survived into the twenty-first century (even if greatly modified), had in effect begun. The Great Rivers were to be the divide that Nature seemed to have designed them to be.

In the vacuum that the obscene horrors of late 1576 had created – horrors that Bruegel in so many of his works had sombrely presaged

– William of Orange strove to bind together the society south of the rivers as he already had that north of it, moving to Brabant to live, even residing in Antwerp itself. He remained in the southern Netherlands until 1583, making the City-on-the-Scheldt a *de facto* anti-Spanish capital.

It has been emphasised throughout this book that both Plantin and Ortelius were thorough-going Antwerpers. The first felt bound to the city by the emotions of adoption; he had chosen Antwerp because he believed in it, he venerated its past and had delighted in the vigour of its present, he had hymned its praises in verse – and had become its greatest entrepreneur who had made money for the community and was now the owner of one of its most illustrious houses. As for Ortelius, personally, intellectually, commercially, he was inextricable from the place. He was even considered (as we've seen) to be 'happy' (LAETUS) in his city (URBS). Their loyalty, far more than to Spain or to William of Orange or to HN's Family or even to the great power-house of the Roman Church, inside which they both continued to remain, was to Antwerp itself, a society, a home of people – and of groups of people – for whom they cared deeply, with whom their beings were bound up. So we shouldn't wonder that Plantin, who had protested his devout Catholicism and loyalty to its regal Spanish upholder, also accommodated himself to William of Orange when he came to the city and wrote verses in *his* honour, or that – as before in his life – he issued from his own printing house books of a Calvinist nature while retaining that cumbersome and imposed title of *Prototypographus*. Nor do I think these activities mutually incompatible. Ortelius and Plantin believed in tolerance. And tolerance means (or should mean) not just accepting but having relationships and doing business with those who think differently from oneself.

In no instances did either man betray any other's confidence or compromise him; their private and societal selves were, without exception, honourable, and in that, their virtuous natures and sincere Christian principles show themselves. Dirk Volckertsz. Coornhert (1522–1590), religious writer, advocate of the inner life (Spiritualism) and of tolerance, memorably took Ortelius to task for being too devoted to the quiet way, to the ordered book-lined study, in inclement times when, if ever, a more active approach was needed.

But when one thinks of the uselessness or the sorry ends of so much confrontationalism, it's tempting to think Ortelius' approach to the life around him – given his nature and particular talents – has a good deal to

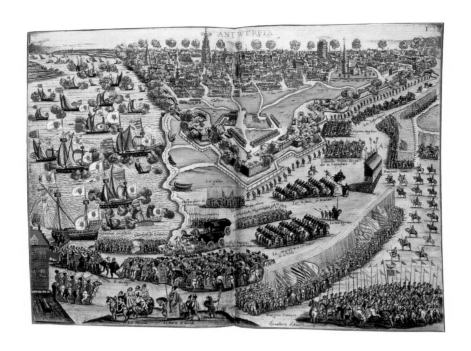

The triumphal entrance of William of Orange and the Duke of Anjou in 1582.

*Frans Hogenberg's engraving of the Spanish and Netherlands armies
in conflict outside Antwerp, 1583.*

be said in its favour; he eschewed violence of all kinds, loathing extremism and aggression, and continuously, unstintingly practised the arts of friendship (which has to include general friendliness).

And for this, even remembering Coornhert, he was to be admired right through to old age. His biographer-to-be, Frans Sweerts (Franciscus Sweertius) the younger, 'apologised' in 1593 for his temerity in writing in the (by this time) wise old man's *Album amicorum*:

> To live well is to live twice over.
> Forgive me, master Ortelius, for having written my name in the album of your friends without having been asked but of my own accord. It's love which attaches me and will always attach me to wise people, which pushes me towards them while I hesitate, I've wanted to say this to you so that you won't be ignorant of it.

And Justus Lipsius, writing in the same book, addressed him as 'Abraham Ortelius, sun not only of your town but of the world' (this is wittier in Latin – *non urbis tuae, sed orbis sol*) 'which you have illustrated with eternal monuments. Justus Lipsius has written these words as a sign of a pious and eternal friendship ... I consider wise those who drink the old wine and who read with pleasure the writings of the ancients. The good glory is that which comes from the Muses.'

CHAPTER
NINETEEN

It was not until 1577/8 that Ortelius took up residence in Antwerp again. The departure of the Spanish garrison from his city had to be described to him in his London exile by his friend, poet, educationalist and Calvinist Pieter Heyns: 'Peace was proclaimed in front of the burned Town-hall, on the stage where they played in 1562 for prizes but which was now hung with tapestry. After this I learned also that, yesterday, the Spaniards had been ordered by beat of drum, to collect, every man under his own banner, to muster and depart. Believing this to be true, I travelled no further, and went to see the stage at Antwerp. The Spaniards, who had stood in battle-array on the market-place, departed quickly, frequently discharging their guns.'

A wonderful moment. Now, as a result of the Pacification of Ghent, and also of the will of an exhausted public, a freer atmosphere, far more conducive to creative activity than for many years, could – and did, if only temporarily – flourish. For the ongoing maps of the *Theatrum* Ortelius worked closely with his friend Filips Galle (whose portrait of him has brought him alive for later generations), and Galle and Pieter Heyns created a pocket edition of the atlas known in Dutch – the first language in which it was produced – as the *Spieghel der werelt* (*Mirror of the world*) and elsewhere as the *Epitome* (reduction to essentials). Heyns, accomplished at such things, wrote a rhyming commentary for it, a popular device for such a book. The *Epitome* was immensely successful, translated into as many languages as the

EPITOME

DV THEATRE DV MONDE,

D'ABRAHAM ORTELIVS.

Auquel se represente, tant par figures que characteres, la vraye
situation, nature, & proprieté de la terre vniuerselle.

Reueu, corrigé, & augmenté de plusieurs Cartes, pour la derniere fois.

A ANVERS,
DE L'IMPRIMERIE PLANTINIENNE,
Pour Philippe Galle.
M.D.XCVIII.

Frontispiece of a French edition of the Epitome, *the pocket version of the* Theatrum,
*maps with a rhyming commentary, an idea thought up by Ortelius' friends Filips
Galle and the poet-translator Pieter Heyns. This enterprise was immensely successful
and went into over thirty editions.*

Theatrum itself, and went into over thirty editions. In England the *Epitome* was even to come out in advance of the *Theatrum*.

More and more maps became available for use, and not only because of Ortelius' energetic solicitation of them. In the tense times before the Pacification many maps had been locked away for reasons of safety; these could be now released, and so Ortelius had much more material at his disposal to include in the *Additamenta* (Additions) of the successive editions of the *Theatrum*. It has already been made clear how important to Ortelius, both as atlas editor and antiquarian, was the subject of placenames; they too are epitomes of past cultures. With his younger bookseller friend from Cologne, Arnold Mylius (1540–1604), he now proceeded to work on a dictionary of them, the *Synonymia geographica* (published in 1578), which, following the lead perhaps of his admired Humphrey Lhuyd, gave to every place chosen its contemporary name, its ancient name, and its vernacular (even slangy) name. This book aroused the admiration of that humanist Antwerp doyen, Plantin's old patron, Alexander Grapheus, who wrote him a Latin poem by way of grateful congratulations. He imagines a meeting between himself (Grapheus) and the god of travelling, Mercury, into whose mouth he puts the following:

> Seeing thee on the cross-road in doubt which way to go, I resolved to make thee acquainted with the *Synonymia* just published by Ortelius. This work will guide thee through all the defiles and windings of the roads, over mountains and rocks, and through valleys, woods and forests; it will enable thee to visit seas, ports, rivers, lakes, cities and all nations of the earth. In this work Ortelius has presented the universe, and has sent forth the gifts of his unwearied genius, as the Scheldt or the Rhine supplies countless people with its never-ceasing waves.

How Ortelius must have relished that comparison with the Scheldt, the river whose power to bring commerce and fertility to his own land and people he had known from the year of his birth!

In 1579 a new edition of the *Theatrum* came out, with a handsome quantity of *Additamenta* (making a grand total now of 93 maps). This time the printer, as well as the paper supplier, was Christophe Plantin. Since Ortelius himself financed the printing, as he had before, *he* should perhaps be considered its 'publisher', though distribution, relations with booksellers and foreign rights would all be handled by Plantin. And with this particularly fine and ample volume we have really reached the end of our story. The two most visionary men of Antwerp's exemplary publishing and intellectual community have now, after many severe trials, united themselves in the interests of a book which has already been hailed over all Europe and begotten emulators. But it could now, with their combined energies, do even better still. By the end of the *Theatrum*'s life it had sold an astonishing (for its time) 7,300 copies, and it's been estimated that Plantin was responsible for the sale of half of these.

The 1579 edition contained a new supplement, the *Parergon* (the word indeed is simply the Greek for 'supplement'). Whereas so far Ortelius has been conspicuous as editor, as a conscientious intelligence operating on other minds' work, for the *Parergon* he himself drew the maps and did so after carrying out his own intense research. 'Geography is the eye of history', he told his readers, it will be recalled. But equally now history was the eye of geography; lands could be seen in terms of what they had once harboured and generated, but which had been obliterated by time, confined to monuments, inscriptions and the books that Ortelius read so voraciously (and no work exhibits the range and intent of his reading more thoroughly than the *Parergon*). He surveys (among much else) Ancient Egypt, Ancient Greece and its islands, Magna Graecia, Etruria, Latium, Gaul under different dispensations, the Pontus Euxinus or Black Sea, the routes of the voyages of Alexander the Great, Aeneas, Ulysses, and Jason and the Argonauts and the foundation of the German Empire in the West.

One is inclined at times to see the concentration on the antique world, on its disasters and successes and final loss of staying power, as born of the sufferings that the Netherlanders had so recently endured – and, from the point of prestige, the southern Netherlanders in particular. For whereas north of the Rivers there was a sense of growth, of building up something new, south of them was a different story. Yet Ortelius still finds much cause for exaltation – though it may be an ambivalent exaltation – as he surveys the world as the century now knows it. In his Introduction to the *Parergon* he returns again to the mystery of so much of it having being closed to the cultural forebears, many of them so illustrious, of himself and his readers:

For every story, before the forenamed Columbus, written in Latin, Greek or any other language, exceeded not the limits of the Roman

The title page of the Parergon, *the historical supplement that Ortelius appended to the first edition of the* Theatrum *to be printed by Plantin, that of 1579. It was included, with revisions and additions, in all subsequent editions.*

Tempe. *This depiction in the* 1579 Parergon *of the Vale of Tempe was Ortelius' own, constructed out of his vast classical reading. Tempe was the Greek paradise located beneath Mount Olympus, the home of the gods. Here, having performed appropriate religious duties, humankind could relax and enjoy merry but innocent pleasures.*

Empire, or the conquests of Alexander the Great (if you shall only except the travels of Marcus Venetus by land, into China …) Whereupon we may see how maimed and imperfect the history of the world is, when as it is very apparent that this part of the earth then known, is scarce a quarter of the whole globe of the world that is now discovered to us. And (which is especially to be considered, rather than to be commended) we may truly say that now, which Cicero in his third oration against Verres wrote most falsely when he said of that age: 'There is now no place within the vast ocean, none so far remote and distant from us, none so obscure or hidden, whither, in these our days, the covetous and bad minds of our men doth not cause them to go.'

Yet one can hear the accents of the reader of Las Casas here – or the listener to accounts from the New World brought to Antwerp itself.

More curiously blended still, however, must both his emotions and his thoughts have been when he felt moved – naturally enough, for obvious reasons – to liken the extent and power of the Roman Empire with that of the Hapsburgs. He has been weighing the former against other Empires of history, with all of which it most favourably compares. Yet when he comes to his own times:

But if you shall compare it with that Monarchy which Charles V Emperor of Rome, within the memories of our fathers established in diverse parts of the world, and Philip his son in our age hath enlarged and shall by looking into an universal map of the Earthly Globe, confer and measure the greatness of this with those others by the eye, you shall plainly and truly discern that this for largeness may not only be preferred far before all those other forenamed, but also even before that of the Romans. The kingdom of the Portugals, after that by diverse navigations they had subdued under their obedience the marine tracts and sea-coasts of East India, together with the islands thereabout if it did reach and were extended up as far within the land as it commandeth about the shore, it might doubtless be accounted none of the least Empires. Seeing now that this also at this day is under the obedience of the said King Philip, who doth not see that this is the greatest that ever was in the world.

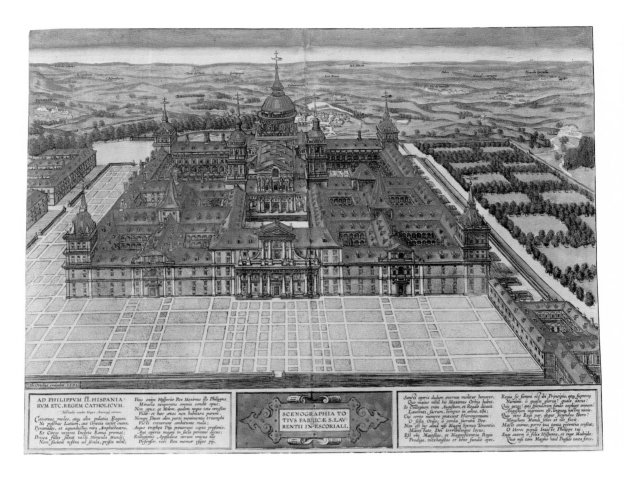

Made by Ortelius in 1591 and accompanied by an encomium in verse to Philip II, this picture of the residence the Spanish king had built for himself at El Escorial is deemed by him to rank with the classical seven wonders of the world – church, monastery, university and palace rolled into one. Bearing in mind the sufferings Ortelius and his fellow Netherlanders had endured at Philip's command, one finds it hard to acquit the Antwerper here of calculated sycophancy.

(In the light of this encomium it isn't perhaps surprising that one of the few nods to the present in the *Parergon* maps is a representation of the 'King's Monastery', Philip's own new palace, splendid and gaunt both at once, of El Escorial, high above the basin in which Madrid lies.)

Certainly to praise Philip's empire for its dimensions (now, as Ortelius reminds us, including, by dint of judicious marriage, Portugal and its colonies) was not to indulge in exaggeration. Ortelius, the student of both the history of empires and of the surface of the Earth, is entitled to his observation, we feel. But when one considers the appalling pressures and pains that this impressive empire had inflicted on his own kin and neighbours (and for that matter on himself), the slaughter, the repressions, the exoduses that were to continue, transferring a whole intelligentsia to the northern Netherlands, one cannot but feel aghast at these words. But then Ortelius was *Royal* Geographer still, just as Plantin was *Prototypographicus Regis*, and maybe both had reason to doubt the ultimate ability of William of Orange to hold on to the south, and of the south itself to maintain any cohesive ideological and political pluralism.

They were right thus to doubt. In 1583 William departed to take up royal residence in Holland, in the Prinsenhof near Delft. What of the south was not directly under Spanish control was exposed to its probable reinstatement.

The tributes to Philip, however, do somewhat vitiate that objectivity of vision we desire in atlas-makers, in geographers and in promoters of the humane arts generally. They cannot have been made in innocence. Whatever Ortelius as a non-Calvinist, closely connected to Spanish intellectuals such as Benito Arias Montano, may have felt about the desirability of an Orange-dominated Protestant hegemony, he was perfectly aware of what the alternative had entailed and would entail. The *politique* nature of Plantin and Ortelius can be easily understood, but I wonder if they can be altogether acquitted of moral compromise. In the same way, just as it is indeed hard to imagine how the atlas could properly have shown the contemporary plights of America and Africa, the distress inflicted by the greedy on the innocent and indigenous of these cruelly plundered continents, it is not impossible to envisage a mentality so fiercely outraged, or so profoundly disillusioned – a Montaigne, to cite a man writing at exactly this time – that at least a tacit attack would be made. This Ortelius could not manage. Nor Plantin, either. Coornhert may have been harsh to chide Ortelius as he did, and we have defended him – but this is not to go wholly along with his extolling of the powerful, who didn't need help, in preference to saying something, to conveying some unforgettable image or fact, that would have highlighted the predicaments of those who really did need it. Truly some work can only be done in the peaceful book-lined study, but one doesn't have to flatter the conqueror outside, not least at the expense of articulations on behalf of the conquered.

But then Plantin and Ortelius themselves, and their families, were soon to come into that category.

In 1583 Ortelius made a tour of the southern Netherlands with his friends Johan Vivianus and Johan Iuliers. Plantin published the edition of Barrefelt's (Hiel's) *Imagines*, that work of pietistic mystical tendency with illustrations by Pieter van der Borcht. The next year Ortelius produced another work on placenames, the *Nomenclatur*, one of his most popular productions, to be reissued repeatedly; it was dedicated to his good friend Mercator. But in the winter of 1584 Spanish forces moved in on Antwerp.

Winter seems to be peculiarly associated with distress in Antwerper history. Eighteen years after the *Beeldenstorm*, eight years after the Spanish Fury, the city suffered again as the winter months harshly drew in. The Spaniards had built forts on either side of the Scheldt, and their commander, the Duke of Parma, spanned them with a bridge of boats. The city was thus under siege, the richest cosmopolitan European nerve-centre enduring weeks which turned into months of cruel cold isolation from the world in which it had played so dominating a part. Its inhabitants went hungry, and the state of demoralisation in which they were forced to go about their daily business can no way have been relieved by the news (in March) of the capitulation of the other great besieged Brabantine city, Brussels, or by the failure of aid forces sent by the States of Holland and Zeeland to make any proper impact on the Spanish. Winter turned into spring, spring turned into summer. Finally, in August, the city surrendered. The sufferings, so long in duration and of so many people, were over at last, but there was no pluralism now to make its restored life correspond either to the best aspects of the past or to still living desiderata. Spanish Catholicism held sway again, and eventually as many as 40,000 Protestant Antwerpers made their way north, to make new lives for themselves where a greater amplitude, a liberty of mental activity was appreciated.

The irenicism of the *Theatrum* had, it might seem, turned out a broken reed. The variegated Low Countries it celebrated was now split in two, the games of the powerful continued, and religion had sundered groups and individuals alike.

Illustration (showing Jacob's Ladder) by Pieter van der Borcht
to Hendrik Barrefelt's Imagines et Figurae Bibliorum.

Plantin continued life and work as a great printer, bequeathing after his death a mighty inheritance, to be ably managed by his Antwerper Catholic son-in-law, Moretus. But as an enterprising humanist publisher, his last years are not remarkable. More and more he was a printer rather than an originator, and a majority of the books he issued promoted the Tridentine outlook. Under Moretus and his son the House became inextricable from Counter Reformation ideology. It was still an important publishing company drawing on a marvellous tradition of printing and production, and it had the tremendous association of Peter Paul Rubens – but multiplicity of endeavour had vanished with the last century. Just as Antwerp itself ceased being a centre of pluriform activity, and indeed, fading like Alexandria before it, had to wait until the nineteenth century for recovery of vigour and civic creativity.

Though on the surface a successful, eminently prosperous man, Plantin in his last years was weighed down with unremitting and serious money worries which ate into his peace of body as well as peace of mind.

Ortelius' life was ordered, sociable, busy; always he occupied himself with getting new maps, and his eliciting from the Portuguese priest and authority on China and Japan, Father Texeira, his finest cartographic work was a triumph indeed. While he never ceased to add new friends to his cast of distinguished old ones, emotionally he was devoted above all others to his nephew Ortelianus, whom he made his heir. (The younger's Calvinism prevented him from coming back to Antwerp to claim his inheritance.)

In 1593 Ortelius' intimate friend Joris Hoefnagel, whose artistry had long delighted him, made a picture, known as the *Hermathena*, which he dedicated to him. Indeed Ortelius himself is its subject. In the very middle, lengthways, of this painting we see a tome supporting a globe on which perches a bird. The book is the *Theatrum*. The globe – which has given the book its subject matter and on which the outlines of Europe, Africa and the Near East can be discerned – sprouts branches, unmistakably the olive-branches of peace. The bird is Athena's owl, wisdom embodied, commandingly rendered by Hoefnagel with one talon (its left) on the globe, the right one clasping one of the objects most associated with Hermes: a caduceus, a white wand which Roman officers would carry with them when pursuing a peaceful course. Entwined round the caduceus are three snakes, to arouse thoughts in us of that O which connotes eternity and is the shape of the Earth, and the symbol for (perpetual) meetings of male and female

Hermathena *by Joris Hoefnagel (1542–1601). Dated 1593, this allegorical picture amounts to a spiritual portrait of Ortelius through an assemblage of items of esoteric significance. The title unites the name of Hermes (see his caduceus) and Athene (see her owl), their respective qualities of peace and wisdom together making up the* Harmonia Mundi *('Harmony of the World'). Ortelius' cartographical instruments occupy the foreground.*

(and, of course, the initial letter of Ortelius' own surname). On closer inspection the rod of the caduceus is seen to be a paintbrush, and now on either side of the book/globe/owl we can find other paintbrushes, together with a pot for mixing paint and a geometer's instruments – compasses, a T-square. These show more memorably than any words could have done the fusion of the artistic and the scientific which informed Ortelius' work. Scattered among these objects are shells, in esoteric terms emblemising the body from which the soul has departed – the soul being responsible for artistic creation and scientific discovery alike. Soul has other representatives in this picture: the two huge butterflies (to English eyes they are 'moths'), depicted with a Dürer-like fidelity and standing on the extreme left and extreme right of the picture. They – in contrast to the shells – represent the immortal parts of our being, yet psyche too has to evolve (caterpillar and larva are shown) and has to undergo death (portrayed here as a long-legged dragonfly able to seize victims at will).

Standing back from the *Hermathena* we find depicted in it a largely harmonious personality, one which, though put to harsh tests by the times, suffers from no significant conflict between concerns for the arts, the sciences and spiritual faith. Yet it would be wrong to entertain a picture of an unworldly man, even from this work; his portraits show him aglow with intelligence, of the kind that transcends the petty, yet he also looks sharp, astute. As indeed he was. He came to maturity in a commercial milieu; one of the main (and highly developed) qualities he shared with Plantin was an ability to understand a business situation in all its potentials and problems. Perhaps it was this, though, from which he was never quite sufficiently to break away, which keeps his achievement from being of the very greatest rank and somewhat mars its legacy, indispensable and admirable though it undoubtedly is. And the consequences of this inability leave a look of sadness on his refined and thoughtful face.

His later years brought him both the contentments of what one might call the active contemplative, and the inevitable sorrows of this stage of life of losing those dear to him. On 26 December 1594 Arnold Mylius wrote to him from Cologne: 'Gerardus Mercator died on the 2nd inst. about midday sitting in a chair as if about to take a nap before the fire.' Only a week later his beloved Ortelianus wrote to him informing him that his own young wife had just died. Ortelius searched how best to comfort the person he loved best in the world: 'Most honourable and dearest nephew, I grieve with you because you are grieving. I have no other cause for sorrow. For what has happened contrary to nature? or even expectation? It was perfectly known to you beforehand that you would some day cause this sorrow to your dear one or she to you. I hope therefore you will bear it with a tranquil mind.'

His faith was perhaps increasingly informed by a Senecan Stoicism, though he was at pains to tell his nephew in another letter that much as he admired the Latin writer, the central Christian teachers were dearer to him still.

On 24 January 1598 Ortelius expressed a wish that Ortelianus might come and live with him in Antwerp, something politically he was quite unable to do. He would be rich as a result, he promised him, he had been a most successful man fiscally. 'Farewell, I write no more for I am dying from day to day.'

In fact he survived another six months. On 7 July Filips Galle wrote to his cousin Emmanuel: 'I therefore inform you that the pious Abraham Ortelius died and rested in the Lord on June 28 and was very decently buried in the Church of St Michael, mourned by many good people who still wished him to live; but his course was to end; he has suffered much pain. His kidneys and many other parts of his body, as the spleen and lung were diseased. He is at rest, we still moving.'

That comparatively recent friend, Frans Sweerts, in his brief biography perhaps gives us the most living and concise account of Ortelius, of the flavour of him as he was known to his contemporaries and fellow citizens:

In company he behaved modestly, courteously and had a pleasant and merry posture. Such was his singular humaneness, that it was surprising to see how easily he won and retained the love and respect of whoever he met. As far as his enemies were concerned, he preferred to meet them with kindness or ignore them, rather than revenge himself because of their malice. He so much hated vice, also in those close to him, that he preferred to appreciate the virtue even in enemies and strangers. Vain questions and empty disputations about divinity or religious disputes he detested and abhorred as being dangerous and pernicious. He preferred deep insight and sound judgement above flattering eloquence or quaint terminology. If dangers or adversity came his way and closed in on him, he endured them with patience, rather than to show any fears. Events that were bitter he endured more successfully than those that were uncertain and hard to assess. During his entire life he was as unselfish as any man could be. He never set his mind on the riches of this world or any of those matters, always keeping in mind the saying CONTEMNO ET ORNO, MENTE, MANU [I scorn and adorn with mind and hand]. Surely this man had some heavenly guidance which withdrew him so completely from everyday worries, that the worst and most upsetting thing that might happen to him was to be interrupted from studying his books, which he preferred above anything in the world. [A list of these follows, many of them familiar by now to the readers of this book.] With all these people and many others he was familiarly acquainted, to these he often wrote and from these he often received kind and respectful letters. He was a great student of antiquities, and collected rare and ancient objects. He had at home in his house images, statues, coins of gold, silver, and copper of the Greeks, Romans and others. Shells, brought from India, and from our antipodes. Marble of all colours. Tortoise shells, some so marvellously large that ten men, sitting around them, might at once eat. Others again so small that they were hardly as large as a pin's head. His library was so well-stocked with all kinds of books that his house might truly be called a shop of all manner of learning, to which men flocked from everywhere, like they did in former times to Plato's Library or Aristotle's Lyceum.

... Being busied in this manner, and having lived now for 71 years, he fell sick in the year of our Lord 1598 and getting worse every day, he finally yielded to nature and died on the 28th day of that month. The physicians declared that he died of an ulcer of the kidneys which Hippocrates writes will hardly ever be cured in old men. In serious business he was very grave and sober, but without any show of arrogant disdain.

His devoted sister did not survive him long. Anne, who had kept house for him, coloured maps for him, including those of the *Theatrum*, and managed his business in his absence, died in 1600.

CONTEMNO ET ORNO – the motto found so fitting for Ortelius is surely one that brings the writer or artist to mind more than the man of science, even though the *Hermathena* shows the geographer as intent on their union. Though such experts as Peter Leurer have rightly insisted that Ortelius was

Portrait of Ortelius by Filips Galle, used in the later Plantin-published editions of the Theatrum.

far more informed and 'insider' as a cartographer than he is often given credit for, it is not among the great map-makers as such that he should be counted. Nor can he be considered an especially effective political or religious presence in his age, since in the end his Nicodemist *politique* position, his aversion to standing up and being counted, must be associated with capitulation – however reluctant and honourable – to power. He was a distinguished collector and antiquarian, yet he was more than either of these vocations, for all their merits, suggest. His *Theatrum*, when all's said and done, effected a change in our world – and of how many other creations can that be claimed? – more in the domain of the human imagination than in those of physical or public activity, but by no means wholly remote from these.

In my view, if we are looking for a context in which, by way of closing, to see Ortelius and his *Theatrum*, we should go to that humanist tradition he was so proud of entering and to its specifically Netherlands manifestation. We should turn (if not exactly for his peers then for his most appropriate companions) not to Peter Apian or Gemma Frisius or Gerard Mercator but to Erasmus and Bruegel, two artists – for the first was that too – concerned with showing forth their vision of humanity in *sui generis* forms, just as the *Theatrum* wasn't like any other book that had hitherto appeared.

In a letter to a fictitious friend, referring to the spiritual tyranny of his schooldays, Erasmus commented: 'Human felicity consists above all in this, that a man should devote himself to what he is fitted by nature. There are men whom one would compel to adopt celibacy or the monastic life with no more success than one would enter an ass for a race at Olympia or take an ox (as they say) to the wrestling school.' So much of what gave him his unique role in the culture of his times is present in these very personal lines: the all-but-instinctual dismissal of cant and lip-service piety in the interests of a more realistic approach to human beings, even to the admission that for most of us a certain amount of home-comfort and bodily satisfaction is necessary for happiness, and that all those artificial rules and shibboleths, all the complex clutter of ancient institutions are not of primary relevance to the education of the mind – or even of the (Christian) soul.

The same spirit permeates what has become – since his lifetime – Erasmus' most enduring book, *Praise of Folly* (begun in 1509, published 1511) – *Moriae Encomium* in Greek, the title punning on the surname of Erasmus' loved friend, Thomas More, and *Stultitiae Laus* in Latin, the language in which it first achieved its fame.

Praise of Folly, so bold and simple in design, is the production of an extraordinary mind which persuades you to see clearly what the duller, timider vision is content to overlook or view only blurredly in the world all round about. And it is the whole world that is its real subject. It's a closely wrought piece in three progressive but linked movements. Folly – 'silliness' would surely be for the most part an apter translation of the Greek or Latin term – begins by presenting herself as ubiquitous – and even beneficently creative. Doesn't silliness play a major part both in the coming together of men and women, and in their conjunctions, responsible after all for the very propagation of the human race? Can we imagine it otherwise, and would we wish to? Silliness is – yes – quite indispensable here. But, people will say, don't concentrate on activities that involve the body, notorious for its defiance of reason, think instead of friendship, of social life. Well, says Erasmus' mouthpiece, 'Go to! Conniving at your friends' vices, passing them over, being blind to them and deceived by them, even loving and admiring your friends' egregious faults as if they were virtues – does not this seem pretty close to folly? ... For the greater number of mankind play the fool; nay, there is no one who does not dote in many ways; and close friendship grows up only between equals.'

Self-love is another manifestation of Folly's universal presence. It's inextricable from anybody trying to forge a path for him- or herself in this world; we couldn't in truth survive without a measure of it. But self-love, often innocent and even comical enough in its expression, shades all too easily into self-importance, a far more destructive and ugly attribute, an overrating of one's own moral or intellectual qualities, with concomitant (and often cultivated) indifference to those of others. Almost all professions provide salutary examples of this.

Now the tone of the work becomes darker. Though the wit is as lively as before, it becomes increasingly barbed and painfully piercing. The religious, the literary, the academic, the scientific, courtiers, lawyers, churchmen, merchants all exhibit what Erasmus terms *Philautia* (love of self), thus putting obstacles in the course of the desirable free and harmonious intercourse among humans: 'But the most foolish and sordid of all are your merchants, in that they carry on the most sordid business of all and this by the most sordid methods; for on occasions they lie, they perjure themselves, they steal, they cheat, they impose on the public. Yet they make themselves men of importance – because they have gold rings on their fingers. Nor do they lack for flattering friars who admire them and call them Right Honourable in public, with the purpose, surely, that some little driblet from the ill-gotten gains may flow to themselves.'

And have the only too present theologians helped to cope with this second aspect of Janus-faced Folly? No more than the men of politics and the court have they done so, their conceit having made them crippledly self-referential, caught up with proving to their and their allies' satisfaction their own cleverness in disputes of their own making, ever more divorced from the interests (or comprehension) of ordinary humanity. They can surely be shown up by invocation of the very highest: 'The apostles knew the mother of Jesus, but who, among them, has demonstrated philosophically just how she was kept clear from the sin of Adam, as our theologians have done? Peter received the keys, received them from One who did not commit them to an unworthy person, and yet I doubt that he ever understood – for Peter never did attain to subtlety – that a person who did not have knowledge could have the key to knowledge ... They worshipped, to be sure, but in spirit, following no other teaching than that of the Gospel, "God is a spirit, and they that worship Him must worship Him in spirit and in truth."'

But for the last part Erasmus makes a most extraordinary and moving reversal of all this. The multiple folly he has just been dealing with has been found among the worldly, among members of the pivotal institutions or those conducting the conventionally approved traffic of rational society, and real folly it has been seen to be. To move away from the ways of the world would be accounted by such slaves to *Philautia* as folly indeed, but try to do so and Janus will swing round and display a virtuous, shining face again. Can't we find homage to Folly not only in classical writers but in the Bible itself? Didn't Christ Himself speak of foolishness, and by doing so exalt the foolish above the wise, especially the worldly wise – the little children, the sheep whom He loved? Following such a teacher, submitting yourself to such risky, unworldly exhortations as the Sermon on the Mount – these could indeed (and have been) thought Silliness/Folly. And just look at men and women at their religious devotions, lost in the ecstasies of communion with Christ, with God. Don't they really look rather crazy, and yet who is happier or more blessed than they?

Praise of Folly is an organic intellectual entity, moving to a conclusion that is as beautiful a celebration of the personal transports of the soul as any written before or since, the more beautiful for being something of a surprise conclusion. Nevertheless, I dare to say that its first part, its *Typus* or world map if you like, presenting the spectacle of humdrum humanity, without doubt often extremely foolish, extremely *silly*, but amusing, interesting, curious, diverse, even lovable, is the most revolutionary, the most forward-pointing. The world lies before us, pluralist, not easy to bring to uniformity let alone justice or judgement. It is what interferes with the varieties of humanities – all the puffed-up priests and lawyers and unscrupulous tycoons – who are the danger, who offend God's creation, not the varieties themselves. One can't expect perfection in any human. Listen to Erasmus on what a model of sense and rectitude would be like:

> Well, if they want it so, I give them joy of this wise man of theirs. They may love him with no fear of a rival, and may live with him in Plato's republic, or, if they prefer, in the world of ideas, or in the gardens of Tantalus. For who would not startle at such a man, as at an apparition or ghost, and shun him? He would be insensible to any natural sympathy, no more moved by feelings of love or pity than as if he were solid flint or Marpesian stone. Nothing gets by him; he never makes a mistake; … there is nothing he does not see; he measures everything with a standard rule … Who would not prefer just anyone from the middle ranks of human foolhood, who, being a fool, would be better prepared either to command fools or obey them; who would please those like himself, that is, nearly everyone; who would be kind to his wife, welcome to his friends, a boon companion, an acceptable dinner-guest; and lastly, who would consider nothing human to be alien to him.

True and profound and comforting. And Erasmus operates on an international scale:

> And now I see that it is not only in individual men that nature has implanted self-love. She implants a kind of it as a common possession in the various races, and even cities. By this token the English claim, besides a few other things, good looks, music, and the best eating as their special properties. The Scots flatter themselves on the score of high birth and royal blood, not to mention their dialectical skill. Frenchmen have taken all politeness for their province; though the Parisians, brushing all others aside, also award themselves the prize

for knowledge of theology. The Italians usurp *belles lettres* and eloquence; and they all flatter themselves upon the fact that they alone, of all mortal men, are not barbarians. In this particular point of happiness the Romans stand highest, still dreaming pleasantly of ancient Rome. The Venetians are blessed with a belief in their own nobility ... The Spaniards yield to no one in martial reputation. Germans take pride in their great stature and their knowledge of magic.

This book will have been written to no purpose if a kinship between the point of view expressed here and that informing Ortelius in his life and in the *Theatrum* isn't immediately evident.

This rejoicing in the diversity of humanity, the rightness of that diversity for all the ugliness and grossness and vice, also informs the most popular masterpieces of Pieter Bruegel. We are speaking now of the paintings for which Bruegel first knew fame, for which he earned the grossly limiting sobriquet of 'Peasant Piet', the author not of the mysterious later symbolical works (though of far closer kin to these than was for years appreciated) but of the *Flemish Proverbs*, the *Children's Games*, the *Wedding Dance*, the *Peasant Dance*. 'The people [of Brabant] are so jocund,' said Ortelius. Bruegel was one of the world's first great celebrants of landscape for its intrinsic interest. But in the above works, it seems to me, he was doing something excitingly new and needed: he was making of human behaviour – in its many bewildering varieties, distressing, comic, sexy, isolated and onanistic or downright gregarious and playful – a landscape. He abolishes the dichotomy between the natural scene and the human subject that has bedevilled us so since. Bruegel is logical and right, because only on the loneliest deserts or tundras are humans not a feature of the physical world that has produced them (and even humans see and feel). The appreciator of woods and fields and clouds and seas must appreciate human beings too; the artist curious about human nature must not, should not, ignore the elements or the intricacies and mysteries of the creature, plant and mineral worlds.

Ortelius is the consort of Bruegel here; his *Theatrum* is a celebration of the many-sidedness, the irreduceability of this world of ours. He is interested in its lands, their contours, their natural beauties and phenomena and in the ways of their inhabitants. His is not a heroic vision of life, just as his wasn't a heroic temperament. The human beings he

Frontispiece to the 1636 Hondius edition of Gerard Mercator's atlas (actually called by this name).

describes on the versos of the maps are on the whole a motley lot, concerned with commerce, indulging in conventions and customs, and the lands he has portrayed are the homes for such beings, whether mountainous or wooded, fertile or desert – the habitations they were born into. Though by no means a foreigner to the mystic outlook, essentially his vision of life was one of quiet acceptance, always interested, sometimes joyful, often sad. He was a good man and the *Theatrum* is itself a work of goodness. Superseded by Mercator's great *Atlas* shortly after his death, it can also ultimately not match the enormous attainment of the society that replaced his own in its cartographic and geographical zeal, that of the northern Netherlands: the monumental atlases of the Blauws. But as a work of art the *Theatrum*, a decidedly southern Netherlands triumph, is quite imperishable.

Zachary Heyns (1566–1638), Pieter's son, wrote: 'As virtue leads us to the celestial paradise, so Ortelius leads us inside the world.' He was right; he does, does so still.

SELECT BIBLIOGRAPHY

APOLLONIUS OF RHODES: *The Voyage of Argo* (translated by E.V. Rieu) London 1959

BAGROW, L.: *Abrahami Ortelii catalogus cartographorum* London 1928–30

——(with Skelton R.A.): *The History of Cartography* London 1964

BARZUN, Jacques: *From Dawn to Decadence – 1500 to the Present: 500 Years of Western Cultural Life* New York 2000

BRAUDEL, Fernand: *The Mediterranean and the Mediterranean World in the Age of Philip II* (translated by Siân Reynolds) Berkeley 1995

BÜTTNER, Nils: 'Abraham Ortelius comme collectionneur' Brussels-Antwerp 1998

COCKSHAW, Pierre and de NAVE, Francine (editors): *Abraham Ortelius 1527–1598 cartographe et humaniste* Brussels-Antwerp 1998

COLUMBUS, Christopher: *Four Voyages* (translated by J.M. Cohen) London 1969

COOLS, Hans: 'Tabula Rasa: the Iconoclastic Fury in the Low Countries' in Volume 10 of *The Low Countries* (q.v. under STICHTING ONS ERFDEEL)

CRANE, Nicholas: *Mercator, the Man who Mapped the Planet* London 2002

CUMMING, W.P., SKELTON, R.A. and QUINN, D.B.: *The Discovery of North America* London 1971

DEKESEL C.D.: 'Abraham Ortelius; numismate' Brussels-Antwerp 1998

DE LAS CASAS, Bartolomé: *Short Account of the Destruction of the Indies* (edited and translated by Nigel Griffin) London 1992

DENUCÉ, J.: *Oud-Nederlandsche kaartmakers in betrekking met Plantijn* (new edition) Amsterdam 1964

DEPUYDT, Dr Joost: 'Le cercle d'amis et de correspondants autour d'Abraham Ortelius' Brussels-Antwerp 1998

DILKE, O.A.W.: *Greek and Roman Maps* London 1985

DUVOSQUEL, Jean-Marie and de GEEST, Joost (editors): *Le Cartographe Gerard Mercator 1512–94* Brussels 1994

ELKHADEM, Hossam (editor and contributor): *Gerard Mercator en de Geografie in de Zuidelijke Nederlanden* Antwerp 1994

——'La naissance d'un concept: Le Theatrum Orbis Terrarum d'Ortelius' Brussels-Antwerp 1998

EISENSTEIN, Elizabeth L.: *Printing Revolution in Early Modern Europe* London 1983

ERASMUS, Desiderius: *Praise of Folly* (translated by Hoyt H. Hudson) London 1998

FERNÁNDEZ-ARMESTO, Felipe: *Civilizations* London 2000

FOSSIER, Robert (editor and major contributor): *The Cambridge Illustrated History of The Middle Ages Volume 3* Cambridge 1987

GEYL, Pieter: *Debates With Historians* The Hague 1955

——*History of the Low Countries* London 1964

GIROUARD, Mark: *Cities and People* New Haven and London 1985

HALE, John: *Civilization of Europe in the Renaissance* London 1993

HAMILTON, Alastair (editor): 'Seventeen Letters from Hendrik Jansen van Barrefelt (Hiel) to Jan Moretus' Antwerp 1979

——*The Family of Love* Cambridge 1981

——'The Family of Love in Antwerp' Antwerp 1987

——*Cronica. Ordo Sacerdotis. Acta HN: Three Texts on the Family of Love* Leiden 1988

HESSELS, J.H.: *Abrahami Ortelii (geographi Antverpiensis) et virorum eruditorum ad eundem et ad Jacobum Colium Ortelianum... epistulae* Cambridge 1887

HIBBERT, Arthur and OEHME, Ruthardt: *Old European Cities: Maps and Texts from Civitates Orbis Terrarum of G. BRAUN and F. HOGENBERG* London 1955

HODGKISS, Alan: *Understanding Maps: A Systematic History of Their Use and Development* Folkestone 1981

HOSKIN, Michael (editor): *The Cambridge Illustrated History of Astronomy* Cambridge 1997

HOURANI, Albert: *A History of the Arab Peoples* London 1991

HUIZINGA, Johan: *The Waning of the Middle Ages* London 1924

——*Erasmus of Rotterdam* London 1952

——*Dutch Civilisation in the 17th Century* London 1968

IMHOF, Dirk: *De wereld in kaart: Abraham Ortelius en de eerste atlas* Antwerp 1998

ISRAEL, Jonathan I.: *The Dutch Republic 1477–1806: Its Rise, Greatness and Fall* Oxford 1995/1998

JARDINE, Lisa: *Erasmus, Man of Letters* Princeton 1993

KARROW, R.W. Jr: *Mapmakers of the Sixteenth Century and Their Maps. Bio-Bibliographies of the Cartographers of Abraham Ortelius, 1570* Chicago 1993

KOEMAN, Cornelis: *The History of Abraham Ortelius and his Theatrum Orbis Terrarum* Lausanne 1964

——*Atlantes neerlandici: Bibliography of Terrestrial, Maritime and Celestial Atlases and Pilot Books, Published in the Netherlands up to 1990* Amsterdam 1967–1970

LISTER, Raymond: *Old Maps and Globes* London 1979

LYNAM, Edward: *The first engraved atlas of the world, the Cosmographia of Claudius Ptolemaeus, Bologna 1477* London 1941

MANGANI, Giorgio: *La signification providentielle du Theatrum orbis terrarum* Brussels-Antwerp 1998

MEEUS, Prof. Dr Hubert: 'Abraham Ortelius et Peeter Heyns' Brussels-Antwerp 1998

MENZIES, Gavin: *1421, the Year China Discovered the World* London 2002

MEURER, P.H.: *Fontes Cartographici Orteliani. Das 'Theatrum Orbis Terrarum' von Abraham Ortelius und seine Kartenquellen* Weinheim 1991

——'Abraham comme cartographe' Brussels-Antwerp 1998

MORE, Thomas: *Utopia* (edited by Susan Bruce) Oxford 1999

de NAVE, Francine and VOET, Leon: *Plantin-Moretus Museum – Antwerp* Antwerp 1989/1995

PAGANI, Lelio (editor): *Claudii Ptolemaei Cosmographia Tabulae* Torriana/Leicester 1990

PING Yan (editor): *China in Ancient and Modern Maps* London 1998

POLO, Marco: *Travels* (translated by Ronald Latham) London 1958

PURAYE, Jean (editor): *ABRAHAM ORTELIUS: Album amicorum* Amsterdam 1967

SABBE, M.: *L'oeuvre de Christophe Plantin et de ses successeurs* Brussels 1937

SARAIVA, José Hermano: *Portugal, a Companion History* Manchester 1997

SCHAMA, Simon: *The Embarrassment of Riches: An Interpretation of Dutch Culture in the Golden Age* London 1987

——*Rembrandt's Eyes* London 1999

SKELTON, R.A.: *Explorers' Maps: Chapters in Cartographic Record of Geographical Discovery* London 1958

——*Ortelius' Theatrum: Facsimile edition with commentary* Amsterdam/Antwerp 1964

——*Decorative Printed Maps of the 15th to 18th Centuries* London 1966

——*Maps, a Historical Survey of their Study and Collecting* Chicago 1972

SMITH, Michael E.: *The Aztecs* Oxford 1996

STICHTING ONS ERFDEEL: *The Low Countries: Art and Society in Flanders and the Netherlands* (Volumes 1–10 inclusive) Rekkem 1992–2002

THOMAS, Hugh: *The Slave Trade: The History of the Atlantic Slave Trade 1440–1870* New York 1997

VAN DEN BROECKE, M.P.R.: *Ortelius Atlas Maps: An Illustrated Guide* Utrecht 1996

——, VAN DER KROGT, P. and MEURER, P.H. (editors): *Ortelius and the First Atlas* Utrecht 1998

VANDENBROECK, Paul (editor and contributor): *The Fascinating Faces of Flanders* Antwerp 1999

VANDERPUTTE, O., VINCENT, P. and HERMANS, T.: *Dutch, the Language of twenty million Dutch and Flemish people* Rekkem 1997

VOET, Leon: *The Golden Compasses. A history and evaluation of the printing and publishing activities of the Officina Plantiniana at Antwerp in two volumes: I. Christophe Plantin and the Moretuses, their lives and their world; II. The management of a printing and publishing house in Renaissance and Baroque* Amsterdam-London-New York 1969–72

VOET, Leon and VOET-GRISOLLE, J.: *The Plantin Press (1555–1589): A Bibliography of the Works printed and published by Christopher Plantin at Antwerp and Leiden* Amsterdam 1967–1970

VÖHRINGER, Christian: *Pieter Bruegel* Cologne 1999

WALLIS, Helen M. and ROBINSON, Arthur H. (editors): *Cartographical Innovations* London 1987

WHITFIELD, Peter: *Images of the World: 20 Centuries of World Maps* London 1994

——*New Found Lands: Maps in the History of Exploration* London 1998

——*Mapping the World* London 2000

ACKNOWLEDGEMENTS

Ifirst must thank St Antony's College, Oxford, for making me a Senior Associate Member and so enabling me for two academic terms to work steadily and peacefully at this project. I particularly thank there Dr Theodore Zeldin who has encouraged my work. Also in Oxford Dr Christopher Brown, director of the Ashmolean, was much help.

I owe a great debt to His Excellency Lode Willems, the Belgian Ambassador to the Court of St James, for facilitating studies in Belgium without which this book could never have been realised. In particular the Ministerie van de Vlaamse Gemeenschap were generous with money and administrative arrangements, organising for me extensive visits to places and institutions and meetings with experts. The Ministry's Chris De Hondt provided an invaluable service here.

Pride of place among Belgian institutions has to go to the Museum Plantin-Moretus en Stedelijk Prentenkabinet in Antwerp, surely one of the finest individual museums anywhere. I thank its director, Francine de Nave, and also Dirk Imhof of its book and print assemblages (for both his learning and for an act of remarkable thoughtfulness to me), Pierre Meulepas for his many kindnesses, Maria Flechten at its excellent library, and photographer Peter Maes for his work at the museum on our behalf. In Antwerp I benefited inestimably from my conversations with Dr Paul Huvenne, director of the Koninklijk Museum voor Schone Kunsten (KMSKA), Dr Hans Nieuwdorp, director of the Museum Mayer van den Bergh, and Daniel Christianson of the Maagdenhuis, and at Antwerp's university UFSIA Prof. Dr Guido Marnef, Prof. Dr Hubert Meeus and Dr Joost Depuydt, now of the Katholieke Universiteit, Leuven. At Leuven itself a meeting with Dr Chris Coppens of the university library's rare and old printed books department was extremely helpful.

Like all who have concerned themselves with sixteenth-century maps and atlases I am greatly indebted to Professor Dr Hossam Elkhadem, head of cartography at the Koninklijke Bibliotheek/Bibliothèque Royale de Belgique in Brussels, who not only spared me much time but provided me handsomely with books and offprints. At the same institution I have to thank also Mr Bart Op de Beeck, head of the Division of Valuable Works. Mrs Helena Bussers, head of the department of Old Art at Brussels' Koninklijke Musea voor Schone Kunsten/Musée des Beaux Arts provided interesting information and much-appreciated guides.

At Sint-Niklaas I was received with real consideration for my intellectual needs by Mrs Greet Polfliet and Mr Alfred van der Gucht, of the Mercator Museum and the Koninklijke Oudheidkundige Kring van het Land van Waas.

The Stichting Ons Erfdeel is an organisation devoted to the Netherlands and Flanders heritage and produces a yearbook that is a matchless source of facts and ideas. Its director, Luc Devoldere, has, during the course of my work on *Imagined Corners*, become a cherished friend, and he and his wife Hildegard have given me much-appreciated hospitality. The same is true of Tiziano Perez of the Nederlands Literair Produktie – en Vertalingenfonds (Foundation for the Promotion and Translation of Dutch Literature) and his partner Marijke. Tiziano also made possible for me useful periods in a Dutch-speaking and -studying environment, Het Vertalershuis (Translators' House), in Amsterdam. In the Netherlands I found stimulation for my project from talk with internationally distinguished writers Margriet de Moor, Connie Palmen, Midas Dekkers, Rutger Kopland, Arthur Japin and Marcel Möring, and from the company of Dr Anthony Paul and his partner, Olga.

Alastair Hamilton, Professor of the History of Ideas at Leiden University, has been the most stimulating and personally considerate of expert guides to the period and society under review. Discussion with Dr Peter Barber, head of the map department of the British Library, made for much clarification and information; and many thanks go to Dr Anne Woollett of the Getty Museum in Los Angeles, USA. I must also express my gratitude to the following friends for help of many and needed kinds – Mark Todd, Jaroslav Izavčuk (who acted as an indispensable amanuensis during the summer of 2001), Stephen and Ljuba Morris, Richard Mallette, Jonathan Gathorne-Hardy and Nicky Loutit, Hugh and Mirabel Cecil, and Paul and Jean Nicholls of Ludlow who, during a time of domestic difficulties, gave me a room in their house to work in.

I am extremely grateful to my agent Christopher Sinclair-Stevenson, and at Headline to the book's commissioning editor, Heather Holden-Brown, and to Lorraine Jerram. Mia Stewart-Wilson has proved the most imaginative of picture researchers. Matthew Parker has given the text the kind of intelligent editorial attention all writers require and rejoice in.

PICTURE CREDITS

The publishers would like to thank all those who have kindly given permission to use the illustrations on the pages listed:

210 www.antiquarianimages.com; **216–7** Royal Geographical Society, London; **226** Royal Geographical Society, London; **230–1** Royal Geographical Society, London; **233** cartouche from map on page 247; **236** Museum Plantin-Moretus, Antwerp/Peter Maes; **241** Royal Geographical Society, London; **247** Museum Plantin-Moretus, Antwerp/Peter Maes; **249** AKG London; **254** cartouche from image on page 286; **257** Museum Plantin-Moretus, Antwerp/Peter Maes; **260** detail from map on page 249; **264** AKG London; **267** Museum Plantin-Moretus, Antwerp/Peter Maes; **269** cartouche from image on page 284; **270** AKG London; **272** AKG London; **277** *top* AKG London/British Library *bottom* Man.1555.a.4 British Library, London; **279** detail from map on pages 230–1; **280** Museum Plantin-Moretus, Antwerp/Peter Maes; **283** www.antiquarianimages.com; **284** www.antiquarianimages.com; **286** AKG London; **289** Museum Plantin-Moretus, Antwerp/Peter Maes; **291** Museum Plantin-Moretus, Antwerp/Peter Maes; **295** Royal Geographical Society, London; **301** www.antiquarianimages.com; **303**, **308**, **310** cartouche from image on page 17.

INDEX

Note: Page numbers in *italic* denote illustrations, '(m)' denotes a map or maps and/or (where applicable) the accompanying *Theatrum* text. The letter *c* appended to a page number denotes text in captions to illustrations. English map titles only are indexed. Maps in lists are indexed only if discussed elsewhere in the text.

Additamenta (*Theatrum*) 281
Aegidius (Gillis Hooftman) 68, 73–4, 76–8, 87
Africa: maps 31, 187, 188, 190, 227, *230–31*, 248; in *Theatrum* frontispiece 209, *210*, 212–14
Akbar (Mughal emperor) 213
al-Khwarismi (mathematician) 193
Album amicorum (of Ortelius) 29, 44, 72, 74, 209, 255–6, 278
Alexander the Great 177
Alexandria 176–7, 179, 192
Alva, Ferdinand Alvarez de Toledo, Duke of 154, 156–8, *157*, 196, 262
Americas 218–20, 243–5; maps *see* maps; in *Theatrum* frontispiece 209, *210*, 214–19
Anabaptism 55–8, *see also* Family of Love; Protestantism; religion
Anna of Saxony 123
Antwerp 7–18; *Beeldenstorm* (Iconoclastic Fury) *142*, 143–6, 149; commercial centre 9–11, 43; cultural centre 5–6, 11–15; other conflicts 263, *277*, 288; pictures and maps of *vi–1*, 8, 15–16, *17*, 21, *115*, 195–6, *198*; Spanish Fury 269–75, *270*, *272*
Apian, Peter (Petrus Apianus) 35, 36
Apollonius of Rhodes 180–81
Arab map-making 193
Argonautica (Apollonius of Rhodes) 180–81
Aristotle 179, 182
Arnolfini and His Wife (van Eyck) 48
Arsenius, Ambrosius 125
Arsenius, Ferdinand 125
Asia: maps 77, 84, 152, 190, 227, 245–6, *247*; in *Theatrum* frontispiece 209, *210*, 212, 213
Atlantic Ocean (m)31
atlases 222; Lafreri's 85–7; Mercator's 85, 128–9, *301*;

Ortelius' for Gillis Hooftman 76–9, 87; *Theatrum see Theatrum orbis terrarum*
Aventinus, Joannes 171
Aztecs 237, 238

Baldin, Clement 107
Barbary and Biledulgerid (m)248, *249*
Barrefelt, Hendrik Jansen van *267*, 268, 288, *289*
Bavaria (m)171, 172
Beans, George 87
Becanus, Joannes Goropius 116, 118, 148, 154
Beeldenstorm (Iconoclastic Fury) 141–6, *142*, 149
Behaim, Martin 31, 194
Belon, Pierre 125
Beuckelsz, Jan (Jan of Leyden) 56
Bible 20, 21, 159–60, 161, 266
Biblia Polyglotta 159–60, 161, 266
Bizzari, Pietro 6, 253, 255
Boethius 192
Bogart, Jacques 108
Bollaert, Roeland 96
'Book of Martyrs' (Foxe) 25
bookselling (Antwerp) 11
Borcht, Pieter van der 288, *289*
Bouchery, Dr 156
Bourse (Antwerp) *115*
Brabant (m)*178*, 227, 252
Braun, Georg 45, 81, 125, 258–9
Brès, Guy de 119, 123
British Isles 211; maps 189, *191*, *216*, *226*, 227, *see also* England
Broecke, M.P.R. Van den 254
Bruegel, Pieter (the Elder) 43, 44, 80–81, 195; paintings 50–53, *52*, 122–3, *134–5*, *137*, 140, 141, 195–9, *198*, 300
Bruto, Jean Michel 119
Byzantine Empire 193

Cabot, John 31

Caesarion (Ptolemy XVI) 177
Calais and Boulogne (m)171, 172, 227
Callimachus (Kallimachos) 179–80, 181, 193
Calvinism 123, 136, 140, 143, 144–5, 148, 149, 154–5, 262–3, *see also* Protestantism; religion
Camden, William 26, 271
Campin, Robert 45–6
Cartier, Jacques 34
cartography *see* map-making
Casallo, Dr 122, 123
Casas, Bartolomé de Las 243–4
Cassiodorus 192
Catalogus auctorum (list of contributors) (*Theatrum*) 207, 225
Cavafy (Constantine Peter Kavafis) 192
Çayas, Gabriel de 116, 156, 159
Cecil, Sir William 26, 255
Ceylon (m)188, 190
Charles V, Holy Roman Emperor 10, 21–3, *22*, 116
China 213; maps 190, 246, *247*
Chrysoloras, Manuel 193
Cicero 206
City of Antwerp with Two Monkeys, The (Bruegel) 195–6, *198*
city maps *vi–1*, 21, 45, *86*, *89*, *130*, *131*, 258–9
Civitates orbis terrarum (Braun and Hogenberg) *vi–1*, 45, 81, *86*, *89*, 125–6, *130*, 258–9
Clément, Nicolas (Trellaeus) 6
Cock, Hieronymus 43, 80, 84
Cock, Matthys 43
colonisation *see* exploration and colonisation
colour, in maps 38–9
Columbus, Christopher 4, 31, 219–20, 245
Contarini, Giovanni 31, 81
contributors, list of (*Theatrum*) 207, 225
Cool, Elizabeth (*née* Ortel, sister of Ortelius) 24, 37, 69, 150

Cool, Jacob 24, 69, 150, 271
Cool, Jacob (Ortelianus, son of
    Jacob) 24, 67, 72, 78–9, 290,
    292–3
Coornhert, Dirk Volckertsz. 276
Corte-Real, Gaspar 31
Corte-Real, Miguel 31
Cortés, Hernán 244
Cory, William (Johnson) 180
Country Feast (van
    Valckenborch) *151*
Coverdale, Miles 21, 69
Cranmer, Thomas 70
Cuba (m)31
Cuzco (m)*130*, 131

dedication (*Theatrum*) 207,
    220–21
Dee, John 6, 26, 126
Delphinas, Nicolaus Nicolaius
    171
Deventer, Jacob van 82, 172,
    178c, 256
Devotio Moderna (Modern
    Devotion) movement 54–5,
    95
Dias, Bartholomeu 9, 31
Dienst, Gillis (Egedius)
    Coppens van 201
Dilke, O.A.W. 186
Dodoens, Rembert
    (Dodonaeus) 160
Donne, John 224
Douai, Joannes Venduillius
    170–71
Drake, Sir Francis 238
Droz, Eugénie 108–9, 118, 119
Dubois, François *264*
Dulle Griet (Bruegel) 132–3,
    134–5
Dürer, Albrecht 21

Earth: circumference 182, 183;
    sphericity 181–2, 190,
    199–201
Edwards, Richard 205
Egmont, Count of 158
Egypt (m)131, 190, 229, 248
Emblem books 207, *208*
England 24–6, 69–71, *see also*
    British Isles
engraving, influence on
    cartography 43–4
Epitome (Ortelius) 279–81, *280*
Erasmus, Desiderius 12, 19, 30,
    55, 88–90, 96, 97, 103; *Praise
    of Folly* 296–300
Eratosthenes 181–3, 193
Estienne, Robert 61, 107, 108

Etzlaub, Erhard 39
Europe: maps 98, 100, 103,
    216–17, 227, 248; in *Theatrum*
    frontispiece 209, *210*, 211–12,
    218
Exchange (Antwerp) *115*
exploration and colonisation
    4–5, 9–10, 30–35, 53–4, 84,
    187, 188, 219–20, 243–5;
    questions posed to religion by
    voyages of discovery 237–42
Eyck, Jan van 45, 48, *49*

Faber, Conrad 89
Fabius, Scipio 131
Family of Love 54, 58–63, 108,
    113–14, 117–18, 148, 163, 205,
    268, *see also* Anabaptism;
    religion
Finé, Oronce 98, 152, *153*
Fisher, John 26
Flanders (m)82–4, 98–100, *99*,
    227
Floris, Cornelis 141
Foxe, John *25c*
France 79, 125–8, *127*; maps
    225, 227, 248–50, *257*
Franck, Sebastian 58–9
François I, King 107
Frankfurt 79, 88–91, *89*
Friesland (m)172, 227, 235,
    236, 239
Frobisher, Martin 245
frontispiece (*Theatrum*) 207,
    209–19, *210*
Fugger family 10, 23

Galle, Filips (Philippe) 43–4,
    63, *104*, 125–6, *127*, 136, 207,
    209, 221, 279, 293, *295*
Gama, Vasco da 242
García Lorca, Federico 18
Gastaldi, Giacomo (Jacopo) 76,
    77, 81–4, *83*, 129–31, 152, 194,
    232c
Gemma Frisius, Regnier 35–7,
    96, 97, 98, 131, 194
Geographia (Ptolemy) 36,
    176–9, 183–94, *184–5*
geographical information,
    assumptions about 235–7
geography, ancient 176–94
Germany (m)189, 227, 251
Ghim, Walter 92, 95, 100, 126,
    128
Gillis, Pieter 12–14, 18
globes 31, 96–7, 100–101, *see
    also* maps
Goltzius, Hubertus 209

Granvelle, Cardinal 156, 196
Grapheus, Alexander
    (Scribonius) 14, 113–14, 281
Grapheus, Cornelius
    (Scribonius) 12, 14, 21
Greece (m)187, 190, 228
Groote, Geert 54–5, 95
Guild of St Luke 39–41, 114
Guttierez, Diego 233

Hakluyt, Richard 26
Hamilton, Alastair 61, 163, 268
Harrewayers, Anne (*married
    name* Ortel, mother of
    Ortelius) 19, 28, 37, 69
Harvesters, The (Bruegel) 52, 53
Hasselt, Augustijn van 56, 136,
    154–5, 156
hedge preachings 133–6, *137*,
    140–41
Henry VIII, King 26
Hermathena (Hoefnagel)
    290–92, *291*
Heyns, Pieter 136, 279
Heyns, Zachary 302
Hispaniola (m)31
Hoefnagel, Joris 45, *64–5*, 126,
    136, 209, 259, 290, *291*
Hogenberg, Frans 79, 125–6,
    127; *Civitates orbis terrarum*
    vi–1, 45, 81, *86*, 89, 125–6,
    130, 258–9; other maps and
    engravings *64–5*, 92, *93*, 126,
    171, 174, 209, *210*, 233, *270*,
    271, *272*, 277
Holbein, Ambrosius 12, *13*
Holy Land (m)97, 131, 190
Hooftman, Gillis (Aegidius) 68,
    73–4, 76–8, 87
Hooren, Melchisedek van 16,
    17
Horn, Count of 158

Iberia (m)187
ibn Hunayn, Ishaq 193
Iceland (m)*241*
Iconoclastic Fury (*Beeldenstorm*)
    141–6, *142*, 149
Imagines et Figurae Bibliorum
    (Barrefelt) *267*, 268, 288, *289*
Imitation of Christ (Kempis) 55,
    57, 62
Index tabularum (table of
    contents) (*Theatrum*) 207,
    227–9
India (m)190, 229, 246
Indian Ocean (m)31, 183
Inquisition 23–4, 122–3

Introduction (*Theatrum*) 207, 222–5
Italy 80–87, 266; maps 82, *83*, 187, 189, 228
Iuliers, Johan 288

Jan of Leyden (Jan Beuckelsz.) 56
Janssen, Gerraert 271–4
Japan (m)152, 246, *247*
Jenkinson, Anthony 172, *173*, 236c, 246
Jode, Gerard de 131
Joris, David 56–8

Kallimachos (Callimachus) 179–80, 181, 193
Kavafis, Constantine Peter (Cavafy) 192
Kempis, Thomas à 55, 57, 62
Key, Adriaen Thomasz. *42*
Kremer, Emerentia 94, 95
Kremer, Gerard *see* Mercator, Gerard
Kremer, Ghisbrecht 94–5
Kremer, Hubertus 94, 95

Lafreri, Antonio 81, 82, 85–7, 126
Lalaing, Count de 170–71
landscape painting, influence on cartography 45–53
latitude 199
Leeward Islands (m)31
Leonardo da Vinci 45
l'Escluse, Charles de (Carolus Clusius) 225, *257*
letter of Gerard Mercator (*Theatrum*) 207, 225
lettering (maps) 96–7, 172
Leurer, Peter 294
Lhuyd, Humphrey 26, 126, 167–70, *169*, 207, 226c, 266
Lipsius, Justus 110, 120c, 278
longitude 199
Lopez, Martin 265
Luther, Martin 21, 23, 90

Macé, Robert 107
Madeburgus, Hiobus 258
Magellan, Ferdinand 34, 215–18, 219
Magnus, Olaus 218c, 248
Man Reading (or *St Ivo*, workshop of van der Weyden) 46, *47*
Mander, Karel van 136c, 195
Mangani, Giorgio 206
Manutius, Aldus 107

map-making 193; influence of painting and engraving 43–53; Italy 81–7; lettering 96–7, 172; placenames 281, 288; production and colouring 37–9
maps: Africa 31, 187, 188, 190; Americas *32*, 34c, 84, 98, 103, 129–31; Asia *77*, 84, 152, 190; British Isles 189, *191*; Ceylon 188, 190; China 190; cities *vi–1*, 21, 45, *86*, *89*, *130*, 131, 258–9; Cuba 31; Egypt 131, 190; Europe 98, 100, 103; Flanders 82–4, 98–100, *99*; Germany 189; Greece 187, 190; Holy Land 97, 131, 190; Iberia 187; India 190; Italy 82, 187, 189; Japan 152; Leeward Islands 31; Newfoundland 31; oceans and seas 31, 34–5, 100, 183; Persia 190; Sicily 82, 189; Spain 82, 189; world *see* world maps, *see also* globes
maps (*Theatrum*) 227–9; Africa 227, *230–31*, 248; Americas 5, *164–5*, 227, 239–42, 245; Asia 227, 245–6, *247*; Barbary and Biledulgerid 248, *249*; Bavaria 171, 172; Brabant *178*, 227, 252; British Isles *216*, *226*, 227; Calais and Boulogne 171, 172, 227; China 246, *247*; Egypt 229, 248; Europe *216–17*, 227, 248; Flanders 227; France 225, 227, 248–50, *257*; Friesland 172, 227, 235, *236*, 239; Germany 227, 251; Greece 228; Iceland *241*; India 229, 246; Italy *83*, 228; Japan 246, *247*; Mediterranean 228; Mexico 244; Northern Regions 229, *236*; Persia 229, 246; Portugal 171, 172, 227; Russia, Muscovy and Tartary 171–2, *173*, 229, 246; Saxony, Meissen, Thuringia 228, 258; Siena 258; Silesia 171, 228; southern regions 234; Spain 227, 250–51; Tartary and the Grand Cham 229, 246; Transylvania 39, *40*, 172, 228; Turkish Empire 229, 246; Utopia (*Parergon*) *13*; Wales 167, 168, *169*, 170, 266; world 227, 233–5, 238–9, 242–3; Würtemberg 171, 172

Margaret of Parma 138–40, *139*, 148, 149, 158
Marinus of Tyre 199
Marlowe, Christopher 233
Massys, Cornelis 43, 50
Matte, Sebastian 141
Matthijsz., Jan 56
Maximilian II, Holy Roman Emperor 172
Mediterranean (m)100, 228
Meetkerke, Adolf van (Mekerchus) 207, 209, 211, 220
Mekerchus (Adolf van Meetkerke) 207, 209, 211, 220
Menzies, Gavin 213
Mercator, Arnold (son of Gerard) 97
Mercator, Barbara (*née* Schellekens, wife of Gerard) 96
Mercator, Gerard (Gerard Kremer) 92, 97; atlas 85, 128–9, *301*; birth and childhood 94–5; comparison with Ortelius 91–2; cylindrical projection 199–201; death 292; edition of Ptolemy's *Geographia* 194; education 95–6; globes 100–101; letter in *Theatrum* 207, 225; lettering (maps) 96–7; maps 82–4, 97–100, *99*, 103, 199–201, 226c, 232c, 233, 234, 236c, 239, 248, 256; part in beginnings of *Theatrum* 126–9, 152; portrait 92, *93*; relationship with Ortelius 90–91, 256, 288; and religion 95–6, 101–2; trip to France with Ortelius 79, 125–8, *127*
Mercator, Rumold (son of Gerard) 97
Meteren, Emmanuel van 24, 28, 35, 68, 150; and beginnings of *Theatrum* 68, 71, 72; Ortelius' letters to 122, 143–5, 260–62
Meteren, Jacob van 21, 23, 24, 26, 28, 35, 69
Mexico (m)244
Mexico City (m)*130*, 131
Moded, Hermannus 144, 146
Modern Devotion (*Devotio Moderna*) movement 54–5, 95
Moflin, Joannes 256
Monachus, Franciscus 96
Montaigne, Michel de 119

Montano, Benito Arias (Arias Montanus) 161–3, *162*, 266, 287
Mor, Antonis 75, *124*
More, Thomas 12–14, 15, 16, 18, 26, 296
Moretus, Balthasar I 110, *111c*, *112c*, 117, *162c*
Moretus, Jan 156, 265–6, 290
Moretus, Martina (*née* Plantin) 156
Mulcaster, Richard 26
Münster, Sebastian 36, 194
Mylius, Arnold 234, 281, 292

Neissensis, Martinus Helwig 171
New World *see* Americas
Newfoundland (m)31
Niclaes, François 118
Niclaes, Hendrik (HN) 58, 59–60, 61–3, 108, 117–19, 148, 155, 268
Nomenclator (Ortelius) 288
North Africa (m)187, 190
Northern Regions (m)229, *236*

oceans and seas (m)31, 34–5, 100, 183, 228
oikoumene (m)183–9, *184–5*
Onze Lieve Vrouwekathedraal (Antwerp) 16–18, 143–4
Orlandi, Caesar (Orlandius) 258
Ortel, Anne (*née* Harrewayers, mother of Ortelius) 19, 28, 37, 69
Ortel, Anne (sister of Ortelius) 24, 37, 69, 271, 294
Ortel, Elizabeth (*married name* Cool, sister of Ortelius) 24, 37, 69, 150
Ortel, Leonard (father of Ortelius) 19, 21, 23, 24, 26
Ortelianus (Jacob Cool) 24, 67, 72, 78–9, 290, 292–3
Ortelius, Abraham (Abram Ortel): *Album amicorum* 29, 44, 72, 74, 209, 255–6, 278; association with painters and graphic artists 43–5; birth 6, 19; businessman 41–3, 68, 221–2; character 4, 14, 28–9, 71–2, 73, 123, 146, 276–8, 287–8, 292, 293–4; comparison with Gerard Mercator 91–2; connections with England 24–6; death 6, 293, 294; description of

Iconoclastic Fury 143–5; early atlas for Gillis Hooftman 76–9, 87; early involvement in map-making 37; education 28, 35–6; Guild of St Luke 39–41; health 175, 293, 294; *Hermathena* (Hoefnagel) 290–92, *291*; influence of Italy 80–87; intellectual frustration 68–9; letters to Emmanuel van Meteren 28, 122, 143–5, 260–62; maps 129–31, 152; memorial to Cornelius Grapheus 14; *Nomenclatur* 288; portraits 28–9, 41, *42*, *151*, 207, 221–2, *295*; relationship with Christophe Plantin 103, 255–6; relationship with Gerard Mercator 90–91, 256, 288; relationship with Ortelianus 72, 290, 292–3; and religion 23–4, 54, 58–9, 60, 63, 72, 122–3, 136–8, 145–6, 293; Royal Geographer 221; scholarship 29–30; *Synonymia geographica* 281; *Theatrum see Theatrum orbis terrarum*; travels 79, 80–81, 88–91, 125–8, *127*, 266, 288

Pacific Ocean (m)34–5
painting, influence on cartography 44–53
Palladio, Andrea 203
Parergon (Ortelius) *13*, 282–7, *283*, *284*
Parma, Duke of 288
Patenier, Joachim 43, 45, 48–50, *51*, 53
Persia (m)190, 229, 246
Peters, Arno 200–201
Pfeiffer, Rudolph 181
Phaeton 212
Philip II, King 74, 75, 116, 123, 138, 140, 141, 159–60, 161, 207, 220–21, 243, 245, 255, 262, *286*, 287
Pierre Levée (rock) 126, *127*
Pinet, Antoine du *130*
placenames 281, 288
Plantin, Christophe 5, 103–21, *112*, 175, 276; birth and early years 105–6; business 98, 103–5, *104*, 107, 110–21, 147–8, 154, 160–61, *208c*, 263–6; Frankfurt Book Fairs *89c*, 90; and Gerard Mercator 5, 98, 100; king's printer 221;

last years and death 43–4, 290; Polyglot Bible 159–60, 161, 266; and printing of Calvinist books 148, 154–6, 158–9, 276; relationship with Ortelius 103, 255–6; and religion 54, 59–61, 63, 108–9, 113–14, 117–18, 136–8, 148, 155, 276; in Spanish Fury 274; stabbing 116–17; and *Theatrum* 103, 201, 202–3, 250, 254, 255, 281–2
Plantin, Christophe (son of Christophe Snr.) 156
Plantin, Henrica (daughter of Christophe Snr.) 156
Plantin, Jean (father of Christophe Snr.) 105, 106
Plantin, Jeanne (*née* Rivière, wife of Christophe Snr.) 107, 108, 109–10, *111*
Plantin, Margareta (*married name* Raphelengius, daughter of Christophe Snr.) 107, 156
Plantin, Martina (*married name* Moretus, daughter of Christophe Snr.) 156
Planudes, Maximus 193
Plato 240
Pliny *83c*, 243, 248
Plutarch 240
poem, Mekerchus' (*Theatrum*) 207, 209, 211, 213, 214–15, 220
Polo, Marco 234
Polyglot Bible 159–60, 161, 266
Porret, Antoine 105
Porret, Pierre 105–6, 107, 108, 109, 110
Portugal (m)171, 172, 227
Postel, Guillaume 60, 152–4, 205, 212
Praise of Folly (Erasmus) 296–300
print-making, influence on cartography 43
printing (Antwerp) 11, 43
projection (maps) 97–8, 199–201, 233
Protestantism 19–23, 26, 27, 69–71, 72, 133–46, 149–50, 275, *see also* Anabaptism; Calvinism; religion
Ptolemy (geographer) 31–4, *32*, 36, 53, 81, 87, 100, 172, 176–9, 182–94
Ptolemy III 181
Ptolemy XVI (Caesarion) 177
Ptolemy Soter 177, 179

Puppier, Pierre 106
Pythagoras 182, 205
Pytheas 187

Rabelais, François 106
Radermacher, Jan 44, 67–8,
    71–2, 73–9, 150–52, 175
Ramusio, Giovanni Battista 84,
    129–31, 130c
Raphelengius, Frans 107, 136,
    156, 161, 265
Raphelengius, Margareta (née
    Plantin) 107, 156
religion 237–42, 298, see also
    Protestantism
Rest in the Flight into Egypt
    (Patenier) 50, 51, 53
Ribera, Diego 34
Rivière, Jeanne (married name
    Plantin) 107, 108, 109–10,
    111
Robinson, Ralph 14
Rogers, Adriana (née de
    Weyden) 70
Rogers, Daniel 24, 70, 71, 72,
    150, 168, 269
Rogers, John 68, 69–71, 72
Rosselli, Francesco 81
Rubens, Peter Paul 41, 105,
    110, 111, 112, 120, 161, 162,
    290
Rudolph II, Holy Roman
    Emperor 172
Russia, Muscovy and Tartary
    (m)171–2, 173, 229, 246

St Bartholomew's Day massacre
    263, 264
St Ivo (or Man Reading,
    workshop of van der Weyden)
    46, 47
Sambucus, Johannes 40, 91,
    172, 256, 266
Santa Barbara (van Eyck) 48,
    49
Saxony, Meissen, Thuringia
    (m)228, 258
Saxton, Christopher 226c
Scarperia, Jacopo d'Angelo da
    193
Schellekens, Barbara (married
    name Mercator) 96
Scholiers, Hieronymus 256, 259
Scribonius see Grapheus
Seneca (the Younger) 119, 120,
    204, 206, 240, 293
Sermon of John the Baptist, The
    (Bruegel) 133, 137, 140, 141
Seville 250–51

Shakespeare, William 205
Sicily (m)82, 189
Siena (m)258
Silesia (m)171, 228
Skelton, John 26
Skelton, R.A. 129, 206
Soto, Hernando de 34
southern regions (m)234
Spain (m)82, 189, 227, 250–51
Spanish Fury 269–75, 270, 272
Stevenson, Robert Louis 38,
    168
Strabo 181
Susato, Tielman 160
Sweerts, Frans (Franciscus
    Sweertius) 28, 35, 43, 278,
    293–4
Synonymia geographica
    (Ortelius) 281

table of contents (Theatrum)
    207, 227–9
Tartary and the Grand Cham
    (m)229, 246
Tempe (Parergon illustration)
    284
Tenth Penny tax, unrest
    following 262–3
Texeira, Father Luis 247c, 290
theatre 202–6
Theatrum orbis terrarum
    (Ortelius) 3–4, 201;
    Additamenta 281; beginnings
    67–79, 126–9; Catalogus
    auctorum (list of contributors)
    207, 225; dedication 207,
    220–21; Epitome 279–81, 280;
    frontispiece 207, 209–19, 210;
    Index tabularum (table of
    contents) 207, 227–9;
    Introduction 207, 222–5;
    language editions 4, 254;
    letter of Gerard Mercator
    207, 225; maps see maps;
    Mekerchus' poem 207, 209,
    211, 213, 214–15, 220; Ortelius
    begins work on 150–52;
    Ortelius gathers maps for
    129, 167–70, 171–5; Parergon
    13, 282–7, 283, 284; portrait of
    Ortelius 207, 221–2, 295;
    print-runs and sales 254, 282;
    public contributions (maps
    and information) 256–8; title
    202–7
Theodoric the Goth 192
Theologia Germanica 55, 59
Thorius, Johannes (John) 150,
    175

Titian 22, 23
Toledo, Ferdinand Alvarez de,
    Duke of Alva 154, 156–8, 157,
    196, 262
Tramezzini, Michael 78, 172
Transylvania (m)39, 40, 172,
    228
Trellaeus (Nicolas Clément) 6
Turkish Empire (m)229, 246
Tyndale, William 20, 21, 25, 69

Utopia (More) 12–14, 15, 16;
    map 13

Valassopoulo, George 192
Valckenborch, Lucas van 151
Venice (m)86
Verhaeren, Emile 9
Vermeer, Jan 37
Vespucci, Amerigo 33, 34, 215,
    219, 220
Vianen 154–6
Virgin with Firescreen (School of
    Campin) 46
Vitruvius 203
Vivianus, Johan 288
Vodel, Anders Sorensen 241c
Voet, Leon 11, 117, 155, 161,
    265
Vopelius, Caspar 131

Waldseemüller, Martin 31–4,
    194, 219
Wales (m)167, 168, 169, 170,
    266
Weyden, Adriana de (married
    name Rogers) 70
Weyden, Rogier van der 45–6
William of Orange (William the
    Silent) 123, 124, 138, 145,
    149, 154, 262, 276, 277, 287
Wolsey, Thomas 19
world maps 31–4, 32–3, 36, 84,
    97–8, 129–31, 153, 199–201;
    globes 31, 96–7, 100–101;
    oikoumene 183–9, 184–5;
    Theatrum 227, 233–5, 238–9,
    242–3
Würtemberg (m)171, 172

Zaltieri, Bolognino 84, 86c
Zeccus, Fernandus Alvares 171,
    172
Zeno, Nicolao 235, 236c
Ziegler, Jacob 97

TYPVS ORB

TERRA SEPT

CIRCVLS ARCTICVS.

AMERICA SIVE IN-
DIA NOVA. Ao 1492. a Chrystophoro
Colombo nomine regis Castellæ primum detecta.

Noua
Fran-
cia.

Chilaga

Flori-
da.

Calicuas

Marata

TROPICVS CANCR

Archipelago di

MAR DE
NORT

S.Lazaro.

CIRCVLVS AEQVINOCTIALIS

Caribana

Tisnada

MAR DEL ZVR.

Peru. Amazones. Brasil.

Noua Guinea
quæ ab alijs insula
aut parti continentis
Australis, incertum.

Islas de Salomon.

TROPICVS CAPRICORNI

EL MAR
PACIFICO.

Hanc continentem
Australem, nonnulli
Magellanicam regionem ab
eius inventore, nuncupant.

Chica.

Archipelago
de las islas

Terra del Fuego.

CIRCVLVS ANTARCTICVS.

190 200 210 220 230 240 250 260 270 280 290 300 310 320 330

TERRA AVSTR

QVID EI POTEST VIDERI MAG
NITAS OMNIS TOTIVSQVE